LEAVING CERTIFICATE

LATER MODERN IRISH HISTORY TOPIC 3

Sovereignty and Partition
1912–1949

M.E. COLLINS

THE EDUCATIONAL COMPANY

First published 2008
The Educational Company of Ireland
Ballymount Road
Walkinstown
Dublin 12

A member of the Smurfit Kappa Group plc.

The paper used in this book comes from Managed Forests in Northern Europe For every tree felled, at least one new tree is planted

© M.E. Collins 2008

Editors: Aengus Carroll, Celine Clavel
Design: Design Image
Layout: Design Image
Maps illustration: Michael Phillips
Indexing: Kristin Jensen
Cover Design: Design Image
Origination: Impress Digital

Acknowledgements

Allen Library, Anne Matthews (historian), Bridgeman Art Library, Emma Philbin Bowman, GAA Museum, Corbis, Garda Síochána, Hulton Picture Archive, National Gallery of Ireland, Images Courtesy of the National Library of Ireland, National Photographic Archive, Royal Society of Antiquaries of Ireland, RTÉ Stills Library, Trinity College Library, Ulster Museum, Voices of Ireland, Father Brown Collection, Science and Society Picture Library.

FOREWORD

The content of this book is intended to meet the requirements for Topic 3 in the Later Modern Ireland section of the new Leaving Certificate History syllabus – The Pursuit of Sovereignty and the Impact of Partition 1912 to 1949.

In line with syllabus requirements, the author has approached this Topic from a number of perspectives – politics and administration, society and economy, culture and religion. These perspectives are explored in each chapter with definitions of the key concepts (and other difficult words) that a student should know at the end of the book. These concepts are developed more fully where they are relevant to the content of the Topic.

The Case Studies listed in Topic 3 – the negotiations for the Anglo-Irish Treaty, October to December 1921, the Eucharistic Congress in 1932 and Belfast during the second World War – are treated in depth within the wider perspectives to which they belong. Similarly the achievements of the Key Personalities are also discussed in the context of the events and movements within which they made their contributions.

For ease of study all chapters are divided into sections. Every section is followed by short questions which will help students extract the essential information from each section. Short paragraphs like these can then be built up into more extended essays. Exam type questions for Ordinary and Higher Level Leaving Certificate students are given after each chapter.

Sources and the development of the skills needed to locate, understand, evaluate and contextualise them are central to the new syllabus. Students can learn these skills on the large number of sources, written and visual, spread throughout the book. The questions accompanying them are carefully designed to help students understand, evaluate, compare and contextualise the sources. Questions like these form an essential component of the new Leaving Certificate history examination.

The new history syllabus aims to help students develop the skills of the historian. But these skills – of research, note-taking, reading for meaning, critical analysis and report writing – are skills which are useful for many walks of life, not just for the study of history. It is hoped that this book will make the acquisition of these skills an enjoyable and rewarding experience.

M.E. Collins
February 2008

WEBSITES

RTÉ
http://www.rte.ie/
BBC
http://www.bbc.co.uk/history
Channel 4
http://www.channel4.com/history/
GAA
http://www.gaa.ie
Ulster Folk and Transport Museum
http://www.uftm.org.uk
National Museum of Ireland
http://www.museum.ie
National Library of Ireland
http://www.nli.ie
National Archives of Ireland
http://www.nationalarchives.ie
http://www.clarelibrary.ie
http://www.islandireland.com/Pages/history.html
http://www.ucc.ie/ucc/depts/history
http://multitext.ucc.ie/
http://www.hist.ie
Edco
http://www.edco.ie/
Scoilnet
http://www.scoilnet.ie/hist/

WEBSITES OF KEY PERSONALITIES

Dawson Bates
http://multitext.ucc.ie/d/Richard_Dawson_Bates
Michael Collins
http://multitext.ucc.ie/d/Michael_Collins
http://www.bbc.co.uk/history/british/easterrising/profiles/po03.shtml
http://www.britannica.com/ebc/article-9361146
http://www.generalmichaelcollins.com/
W.T. Cosgrave
http://multitext.ucc.ie/d/William_T_Cosgrave
http://www.generalmichaelcollins.com/Fine_Gael/W_T_Cosgrave.html
Sir James Craig, Lord Craigavon
http://multitext.ucc.ie/d/James_Craig
http://en.wikipedia.org/wiki/James_Craig,_1st_Viscount_Craigavon
Arthur Griffith
http://multitext.ucc.ie/d/Arthur_Griffith
http://en.wikipedia.org/wiki/Arthur_Griffith
http://www.bbc.co.uk/history/british/easterrising/profiles/po07.shtml
Evie Hone
http://multitext.ucc.ie/d/Eva_Sydney_Hone
http://en.wikipedia.org/wiki/Evie_Hone
Constance Markievicz
http://www.spartacus.schoolnet.co.uk/Wmarkiewicz.htm
http://multitext.ucc.ie/d/Countess_Constance_Markievicz
J.J. McElligott
http://multitext.ucc.ie/d/James_J_MacElligott
Pádraig Pearse
http://en.wikipedia.org/wiki/Patrick_Pearse
http://multitext.ucc.ie/d/Patrick_Henry_Pearse
http://www.ucc.ie/celt/pearse.html
Eamon De Valera
http://en.wikipedia.org/wiki/%C3%89amon_de_Valera
http://multitext.ucc.ie/d/Eamon_de_Valera
http://www.ucd.ie/archives/html/collections/devalera-eamon.htm
http://www.president.ie/index.php?section=35&lang=eng

CONTENTS

INTRODUCTION

The years from 1912 to 1949 say huge changes in Ireland.

In 1912, the whole island was part of the United Kingdom of Great Britain and Ireland. MPs from Ireland travelled to the British Parliament in Westminster where they played a part in governing what was then the world's greatest power with a world-wide empire.

A minority of Irish people were unionists who approved of Ireland's membership of the United Kingdom and wanted it to continue, but the majority were nationalists. They thought Ireland would be better if it was an independent, sovereign state.

A period of revolutionary unrest, between 1912 and 1922, led to the partition of the island. The north-east, where unionists were in a majority, became Northern Ireland and remained within the United Kingdom. The rest of the island became the Irish Free State which was a self-governing dominion of the British Empire. But nationalists were not satisfied to remain part of the British Empire and by 1949 the Free State had evolved into the Irish republic, a completely sovereign and independent state.

This book gives an account of these changes, of the men and women who brought them about, and of the various ways in which they affected the lives of the people living on this island.

Note
Pounds, shillings and pence
Our currency was different in the 19th century. You will need to understand it to read documents. It was rather complicated:

      1 pound (£1) contained 20 shillings (20s)

and   1 shilling (1s) contained 12 pence (12d).

It was written like this: **£2. 3s. 6½d** which means two pounds, three shillings and six pence halfpenny.

Inflation has greatly changed the value of money. In 1910, £1.10s was a reasonable weekly wage and the old age pension was 5 shillings a week. To get a rough equivalent of modern values in euro, multiply all pounds by 300.

Personalities
Introductions to several historical figures are given in purple boxes (key personalities) and green boxes (other personalities) throughout the chapters, with more details in the text about their life and contributions. Biographies of key personalities are also available at the end of the book (see pages 203–210).

	Ireland today	Ireland 1910
		UNITED KINGDOM OF GREAT BRITAIN AND IRELAND
Head of state	President, elected by Irish people.	King George V who lived in Britain. By law he had to be a Protestant.
Flag	Irish tricolour	Union Jack
Our parliament	The Oireachtas (Dáil and Seanad) elected by Irish voters. Meets in Dublin.	Parliament (Commons and Lords) which met in Westminster (London). ■ British voters elected 565 MPs; ■ Irish voters elected 103 MPs.
How laws are made	Passed by the Oireachtas; signed by the President.	Passed by Commons and Lords; signed by the King.
How the government is formed	Dáil elects Taoiseach (Prime Minister) and his Ministers. They live and work in Ireland.	King appointed leader of biggest party as Prime Minister. He lived in London and appointed two ministers to run Ireland – Lord Lieutenant who lived in Dublin and Chief Secretary who lived mostly in London.
How the government works	One minister in charge of each area of government, e.g. Finance, Foreign Affairs, Education, Health, etc.	From Dublin Castle, the Chief Secretary was responsible for about fifty departments, boards and commissions. Some he controlled, some were independent, some had their headquarters in Britain.
How taxes are decided	Decided by Irish Minister for Finance to suit Irish conditions.	Decided by British Chancellor of Exchequer to suit Britain whose economy was very different from Ireland's.
Who are the police?	Garda Síochána, who do not carry guns.	Armed Royal Irish Constabulary (RIC). As well as dealing with ordinary crime, they watched Irish nationalists.

① Ireland at the Start of the 20th Century

1.1

IRELAND IN THE UNITED KINGDOM

Ireland in the early 1900s was a very different place from Ireland today:

- Today the island of Ireland is divided into **two states** – Northern Ireland with six counties and the Republic of Ireland with twenty-six counties. Then the whole island (thirty-two counties) was **a single unit**.

- Today, twenty-six counties of Ireland form an **independent republic** while the six counties of Northern Ireland are part of the United Kingdom of Great Britain and Northern Ireland. Then the whole of Ireland was **part of the United Kingdom** of Great Britain and Ireland.

- Today Ireland is an **urbanised** country where most people live in towns and cities. Then Ireland was a **rural** country in which over 60 per cent of the people lived in the countryside.

- Today Ireland is an **industrial country**, producing a range of industrial goods like drugs, computers, etc. Then it was mainly agricultural with over 60 per cent of the people working on the land. The only area where there was much industry was around Belfast.

In this book we will trace the main events which changed Ireland so profoundly and helped to form the country we know today.

THE ACT OF UNION OF 1800

The Act of Union, passed in 1800, united the kingdom of Ireland to Britain to form the **United Kingdom of Great Britain and Ireland**. As you can see from the table opposite that affected every aspect of Irish life:

- Important decisions affecting people's lives – about taxes, trade, the economy, social welfare and education – were made in London.

- Many of the people who made these decisions knew little about Ireland. They did not mean to do Ireland any harm, but often their lack of knowledge and understanding caused damage.

- Irish people who wanted to influence these decisions had to go to London and take part in politics there.

THE UNITED KINGDOM PARLIAMENT AT WESTMINSTER

The main source of power in the United Kingdom was the parliament that met in Westminster in London. It consisted of two houses, the **Lords** and the **Commons**:

The House of Lords

After the Union, Irish lords elected twenty-eight of their number to sit in the Lords. Most members of the Lords were wealthy men, many of them landlords. They saw little reason to change society. Therefore, they were usually conservative and supported the Conservative Party. It always had a majority in the Lords.

The House of Commons

The Commons contained 665 Members of Parliament (MPs) who were elected by the voters of England, Scotland, Wales and Ireland. Irish voters chose 103 of them. Although that might seem like a small proportion, it was more than Ireland was entitled to on a population basis.

> The number of Irish seats in the Commons fluctuated between 103 and 105.

The palace of Westminster where the UK parliament meets

Courtesy: Corbis

WHO COULD VOTE FOR MPs?

MPs were elected at **general elections**. The right to vote for them (also called the **franchise** or **suffrage**) was limited to men over twenty-one who occupied a house. Men who were not householders and all women were not allowed to vote.

PASSING AN ACT OF PARLIAMENT

Parliament made the laws for the United Kingdom. First a proposal, called a **bill** was introduced into the Commons or the Lords. When both Houses had passed it, the bill became an **Act of Parliament** (i.e. became the law). Up to 1911 the Lords could stop any bill from becoming an act but after that they could only delay it for two years.

THE GOVERNMENT OF THE UNITED KINGDOM

Parliament also controlled the **government**, which was headed by the **Prime Minister**. He was the leader of whichever party won most seats in a general election. He appointed ministers to take charge of various aspects of the government and together they formed the **Cabinet**, which decided about laws and taxes for the whole United Kingdom.

THE GOVERNMENT OF IRELAND

The Prime Minister appointed two ministers for Ireland. They were:

- The **Lord Lieutenant** or **Viceroy** who was the king or queen's representative. Always a member of the Lords, he lived in the **Viceregal Lodge** in Dublin (now Áras an Uachtaráin) and carried out the ceremonial tasks of a head of state.

- The **Chief Secretary** was always an MP and Cabinet Minister. He had to go regularly to the Commons and answer questions from MPs about the government's Irish policy. Although the Viceroy sounded more important, the real power lay with the Chief Secretary.

DUBLIN CASTLE: THE BRITISH GOVERNMENT IN IRELAND

The Chief Secretary moved constantly between London and Dublin. He had his Irish office in **Dublin Castle**. His main assistant there was the head of the Irish civil service, the **Under-Secretary**.

From Dublin Castle these men governed Ireland. They collected the taxes, controlled the police, supervised the education system, administered the Poor Laws and so on. They did none of these things very well, partly because the government in

Dublin Castle where the Chief Secretary for Ireland had his office. In 1910 people used the words 'Dublin Castle' to mean the government

London had the final say in every decision and this caused confusion and uncertainty.

POLICE

Dublin Castle's main concern was keeping order. It had two police forces. The unarmed **Dublin Metropolitan Police (DMP)** were responsible for

A Constable in the Dublin Metropolitan Police (DMP)

Dublin. The armed **Royal Irish Constabulary (RIC)** dealt with the rest of the country.

Popularly known as 'Peelers', the constables in the DMP and the RIC were ordinary Irishmen, though their officers were usually British. Most of their time was spent dealing with petty criminals and minor breaches of the law like *poitín* making and unlicensed dogs.

They were also expected to keep watch on possible troublemakers. They had a special branch which spied on various nationalist and socialist organisations. They sent an endless stream of reports about their activities to Dublin Castle. These reports are now a valuable source of information for historians.

THE DEBATE ABOUT THE UNION

Was it good for Ireland to be in the United Kingdom? Irish people were divided about this.

- **Unionists** believed that the Union was good for Ireland and wanted to keep it. They argued that it put the country at the heart of the British Empire which was then the greatest empire in the world. Unionists believed that Irish people benefited by sharing in the control of that empire. It gave them far more power and prestige than Ireland would enjoy as a tiny independent country.
- **Nationalists** did not think that being in the United Kingdom had been good for Ireland.

They pointed out that since 1800 the country had experienced famine, emigration and economic decline. In Westminster, Irish MPs were in a minority and found it hard to make British MPs and ministers listen to their concerns. Ireland, they felt, would be better off if Irish people were allowed to rule it.

We will look at these views in more detail in the following sections.

QUESTIONS

1 From 1800 to 1920 Ireland was part of the United Kingdom. Explain four ways in which this affected life in Ireland.

2 Name the two United Kingdom ministers who were responsible for Ireland. Write a brief account of what each one did.

3 How many Irish MPs were elected to the Westminster parliament? How many British MPs were there? Do you think this would make any difference to the way Ireland was run? Explain your answer.

4 Name the two Irish police forces. List some of their duties.

5 'Irish people were divided about being in the United Kingdom.' Explain briefly what these divisions were.

1.2

UNION OR SELF-GOVERNMENT? THE UNIONIST VIEW

WHO WERE THE UNIONISTS?

Unionists were people who believed that it was good for Ireland to be in the United Kingdom and who wanted to keep it there. There were three main reasons why a person might be a unionist – ethnic identity, religion and economic considerations.

○ Ethnic identity

Many unionists were descended from British people who settled in Ireland in the 16th and 17th centuries. They **felt British as well as Irish**. They were loyal to the king and wanted to remain part of the British state in which they felt at home.

○ Religion

Most Irish Protestants were unionists. They felt comfortable in the United Kingdom because it was a Protestant state. In Britain, the vast majority of the people were Protestants. The king or queen had to be a Protestant and Protestant Churches enjoyed a privileged position.

But in Ireland, as Table A shows, only a quarter of the population was Protestant. The rest were Roman Catholic. If Ireland were to break away from the United Kingdom and have its own parliament, Protestants would be heavily outnumbered by Catholics.

Table A

Distribution of religion in Ireland in 1911		
	Roman Catholics	Protestants
All of Ireland	3,242,670	1,147,549
Ulster	690,816	890,880
Three southern provinces	2,551,854	256,669

For that reason most Irish Protestants wanted to stay in the United Kingdom. They felt safe there, whereas in an independent Ireland they feared they might suffer discrimination in jobs and even religious persecution.

However, while most Protestants were unionists, there were exceptions. For example, the founders of the Home Rule Party, Isaac Butt and Charles Stewart Parnell, were Protestants. So were Douglas Hyde, founder of the Gaelic League, W.B. Yeats and Lady Gregory, founders of the Abbey Theatre, and Bulmer Hobson and Ernest Blythe, both prominent republicans.

○ Economic considerations

(i) Most owners of big Irish businesses (like the Guinness and Jacob families) were unionists.

They sold most of their produce to Britain and its empire. They feared that Irish independence would interfere with that trade.

(ii) In the **north-east of Ulster**, the economy had prospered during the Union while other parts of Ireland declined economically. Protestants, who were in a majority in this area, had also done well, with good jobs in linen and shipbuilding. They feared an Irish parliament (dominated by farmers) would impose barriers on trade with Britain and damage their prosperity.

UNIONIST DIVISIONS

Irish unionists were divided into Southern unionists and Ulster unionists. While both groups were united in their determination to keep Ireland in the United Kingdom, their circumstances were very different.

SOUTHERN UNIONISTS

As you can see from Table A on page 4 and the map below, Protestants were in a small minority in the three southern provinces of Ireland. In 1885 they set

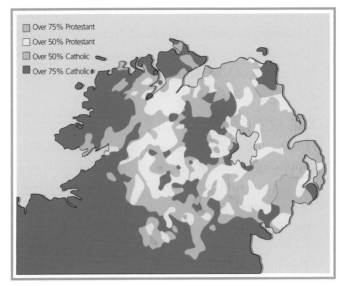

Distribution of Protestants and Catholics in Ulster, 1911

up the **Irish Loyal and Patriotic Union** to fight elections, but due to their small numbers, they seldom won a seat. Only the graduates of Trinity College in Dublin, most of whom were Protestants, always elected two Unionist MPs. They provided Southern unionists with their only guaranteed voice in the Commons.

However, Southern unionists had wealth and influence to make up for their lack of numbers. While some were poor farmers or workers, they also included some of the wealthiest men in Ireland. Many of them, like Lord Iveagh, the head of Guinness, or Lord Lansdowne, a wealthy landlord, had seats in the House of Lords. This gave Southern unionists more influence than their numbers justified. They used their wealth and position to campaign in Britain against self-government for Ireland.

ULSTER UNIONISTS

Ulster unionists were in a much stronger position than Southern unionists. Across the whole nine counties of Ulster they were slightly over 50 per cent of the population but, as the map above shows, in the north-eastern counties they were in a large majority.

Ulster unionists included all classes and several creeds. Farmers, landlords and labourers, factory workers and their bosses, Anglicans, Presbyterians and Methodists were all united in supporting the

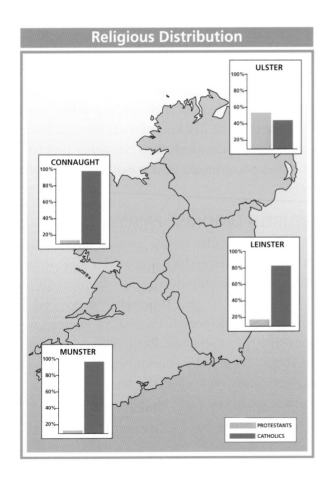

Union with Britain. In 1905 they set up the **Ulster Unionist Council** to maintain unity and organise elections. In the 1910 election, unionists won seventeen of Ulster's thirty-three seats.

THE ECONOMY OF ULSTER

Ulster unionists had strong economic reasons for opposing Home Rule. While the rest of Ireland grew poor under the Union, Ulster, especially the area around Belfast, prospered. This was due to two key industries, linen and shipbuilding.

The linen industry, which had begun in people's homes in the 18th century, had expanded into factories in the 19th century. Most of the factories were located in the 'linen triangle' of towns around Belfast. By 1900, 70,000 people, mostly women, worked in the industry. The hours were long and the wages and conditions bad, but at least they had jobs, unlike people in southern towns.

Shipbuilding, not linen was the main source of Ulster's prosperity. Begun in Belfast in the 1850s this industry was at its peak between 1900 and 1920. The main shipyard, **Harland and Wolff**, was the biggest in the world. It specialised in producing luxury transatlantic liners. It launched the *Olympic*, the biggest passenger ship ever built, in 1910 and its sister ship, the *Titanic*, in 1912. Harland and Wolffe and a second large shipyard employed 20,000 men, most of them highly skilled and well paid.

The success of shipbuilding drew in other industries. There were firms which produced engines, ropes, furniture and fittings for the shipbuilders. The pool of skilled workers also attracted other industries to Belfast, like cigarette-making, brewing and distilling.

All foreign visitors commented on the vigour and bustle of Belfast and the prosperity of its citizens, compared to the poverty-stricken appearance of Dublin and other southern cities. That prosperity was due to the existence of plenty of well-paid work. In many families both men and women could get jobs, and that meant families enjoyed a relatively decent standard of living.

A unionist propaganda postcard. What message does it send?

Ulster unionists feared they would lose that prosperity if Ireland got Home Rule. A Dublin-based parliament, jealous of Belfast's prosperity, might interfere with the free flow of trade between Britain and Ireland upon which their prosperity depended. They were determined to stop that from happening.

THE IRISH UNIONIST PARTY

In 1886 the leader of the British Liberal Party, William Gladstone, had proposed giving Ireland Home Rule. To stop it, unionists from north and south united in the **Unionist Party**. Led by Edward Saunderson, it formed an alliance with the British Conservative Party. This alliance was fortunate for the unionists because the Conservatives controlled the House of Lords. As long as the Lords could block any Home Rule Bill, they were safe.

THE ORANGE ORDER

The Unionist Party drew much of its strength from the Orange Order. This was an exclusively Protestant organisation. Set up first in the 1790s, it revived in the 1880s to resist Home Rule. Its stated aim was to preserve the Protestant constitution of the United Kingdom and its Protestant ruler.

Although the Orange Order had a few branches in the south, its main strength was in Ulster. In each town and village the Orange Hall was the local meeting place, where rich and poor mingled. The Order organised regular marches and demonstrations to commemorate Protestant victories, such as that by the Protestant King William of Orange over the Catholic King James at the Battle of the Boyne in 1691. The purpose of these marches was to demonstrate that Protestants were the dominant faction in Ulster.

The Unionist Party had close links with the Orange Order. Its leaders were usually active Orangemen and the Order was entitled to a place on the Ulster Unionist Council. In elections the Order played an important part in getting Protestant voters out to support Unionist candidates.

Q U E S T I O N S

1 Explain what is meant by a 'unionist'.

2 Give three reasons why a person might have been a unionist in 1910.

3 Who were the 'Southern unionists'? Where did their influence lie?

4 Who were the 'Ulster unionists'?

5 Describe the Ulster economy in 1910. How did economic conditions in Ulster differ from economic conditions elsewhere in Ireland? How did this influence the political views of Ulster unionists?

6 Write a paragraph each about the Unionist Party and the Orange Order.

UNION OR SELF-GOVERNMENT? THE NATIONALIST VIEW

WHO WERE THE NATIONALISTS?

Nationalists were people who felt Ireland would be better off if it left the United Kingdom. As with the unionists, there were three main reasons why a person might be a nationalist.

● Ethnic identity

Many nationalists in the early 1900s believed that they were part of the Gaelic or Celtic race that lived in Ireland before the English conquered it. This was a myth. Today we realise that the Irish are a mixture of the races, Gaelic, Norman, English, Scots, etc, which have settled here over the centuries. But at that time a lot of people firmly believed in this racial identity. It made them feel they were **Irish**, **not British** and they felt Ireland would be a better place if Irish people, not British people, were in charge.

● Religion

Most nationalists were Catholics, who made up over 75 per cent of the population (see page 4). They did not feel comfortable in the predominantly Protestant United Kingdom with its established Protestant Churches and Protestant monarch. They believed that it discriminated against them in jobs and on issues like education. If Ireland had its own parliament, Catholics would be in a majority and could run things to suit themselves.

● Economic and social conditions

Outside of east Ulster, the Irish economy had declined since the Union. In 1900 there were fewer industrial jobs than in 1800, and throughout the 19th century, Ireland had suffered famine, poverty and emigration. At a time when the population of other countries was expanding, the population of Ireland had fallen from over 8 million in 1841 to 4.3 million by 1911 (Table B). Nationalists felt they could manage Irish economic and social affairs better than Britain had and wanted a chance to do so.

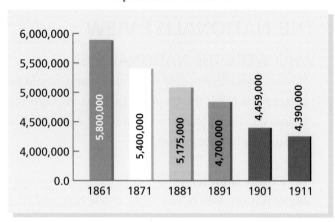

Population Decline

Year	Population
1861	5,800,000
1871	5,400,000
1881	5,175,000
1891	4,700,000
1901	4,459,000
1911	4,390,000

The decline of the Irish population from 1861 to 1911

WHAT DID NATIONALISTS WANT?

All nationalists agreed that Ireland should have **'self-government'**. That meant that Irish people, not British people, would make the important decisions about law, taxation, police, education and the economy, all of which affected the lives of people in Ireland:

- But how should self government be won?
- And afterwards, should the British continue to have any influence in Ireland?

These questions divided nationalists into **moderates** and **extremists**.

MODERATE NATIONALISTS: HOME RULERS

The great majority of nationalists in the early 1900s were moderates. They wanted to win self-government peacefully by persuading the British to agree to it. To achieve that they elected MPs who formed the **Nationalist Party**. Their aim was to persuade the British to let Ireland look after local matters like education, health or roads, while Britain still controlled international issues like trade or war. This was called **Home Rule**, and the Nationalist Party was often called the 'Home Rule Party'.

In the 1880s, under the leadership of Charles Stewart Parnell, the Home Rulers made great progress. But when he was involved in a divorce scandal, the party split and declined into squabbling factions. At the same time, the unionists through their friends in the House of Lords were able to block any proposal for Home Rule. Therefore, in the early 1900s Home Rule still seemed like a distant dream.

EXTREME NATIONALISTS: REPUBLICANS AND THE IRB

Home Rule was not enough for some nationalists. They wanted to cut all links between Britain and Ireland and set up an **Irish republic** that would be completely separate from Britain. Because of these aims they were known as **'republicans'** or **'separatists'**. They believed that peaceful persuasion would never make the British leave, so they planned to drive them out by force.

The main separatist organisation was a secret society, the **Irish Republican Brotherhood (IRB)**. It was led by a **Supreme Council** with a President, Secretary, Treasurer and delegates from regional branches. Men who joined it took a solemn oath to fight for an Irish republic, to keep the secrets of the Brotherhood and to obey the orders of its leaders.

IRB men wanted to lead a rebellion against British rule in Ireland, but they knew they had no hope of defeating the British army and police by themselves. They needed outside help, and that would only come from the enemies of Britain if Britain went to war. They summed up this view in the slogan 'England's difficulty (i.e. England's involvement in a war) is Ireland's opportunity'.

Unfortunately for the IRB's plans, Britain did not get involved in a major European war in the fifty years before 1914. So they had to wait. Meanwhile they tried to win more followers by **infiltrating** (secretly taking over) other nationalist organisations, such as the GAA and the Gaelic League. This policy was successful but it also weakened the IRB by drawing its followers into open nationalist organisations. By 1900 the IRB had shrunk to a small group of plotters who seemed to be going nowhere.

QUESTIONS

1 What was a nationalist?

2 Give three reasons why a person might be a nationalist.

3 Explain what is meant by 'self-government for Ireland'.

4 What two questions divided nationalists?

5 Write a paragraph about moderate nationalists, explaining what they wanted, how they planned to get it, and why, in the early 1900s, they seemed unlikely to achieve their aims.

6 Explain what is meant by the words 'republican' and 'separatist'.

7 Write a paragraph about extreme nationalists, explaining what they wanted, how they planned to get it, and why, in the early 1900s, they seemed unlikely to achieve their aims.

In the early 20th century, nationalists tried to encourage an interest in Irish independence by publishing colourful and highly romantic pictures of the bravery and suffering of earlier patriots. This one shows an episode during the 1798 Rebellion

Courtesy: Allen Library

1.4

CULTURAL NATIONALISM AND THE EMERGENCE OF NEW MOVEMENTS

IDEAS ABOUT NATIONALISM

In the 1890s and early 1900s, many young nationalists grew disillusioned with politics. Home Rulers were always bickering and the IRB had almost vanished. Instead they became involved in a number of new movements that were concerned with Irish identity, Irish race and Irish culture. They tried to answer questions like:

- What makes a person Irish?
- What makes Irish people different from English people?
- What entitles the Irish to demand self-government?

THE IMPORTANCE OF LANGUAGE

Around 1900 all across Europe, nationalism was growing. Nations which had long been ruled by outsiders were demanding the right to rule themselves. The Poles wanted freedom from the Russians; the Czechs wanted independence from the Austrians. In every case these people spoke a different language from their rulers. That, they claimed, was what made them different and entitled them to self-government.

THE ANGLICISATION OF IRELAND

But Ireland's language was vanishing. The 1901 census showed that only 14 per cent of the population spoke Irish and the number was falling every year. This was caused by the **Anglicisation** (adopting English language and customs) in the 19th century.

As the Irish language disappeared, so did many of the customs, stories, music and traditions associated with it. These were the things that made the Irish most obviously different from the British. If they went, could the Irish still claim to be a separate nation with the right to self-government? There were many people in Britain and elsewhere who said no.

Nationalists were dismayed that Ireland was being Anglicised. They wanted to stop it and restore a distinctive Irish culture and language. This led to the development called '**cultural nationalism**'. It produced three important organisations, the GAA, the Gaelic League and Sinn Féin, which had a deep impact on Irish history and have survived into the 21st century.

THE GAELIC ATHLETIC ASSOCIATION (GAA)

When English-invented sports like cricket, soccer and rugby began to spread in Ireland in the 1880s, nationalists set up the Gaelic Athletic Association to protect and develop distinctively Irish sports. After a shaky start, the GAA became a very successful sporting organisation in the early 1900s.

From the start the IRB infiltrated the GAA. These fit young athletes, it believed, were just the kind of men it needed for its planned rebellion against British rule. Many GAA men, like Cathal Brugha, were later involved in the war against the British in 1919–21.

Douglas Hyde (1860–1949): Born in Co. Roscommon, the son of a Protestant clergyman, he learnt Irish from the local people and studied it in Trinity. Later he collected folk tales and poems and published collections of them, which influenced many people.

THE GAELIC LEAGUE

In 1893, when **Douglas Hyde** gave a talk in Dublin. Called *The Necessity of De-Anglicising the Irish People*, it aroused great interest. A short time later Hyde and **Eoin MacNeill** set up the Gaelic League. Its aim was to revive the Irish language, to develop a new literature in Irish and to foster Irish music, dance and customs.

Douglas Hyde was elected President of the League. A Protestant nationalist, he had many unionist friends and relatives, so he wanted a love of Irish to act as a bridge between nationalists and unionists. For many years he tried to keep the League from taking sides.

At first he was successful. The League spread around the country in the early 1900s and both unionists and nationalists joined it. But involvement in the League strengthened nationalists' belief in the need for self-government. They thought that British governments were indifferent to the language and only an Irish government, which controlled education, could stop Irish disappearing completely. This opinion alienated unionists and most of them left the League.

The IRB also infiltrated the Gaelic League. It won recruits among the members and in 1915 they were able to change the constitution of the League to make it support a republic. Hyde then resigned as President.

THE IMPACT OF THE GAELIC LEAGUE

The Gaelic League had a huge impact on Irish history:

- It helped to revive the IRB. Young men like **Bulmer Hobson** and **Seán MacDiarmada** were won over to extreme nationalism as a result of being in the Gaelic League. Between 1910 and 1912 Hobson and MacDiarmada took over the Supreme Council and built a more active movement (see page 26).
- In 1910 few nationalists were separatists. By 1918 the separatists were strong enough to defeat the Home Rule Party (see chapter 3.4). Many of the leaders of this new movement started as members of the Gaelic League. They included Éamon de Valera, Michael Collins, Cathal Brugha and many more.

PÁDRAIG PEARSE AND THE GAELIC LEAGUE

Pádraig Pearse is an example of this development. He joined the Gaelic League at sixteen and learnt to speak and write Irish. An emotional man, he tended to adopt a cause with great intensity, then, when it disappointed him, to move on to a new enthusiasm.

Pearse's first enthusiasm was for the Gaelic League and the revival of Irish. Although trained as a lawyer, he abandoned the law to devote his time to teaching and writing Irish. In 1903 he became editor of the League's newspaper, *An Claidheamh Soluis*.

Pearse worked very hard to make it a good newspaper, publishing news items as well as stories and poems in Irish. He believed that a good paper would convince Irish people to learn Irish. But while many were interested in Irish, few shared Pearse's all-consuming enthusiasm for it. They were not willing to put in the hard work needed to learn much more than *cúpla focail*.

The Gaelic League encouraged Irish music and dance as well as trying to revive the Irish language

Pádraig Pearse (1879–1916): Born in Dublin, the son of an English stonemason. He trained as a lawyer, but worked as a journalist and school master.

PEARSE AND ST ENDA'S

Disappointed, Pearse then turned his attention to the education system. He criticised its limited curriculum, frequent examinations and often fierce corporal punishment. He called it a 'murder machine' which was killing the spirit of young Irish people. In its place he proposed schools based on his very idealised version of education in ancient Gaelic Ireland.

To turn his dream into reality, he set up his own school, **St Enda's**, in 1908. In it, teaching would be mainly through Irish and the students would have freedom to express themselves and time to develop their talents. At first it was a success. His friends and family helped with the teaching and many Gaelic League enthusiasts sent their sons as pupils.

But Pearse was not satisfied. Excited by his success, he moved the school to a bigger house on the outskirts of Dublin. It was a serious mistake. Costs increased while the number of students fell because the school was further away. By 1912 Pearse was almost bankrupt and had to beg and borrow money to keep his dream alive.

PEARSE BECOMES A REPUBLICAN

Up to then, Pearse was a nationalist but only in a general way. He concentrated wholly on the restoration of Irish and paid little attention to arguments about Home Rule or republicanism. When it seemed likely that Ireland would finally get Home Rule in 1912, he supported it.

But in 1912–13 his plans for education failed. At the same time, the conflict between unionists and nationalists reached a crisis point (see chapter 3). These developments turned Pearse the language enthusiast into a republican separatist. In a speech he defined his aims as 'an Ireland not free merely but Gaelic as well; not Gaelic merely but free as well'. Here Pearse showed how the two issues, reviving Irish and winning complete independence for Ireland, had become linked.

He was not alone. This thinking, formed by the Gaelic League, became one of the founding ideas of the Irish state that was set up after 1922.

ARTHUR GRIFFITH

Cultural nationalism also produced a new political party, **Sinn Féin**. Its founder was **Arthur Griffith**. In 1898, he set up a small newspaper. That year was the centenary of the United Irishman Rebellion and in honour of that he called his paper *The United Irishman*.

The centenary aroused interest in republicism and Griffith published articles about Wolfe Tone, Robert Emmet, Thomas Davis and other early republicans which introduced their ideas to a new generation of nationalists. Griffith supported the cultural revival and publicised the activities of the GAA and the Gaelic League in his paper. He also encouraged a 'buy Irish' campaign which cultural nationalists supported.

GRIFFITH'S IDEAS

Griffith was a nationalist, but he disliked Home Rule because he felt it would leave Ireland too much under British control. He also felt the Home Rule Party had been corrupted by the long years it had spent in Westminster.

Arthur Griffith (1872–1922): Born in Dublin, he trained as a printer. In 1896 he went to South Africa, but returned in 1898. From then on he made his living as a journalist.

He would have preferred a republic but he knew that most Irish people did not agree with him. Republicanism meant war with Britain. It would cause great suffering and death and the Irish were unlikely to win. Most nationalists did not want that, preferring the peaceful path of negotiation and Home Rule. What Griffith had to find was a middle way between an inadequate Home Rule and violent republicanism.

He read about the experience of other countries and found an example of what he wanted in the peaceful way the Hungarians had won self-government within the Austrian empire in 1867. In 1904, in a book called *The Resurrection of Hungary*, he suggested that the Irish people should try to win independence by using the same tactics:

- Irish MPs would leave Westminster and return to Dublin. There they would join representatives from local councils to form a Council of Three Hundred.
- The Council would act as an Irish parliament, set up a government, civil service and courts and *peacefully* take over from the British government. The British would be able to do nothing because Irish people would refuse to accept their right to rule.
- Griffith understood that the British might agree to Irish independence more readily if some link remained between the two countries. He was also concerned about the unionists and was aware that they had a strong personal loyalty to the British monarch. For those reasons he proposed that (as in Austria-Hungary) there should be a **Dual Monarchy**, with the British king also being head of the Irish state, instead of a republic which he would have preferred.

GRIFFITH'S ECONOMIC IDEAS

Most nationalists ignored economic issues, but not Griffith. He pointed out that Irish industry had declined since 1800, leading to unemployment, emigration and a falling population. He said that the reason for this was the **free trade** between Britain and Ireland which came with the Union. Larger, more efficient British industries destroyed the smaller and less developed Irish ones. The main reason for wanting an Irish government, in

Griffith's view, was to be able to reverse this trend by **protecting** Irish industries from British competition.

Griffith's economic ideas were popular with small businessmen, but they were deeply flawed. Not all Irish industries in 1900 were small and inefficient. Some – Guinness, Jacobs, the Belfast shipyards and a few others – were among the best in the world. Their success depended on being able to sell their products freely to British and overseas markets. A protectionist policy, such as Griffith wanted, would have damaged them.

The damage would have been worst in Belfast. But Griffith, like most nationalists, knew little and cared less for that Irish city. He also shared the usual nationalist ignorance of the economic reasons why unionists were opposed to Irish self-government.

1905: THE START OF SINN FÉIN

Cultural nationalists were attracted by Griffith's ideas. In 1905, they came together in an organisation called **Sinn Féin**. The use of an Irish name, Sinn Féin (which translates as We Ourselves), shows the impact of the cultural revival. It also caught the mood of self-reliance and self-confidence which it had produced among young nationalists. Other clubs and societies joined Sinn Féin, and the IRB secretly backed it. Griffith renamed his paper, *Sinn Féin*, to spread the message. It was the first Irish political party to admit women as full members.

THE FAILURE OF SINN FÉIN

By 1908 Sinn Féin had 100 branches throughout the country. It won some seats in local councils. William T. Cosgrave held one in Dublin. But before Sinn Féin could build on this good beginning, Home Rule again began to be possible (see page 16). People who had supported Sinn Féin drifted back to the Home Rule Party. At the same time more active members of the IRB grew contemptuous of Griffith's opposition to violence. They set up their own paper, *Irish Freedom*, which took many of Griffith's readers away.

As a result Sinn Féin almost disappeared as a political party. But Griffith would not give up. Over the next few years he went on preaching his ideas to an apparently indifferent world. His persistence paid off. The Sinn Féin Party might be dead, but the name 'Sinn Féin' hung around.

People used it as a catch-all term to describe active Gaelic Leaguers, enthusiastic nationalists, even those suspected of being in the IRB. When the 1916 rising broke out no one knew who started it, so everyone called it the 'Sinn Féin rebellion' even though Griffith was in no way involved. That fact was to have enormous consequences for Griffith and his party.

Table C

The difference between Home Rule, Sinn Féin and the IRB		
What did Home Rule mean?	What did Dual Monarchy mean?	What did a republic mean?
British King as head of state	British King as head of state	Elected President as head of state
British parliament controlling most taxation; able to stop Irish laws it disliked.	British to have no say in Irish decisions.	British to have no say in Irish decisions.
British government to control foreign policy (i.e. overseas trade, war and peace).	Ireland in control of its own foreign policy.	Ireland in control of its own foreign policy.
How to get it?	How to get it?	How to get it?
Send MPs to Westminster to persuade the British to give Home Rule.	Keep MPs in Ireland and set up an Irish parliament and government to take over the the country.	Ignore politics completely: fight the British until they give complete independence.

OTHER NEW MOVEMENTS

In the years from 1900 to 1914 two other new movements made an impact in Ireland. One was socialism, the other feminism.

SOCIALISM

Socialists are people who believe that society is unfair because the rich have more than they need and the poor less. They want to **redistribute** the wealth of the rich to enable the poor to have decent health care, education and housing. Socialism appealed mainly to workers in industry who were usually badly paid and unable to provide these things for themselves.

Two men tried to develop socialism in Ireland – **James Connolly** and **James Larkin**. Connolly had come to Ireland in the 1890s but had little success. In 1903 he left for the United States. Larkin arrived in 1907 to organise a trade union among the dock workers of Belfast. He had some success, but was hampered by the divisions between nationalist and unionist workers which made it almost impossible to get them to co-operate.

THE 1913 LOCKOUT

Larkin then moved to Dublin where he set up the **Irish Transport and General Workers' Union (ITGWU)**. In 1910 Connolly returned from America to become the union's Belfast organiser. In 1913 they led a strike against the Dublin Tramway Company, which was controlled by William Martin Murphy. Murphy, who hated Larkin and all he stood for, united the other employers and persuaded them to lock out any workers who went on strike. This lasted through the winter of 1913/14 and ended in defeat for the workers.

During the strike, there was considerable violence from the police. To protect the workers, Larkin and Connolly formed the **Irish Citizen Army**. It had about 200 members, men and women. When Larkin left for America in 1914, Connolly took over the leadership of both the ITGWU and the Citizen Army. When war broke out in Europe he began to think about using it to start a socialist revolution in Ireland.

'VOTES FOR WOMEN'

In the early 1900s women became more active in politics. They took part in all the political movements of the day, from nationalism and unionism to Sinn Féin and the labour movement.

Women of all shades of political opinion were also demanding that women be given full citizenship rights. By the start of the 20th century they had won equality with men in education and they could vote in local elections, but they still could not vote for or become MPs. That meant they had no influence in parliament where the big decisions affecting women as well as men were made.

Courtesy: National Library of Ireland

Hanna Sheehy Skeffington (1877–1946)

In 1908, **Hanna Sheehy Skeffington**, a university graduate, helped to found the **Irish Women's Franchise League (IWFL)** to campaign for the right to vote. Like the suffragettes in Britain at the same time, they adopted a more violent and aggressive approach than their predecessors.

The issue of votes for women came to the fore after 1910, when it seemed likely that Ireland would get a Home Rule parliament. It would give Irish men a say in how their country was run; but what about Irish women? The leaders of the Home Rule Party refused to discuss the issue. They did not want to embarrass the British government, which was divided on the question of votes for women in the

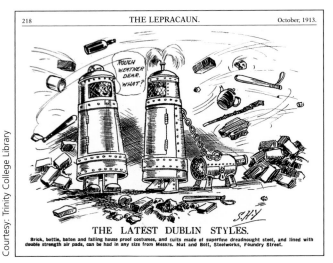

THE LATEST DUBLIN STYLES.

Brick, bottle, baton and falling house proof costumes, and suits made of superfine dreadnought steel, and lined with double strength air pads, can be had in any size from Messrs. Nut and Bolt, Steelworks, Foundry Street.

Courtesy: Trinity College Library

1 When was this cartoon published?

2 What was happening at the time to explain the 'latest styles' shown here?

3 Which side did *The Lepracaun* sympathise with? Explain your answer.

although these tactics won publicity, they did not win sympathisers and in 1914 the Home Rule Bill passed without women getting the right to vote.

CONSTANCE MARKIEVICZ

Constance Markievicz was another woman who became active in politics at this time. Born Constance Gore-Booth, her family were landlords in Sligo. She studied art in London and enjoyed the lavish social life of her class. In 1900 she married a Polish count and they settled in Dublin.

But in her forties, she tired of her life of leisure. She became interested in nationalism and joined Sinn Féin. In 1909 she helped Bulmer Hobson to found **Fianna Éireann**, a boy-scout type organisation for young nationalists. Many of its members fought in the 1916 rising. Some of the boys in the Fianna came from poor homes in Dublin and this drew her to socialism. In the 1913 Lockout she helped to run the soupkitchen which fed thousands of striking workers. She also joined the Irish Citizen Army, set up to protect workers against the police.

United Kingdom. Redmond, the Home Rule leader, told the women they must wait.

This provoked a reaction from a small group of women, mainly in the IWFL. They heckled the speakers at public meetings, smashed the windows in public buildings and were sent to jail. But

QUESTIONS

1 Why did the decline in the use of the Irish language worry Irish nationalists?

2 Explain what is meant by 'Anglicisation' and give two reasons why it happened in the 19th century.

3 Explain what is meant by 'cultural nationalism'. Name the two main cultural nationalist organisations and write a paragraph about each of them.

4 Write a short account of the life of Pádraig Pearse up to 1913.

5 Who founded the Sinn Féin party? Write a short account of his ideas on
(a) Home Rulers and separatists,
(b) how to win independence and what form it should take and
(c) how to manage the economy.

6 Trace the development of Sinn Féin from 1905 to 1912.

7 Explain what 'socialism' means and write a paragraph on the work of James Connolly and James Larkin.

8 What right did women want in the early 1900s? Explain why that was important and say what they did to get it.

The Home Rule Crisis 1910–1914

2.1
OPENING THE WAY FOR HOME RULE

THE HOME RULE PARTIES AND THEIR LEADERS

In 1910, the Home Rule and the Unionist Parties were the main political parties in Ireland. The main Home Rule Party had seventy MPs from every province in Ireland. Since 1900 its leader had been **John Redmond**. He was a skilful politician who enjoyed being in Westminster and negotiating with British leaders. Redmond's weakness was that he tended to forget what his voters in Ireland wanted.

Redmond's second in command was **John Dillon**. The two men made a good team. Dillon disliked London and distrusted the British system of government. He felt it corrupted Irish leaders and encouraged them to ignore the wishes of their voters. He preferred to stay in Ireland and he tried to keep Redmond in touch with Irish feelings.

After 1906 **Joseph Devlin** also emerged as a leading member of the party. Known as 'Wee Joe', he was the MP for West Belfast and was the main spokesman for Catholic nationalists in Ulster.

A few Home Rulers led by **William O'Brien** and **Timothy Healy** (see page 120) had fallen out with Redmond, but the quarrel was about personalities, not about policies. They too wanted Home Rule. In 1910 they held eleven seats, mostly in west Munster.

John Redmond (1856–1918): Born into a prosperous Catholic family, he became a Home Rule MP in 1881. When the Party split over the O'Shea divorce case, he sided with Parnell. In 1900, when the party reunited, he was chosen as leader.

All Home Rulers had only one aim: to persuade British leaders to give Ireland its own local parliament to deal with local Irish issues like transport, education and roads. Westminster would still look after international issues like trade or war.

THE UNIONIST PARTY

The Unionist Party also had only one aim – to prevent Home Rule and keep Ireland in the United Kingdom. In 1910, it chose **Edward Carson** as its leader. By then sixty years old, Carson turned out to be a good leader. Through rallies and speeches he united Irish unionists behind the cause of the Union while also gaining the sympathy of British political leaders.

Sir Edward Carson (1854–1935): A Dublin-born lawyer, he was MP for Trinity College from 1891 to 1918. From 1893 he worked as a barrister in London and between 1900 and 1905 he was a minister in the Conservative government.

Carson's second-in-command was a wealthy Belfast industrialist, **Sir James Craig**. A very energetic man, Craig worked behind the scenes to organise unionist opposition to Home Rule.

WHAT DID THE BRITISH THINK?

Whatever the Irish wanted, it was the 560 British MPs, representing British voters in the House of Commons, who would have the final say on Home Rule:

- Only by convincing a majority of them to agree to Home Rule could nationalists win their own parliament.

- Only by convincing a majority of them to keep the Union could the unionists feel safe.

So what did British people feel about the question of Home Rule for Ireland? Most of them were probably not interested. But among those who were, support for the unionists was probably stronger than support for the nationalists, especially in England.

BRITISH REASONS FOR OPPOSING HOME RULE

British voters had four main reasons for not wanting to give Ireland self-government:

- The most important was **the security of Britain**. Britain faced many possible enemies on the Continent. If it went to war with one of them, that enemy might send troops to Ireland and use it as **a back door into Britain**. The Act of Union was passed in 1800 because the French had attempted to invade Ireland two years before. British people feared that something similar might happen again if Ireland had its own government.

- Many British people opposed Home Rule in order to protect Irish Protestants. Ireland was 75 per cent Catholic and an Irish parliament would be overwhelmingly Catholic. British Protestants feared that Irish Catholics might persecute Irish Protestants.

- Some British people took a racist attitude to the Irish. They regarded them as inferior and doubted if they were capable of self-government.

- In 1910, Britain had the biggest empire in the world. British people feared that self-government for Ireland might encourage other conquered peoples, such as the Indians, to demand the right to rule themselves.

BRITISH SUPPORT FOR HOME RULE

Those British voters who supported Home Rule did so for three main reasons:

- British people were proud of their country and its history of prosperity and freedom. But when they boasted about these, foreigners pointed to Ireland. As part of the United Kingdom, it had suffered poverty, famine and emigration. To keep control of it, Britain had limited Irish people's civil rights in a way it never did to its own people. This embarrassed some British people. They felt it would be better to let the Irish rule themselves, since Britain seemed unable to do it justly and fairly.

- Since 1885, Home Rule MPs never won less than 80 of the 103 Irish seats in Westminster. That overwhelming vote in favour of self-government convinced some British people that they could not keep Ireland in the United Kingdom against the clear will of the majority.

- Since the 1870s, Irish MPs had been disrupting the business of the British parliament with their demands for Home Rule and various reforms for Ireland. Many British people wished they would just go away so that Britain would have time to deal with its own problems.

THE BRITISH PARTIES AND THE UNION

The different attitudes to Home Rule were reflected in the two big British political parties:

- Since 1886 the **Conservatives** had maintained close links with **Irish unionists** and had firmly supported the Union. Since they always had a majority in the House of Lords they were able to block Home Rule, even when they lost elections.

- Officially the **Liberals** were in favour of Home Rule. They had formed an alliance with the Home Rule Party and worked closely with them. But Liberal leaders knew Home Rule was not popular with British voters, so they played down their commitment to it. In the elections of 1900 and 1906 only Liberals with many Irish voters in their constituencies spoke out in favour of it.

- In 1900 a new party, the **Labour Party**, was set up. From the start it strongly supported Home Rule, but in 1910 it was still quite small.

THE LIBERAL VICTORY OF 1906

In the 1906 general election, the Liberals won a huge majority. They had promised social reforms like old age pensions and unemployment and sickness pay. Irish nationalists hoped they would bring in Home Rule but they were quickly disappointed. Liberal leaders told Redmond they did not intend wasting time on a Home Rule bill which the House of Lords would certainly block. There was nothing Redmond could do about this decision because the Liberals had more votes than all the other parties combined an overall majority and did not need his votes (see Table A).

WHO WERE THE LIBERAL LEADERS?

Four leaders of the Liberal party were especially concerned with Irish issues:

- The most important of them was **Herbert Asquith (1852–1928)** who became Prime Minister in 1908. He was not enthusiastic about Home Rule, though he was willing to consider it if he had to.

- Asquith appointed **Augustine Birrell (1850–1933)** as Chief Secretary for Ireland. He was more sympathetic to Home Rule than Asquith but he realised it was not yet achievable. Meanwhile he tried to satisfy Redmond by setting up the National University and Queen's University, by improving arrangements for land purchase and by trying to give more government jobs to Catholics.

- After Asquith, the most important Liberal was the 'Welsh wizard', **David Lloyd George (1864–1945)**. He was Chancellor of the Exchequer (Finance Minister) and his decisions about taxes and spending had a big impact on Ireland.

Table A

Results of the 1906 election				
Liberal Party	Conservative & Unionist Party	Labour Party	2 Home Rule Parties	Others
399	156	29	83	3

1 How many seats did the Liberal Party win in this election? How many did the other parties combined win?
2 Explain the words 'The Liberals had an overall majority' by referring to these figures. Why did that make it difficult for Redmond to get Home Rule?

Herbert Asquith

Augustine Birrell

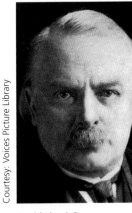

David Lloyd George

Winston Churchill

○ Also important was **Winston Churchill (1874–1965)**. His father, Randolph Churchill, had been a leading unionist. Elected as a Conservative MP, Churchill had quarrelled with the Conservatives in 1904 and joined the Liberals. He became Home Secretary in 1910.

1909–11: THE LIBERALS CLASH WITH THE LORDS

The Liberals brought in important social reforms such as pensions for poor people over seventy and unemployment insurance. They also became involved in a naval race with Germany, building huge and very expensive battleships, the dreadnoughts. These things cost money and in 1909 Lloyd George had to find £16 million to pay for them. To get it, he drew up a budget that increased taxes on the rich. Rich men were numerous in the Lords and as result they rejected his budget.

THE 1910 ELECTION GIVES REDMOND THE BALANCE OF POWER

To deal with this crisis, Asquith called a general election in January 1910. Voters throughout the United Kingdom were asked to approve Lloyd George's budget. The results were everything Redmond could have hoped for. Liberals and Conservatives were neck and neck (see Table B). If Asquith was to go on being Prime Minister he needed Redmond's votes, and Redmond could demand Home Rule in return.

1911: THE PARLIAMENT ACT ENDS THE LORDS' VETO

First the Lords' veto had to go. After another general election in December 1910, which changed little, this was achieved with the **Parliament Act**, passed in 1911:

○ **It reduced the Lords' veto to a delaying power**. Any bill which passed the Commons three times in three years would become law, even if the Lords continued to reject it.

Table B

		Liberal Party	Conservative Party	Unionist Party	Labour Party	2 Home Rule Parties
Results of the 1910 elections						
January	1910	275	252	21	40	82
December	1910	273	252	19	42	84

1 How many seats did the Liberals win in 1910? How did that compare with the number of seats won by the Conservatives and their Unionist allies?

2 How many Home Rule MPs were there?

3 Explain why these results changed the fortunes of the Home Rule Party.

● The Act also brought in payment for MPs and reduced the interval between elections from seven to five years.

1912: REDMOND'S REWARD – THE THIRD HOME RULE BILL

As the Parliament Act went through, Redmond loyally supported Asquith and the Liberal government. Then he claimed his reward: a Home Rule bill. With the Lords' veto gone, it seemed as if nothing could stop Ireland from getting its own parliament in 1914.

QUESTIONS

1 Write a short paragraph on the Irish Parliamentary (Home Rule) Party in 1910, describing its leaders, aims and allies.

2 Write a short paragraph about the Irish Unionist Party in 1910 describing its leaders, aims and allies.

3 Give reasons why some British voters (a) opposed Home Rule for Ireland and (b) supported it. If you were a British voter in 1910, which of those points would seem most convincing to you? Explain your choice.

4 Explain why both Irish political parties had to pay attention to the views of British voters.

5 Describe briefly the Liberal Party's attitude to Home Rule in 1906 and explain why that had changed by 1911.

WHO'S AFRAID?

This cartoon appeared in 1912.

A 1 What does the 'person' represent?
  2 Where is 'he' headed?
  3 Explain what the sheild represented and why 'he' needs it.
  4 Do you think the cartoonist approved of the shield? Support your opinion by referring to the cartoon.

B What did the Parliament Act say?

C How was the Parliament Act passed?

UNIONISTS OPPOSE THE HOME RULE BILL

1912: THE THIRD HOME RULE BILL

In April 1912, Asquith presented the third Home Rule Bill to parliament. It offered Ireland a very limited amount of self-government. Its main points were:

> The first (1886) and second (1893) Home Rule Bills were drawn up by W.E. Gladstone but never passed.

- Ireland was to have a parliament which would elect an Irish government.
- The parliament *'shall have power to make laws for the peace, order and good government of Ireland with the following limitations'*.
- The 'limitations' were a long list of things the Irish parliament **would not control**. They included the monarch, peace and war, the armed forces, relations with foreign governments, treason, trade outside Ireland, postal services, police (for the first six years at least), religion and taxation.
- Taxes would be still be decided in Westminster to which Ireland would still elect forty-two MPs. The money raised would then be given to Ireland in a lump sum to be spent according to the wishes of the Irish government.
- Laws passed by the Irish parliament could be blocked by the British Privy Council (a body of senior politicians and judges who advised the King).

THE PROSPECT OF HOME RULE

When the Bill was introduced everyone knew that the Commons would vote for it but that the Lords would vote against. However, under the terms of the Parliament Act, that would only delay it until 1914.

- Nationalists greeted this prospect with enthusiasm. At last, after forty years of struggle and persuasion, Britain would let Irish people run Irish affairs. For the time being they were willing to overlook the very limited amount of independence Home Rule would bring.

- But for unionists, the Home Rule Bill threatened disaster. Carson and Craig knew that, with the Lords' veto gone, they could not stop it in parliament. They had to organise their resistance outside parliament and they had two years to do it.

ULSTER'S SOLEMN LEAGUE AND COVENANT: SEPTEMBER 1912

Unionist resistance to Home Rule began as soon as the Parliament Act removed the Lords' veto. At first it took the form of mass demonstrations, held in Ulster and around Britain.

The most impressive of these was staged in September 1912. Before it, Unionist leaders drew up a document they called **Ulster's Solemn League and Covenant**. This title was a deliberate echo of the Bible's account of God's covenant (i.e. contract) with the Jewish people. It was meant to convey the message that Ulster Protestants too were God's chosen people.

The Covenant said that unionists opposed Home Rule because it would be:

> *'… disastrous to the material well-being of Ulster as well as of the whole of Ireland, subversive of our civil and religious freedom, destructive of our citizenship and perilous to the unity of the Empire.'*

And those who signed it pledged themselves to:

> *'stand by one another in defending … our cherished position of equal citizenship in the United Kingdom and in using all means which may be found necessary to defeat the present conspiracy to set up a Home Rule parliament in Ireland. And in the event of such a parliament being forced upon us we further solemnly … pledge ourselves to refuse to recognise its authority.'*

On Sunday 28 September 1912, Craig organised rallies throughout Ulster. At them about 470,000 men signed the Covenant. Some even signed it in their own blood. At the same time about 250,000 women signed a separate Covenant, expressing much the same views.

THE ULSTER VOLUNTEER FORCE

The Covenant contained the words *'using **all means** that may become necessary to defeat the present conspiracy'*. It became clear what those words meant when well-drilled and armed men appeared at unionist demonstrations. They were the **Ulster Volunteers**.

In 1911, some Orangemen in Tyrone had begun to drill and arm in secret. Soon after, an old law was unearthed. It allowed Justices of the Peace to permit men to drill 'for the purpose of maintaining the constitution of the United Kingdom as now established'. Since many Justices were unionists, they were happy to give permission. After that Volunteer units sprang up all over Ulster.

For Carson and Craig this development was a mixed blessing. The Volunteers could be used to put pressure on the government but there was a danger that some of them might engage in violence and damage the cause. To bring them under control, the Ulster Unionist Council united the separate Volunteers into one body, the **Ulster Volunteer Force** (**UVF**) early in 1913.

They appointed a retired general, Sir George Richardson, as their commander. Many former British soldiers joined the UVF and began to drill the Volunteers. Wealthy sympathisers set up a secret arms fund which contained £1 million by 1914. Leaders went to Germany to buy arms and meanwhile Volunteers drilled with wooden guns. This allowed Redmond and Asquith to underestimate the threat posed by the UVF.

Carson hoped that the mass demonstrations and the UVF would convince people in Britain that Irish Protestants were vehemently opposed to Home Rule. That might force the Liberals to drop it.

TRUE TO LIFE.

Is the cartoon pro- or anti-Unionist? Explain your choice

THE CONSERVATIVES SUPPORT THE UNIONISTS

British Conservatives enthusiastically supported the unionists, even when they talked of using force. This was strange because traditionally Conservatives prided themselves on upholding the law. But in 1912–14 things were different. The Conservative Party was in disarray. It had lost three general elections and its stronghold, the House of Lords, was weakened. The Party was deeply divided and one of the few issues on which the members could agree was the need to stop Home Rule.

In 1911, the Conservatives got a new leader, **Andrew Bonar Law**. His family came originally from Ulster and that made him more committed to the unionist cause than previous Conservative leaders.

Andrew Bonar Law (1858–1921)
Leader of the Conservative party

In 1912, at a rally of British unionists he proclaimed:

'if an attempt were made, without the clearly expressed will of the people of this country and as part of a corrupt parliamentary bargain, to deprive these men [Irish unionists] of their birthright, they would be justified in resisting by all means in their power, including force … [and] I can imagine no length of resistance to which Ulster can go in which I would not be prepared to support them.' (Robert Blake: *The Unknown Prime Minister*, London 1955, p. 130)

In this speech, Law set out two of the main reasons why British unionists opposed Home Rule in 1912:

- The first was their belief that the Home Rule Bill was part of a 'corrupt bargain' between Redmond and the Liberals. The only legitimate way to decide about Home Rule, they argued, was to let the British people vote on it in a referendum. They wanted a referendum because they believed a majority of British voters would back them.
- The second was that it would be unjust to expel the unionists from the United Kingdom, deprive them of their British citizenship and leave them at the mercy of Irish Catholics. Irish Protestants were, after all, the one section of the Irish people who had always remained loyal to Britain. This was the argument that particularly worried Liberal MPs.

All through 1912, 1913 and 1914, British and Irish unionists issued pamphlets and organised speeches and demonstrations throughout Britain, hammering away at these points. They had many influential supporters including senior army officers, wealthy businessmen and members of the House of Lords.

PARTITION AS A SOLUTION

Unionists hoped to win over enough voters in Britain to persuade the Liberals to give up Home Rule. If that failed Ulster unionists had a fallback position – partition. Ireland would be divided into two parts: Ulster would remain within the United Kingdom while the rest of Ireland could have Home Rule:

- Partition appealed more to Craig than to Carson. A wealthy Belfast businessman, Craig believed that 890,000 Ulster unionists, with their thriving industry, would manage very well without the rest of Ireland.
- Carson, however, was a Dublin man. He did not want partition, which would leave 250,000 southern unionists at the mercy of a huge nationalist majority. But he was willing to talk about partition because he hoped that Redmond would give up Home Rule rather than agree to it.

IGNORING THE UNIONIST THREAT

Asquith and Birrell asked Redmond what to do about the unionist campaign. He advised them to leave the unionists alone and that was what they did. There were various reasons for this:

- Unionists seemed to be a small minority in Ireland as a whole. In 1912, they had only nineteen seats, compared with eighty-four held by Home Rulers. To Liberals and nationalists it seemed undemocratic that such a small minority could block the will of the majority.

- Like most nationalists, Redmond knew little about Ulster unionists. He under-estimated the intensity of their resistance to Home Rule and the strength of the UVF.

- Traditionally, unionists had always been law-abiding. Liberals and nationalists could not believe that they intended to use force. They thought Carson and Craig were bluffing and would accept Home Rule once parliament passed it.

- The RIC (police) had always watched nationalists, not unionists. As a result they had few informers in the unionist community and were not able to tell the government much about the growth of the UVF. So no one in London realised how strong it was.

- Asquith, whose favourite saying was 'wait and see', always preferred to put off problems, hoping they would go away. Birrell, who as Chief Secretary was supposed to be running Ireland, was often absent because his wife was dying. That meant the two men in charge of Ireland did nothing to stop the crisis until it was out of control.

Ulster's
Solemn League and Covenant.

Being convinced in our consciences that Home Rule would be disastrous to the material well-being of Ulster as well as of the whole of Ireland, subversive of our civil and religious freedom, destructive of our citizenship and perilous to the unity of the Empire, we, whose names are under-written, men of Ulster, loyal subjects of His Gracious Majesty King George V., humbly relying on the God whom our fathers in days of stress and trial confidently trusted, do hereby pledge ourselves in solemn Covenant throughout this our time of threatened calamity to stand by one another in defending for ourselves and our children our cherished position of equal citizenship in the United Kingdom and in using all means which may be found necessary to defeat the present conspiracy to set up a Home Rule Parliament in Ireland. ¶ And in the event of such a Parliament being forced upon us we further solemnly and mutually pledge ourselves to refuse to recognise its authority. ¶ In sure confidence that God will defend the right we hereto subscribe our names. ¶ And further, we individually declare that we have not already signed this Covenant.

The above was signed by me at_____
"Ulster Day," Saturday, 28th September, 1912.

1 List the reasons why unionists think Home Rule would be disastrous.
2 What do they pledge themselves to do?
3 What 'means' do they plan to use? What do you think they meant by that?
4 What will they do if Home Rule passes?
5 The Covenant calls the plan to set up an Irish parliament 'a conspiracy'. Why did the unionists think that?

CHRISTMAS NUMBER, 1912.]   THE LEPRACAUN.   95

The Traitor—Which?

Do you think the person who drew this cartoon would sympathise with the people who signed the Covenant? Explain your answer

QUESTIONS

1 List the main points of the third Home Rule Bill. Do you think it gave Ireland enough self-government? Explain your answer.

2 Read the words of the Ulster Covenant and write down the four reasons it gives for not wanting Home Rule.

3 Write a short paragraph about the Ulster Volunteer Force (UVF).

4 Explain the attitude of British conservatives to Irish unionists.

5 What did Carson and Craig hope to achieve by demonstrations and the threat of the UVF? Did they succeed?

6 Why did Asquith and Birrell not try to stop the UVF at an early stage?

PARTITION AND THE NATIONALIST RESPONSE

OPPOSITION TO PARTITION

Unionist resistance to Home Rule worried many British Liberals. As early as 1912 Lloyd George and Churchill had suggested that each county in Ulster be allowed to vote on whether it wanted Home Rule or would prefer to remain in the United Kingdom for a few more years. This idea was called **'county option'**. Redmond turned it down. Like most nationalists, he hated the idea of partition.

In a speech he said:

> 'Ireland for us is one entity. It is one land … Our ideal in this movement is a self-governing Ireland in the future when all her sons of all races and creeds within her shores will bring their tribute, great or small, to the great total of national enterprise, national statesmanship and national happiness.' (Quoted in P. Jalland, *The Liberals and Ireland*, London 1980, p. 108)

But by the autumn of 1913 the Liberals made it clear that he had to choose – either agree to partition or give up on the dream of Home Rule. As a result, secret talks between Carson and Redmond began late in 1913 and continued to the summer of 1914.

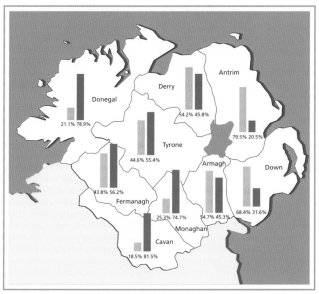

The distribution of Catholics and Protestants in the nine Ulster counties

The two sides soon accepted that the only way to avoid a civil war was to exclude 'Ulster' from Home Rule. But this raised three important questions:

- What exactly was meant by 'Ulster'?
- What was to happen to the excluded area?
- How long would the exclusion last?

WHAT WAS 'ULSTER'?

This was the most difficult issue. Historically Ulster contained nine counties (see map). The 1911 census showed that Ulster Protestants outnumbered Ulster Catholics by 891,000 to 691,000 and the map shows the two communities were not spread evenly over the nine counties:

- Four counties, **Antrim**, **Down**, **Armagh** and **Londonderry** had clear Protestant, unionist majorities.
- But parts of those counties (i.e. Derry city, south Armagh and south Down) had local nationalist majorities.
- Three counties, **Donegal, Cavan and Monaghan**, had very large Catholic, nationalist majorities.
- Two counties, **Tyrone and Fermanagh**, were more evenly divided, though Catholics were in a small majority.

So if 'Ulster' was to be left out of Home Rule, what did that mean? All nine counties? Six counties? Four counties? Or some other division?

By 1914, Redmond had more or less accepted that the four counties with a unionist majority should be left under London rule. But he was determined that the five counties with a nationalist majority must be under a Dublin government.

By then Carson also realised he would have to sacrifice the Protestants in Donegal, Monaghan and Cavan. But he was determined that the remaining six counties must be kept out of Home Rule.

Thus by mid-1914 both sides had agreed to partition, but neither would agree on the fate of Tyrone and Fermanagh.

WHAT WAS TO HAPPEN TO THE EXCLUDED AREA?

Redmond offered Carson 'Home Rule within Home Rule' (i.e. a separate Belfast Parliament under the overall control of the Dublin parliament). The unionists turned that down. They wanted to remain under the direct rule of the Westminster parliament. By 1914, this seemed the most likely solution.

HOW LONG WOULD THE EXCLUSION LAST?

Redmond offered to accept a transition period of six years. Carson rejected this; he wanted a permanent exclusion. By 1914, it seemed they would not put any time limit on the exclusion. This suited both leaders. Redmond could claim that it was a temporary arrangement while Carson could claim that it was permanent.

1913: NATIONALIST ANGER AT TALK OF PARTITION

Word about the secret talks soon leaked out. Up to then most nationalists had not taken unionist resistance seriously. They believed Carson and Craig were bluffing and mocked the UVF when at first it drilled with wooden guns. So it was a shock to hear that Redmond was talking about partition. There was a general feeling that something should be done to stop it, but no one was sure what to do. This played into the hands of the secret republican society, the IRB (see page 8).

THE NEW MEN IN THE IRB

At the start of the 20th century the IRB had almost disappeared, but in the following decade a small group of dedicated revolutionaries had been working to revive it. Two of them were **Bulmer Hobson** and **Seán MacDiarmada**. Inspired by the cultural revival, they at first supported Arthur Griffith's Sinn Féin but then grew disillusioned with his attitude to physical force.

In 1907 an old republican, **Tom Clarke**, returned to Ireland. To the younger men he was a hero because he had spent fifteen years in an English jail for setting off bombs in Britain. He was on the IRB Supreme Council and with his help they took it over in 1912. Then they began to recruit young men. Some who joined them were drawn to republicanism by the cultural revival, others by Redmond's acceptance of partition. One of their

Bulmer Hobson (1883–1969): Was born into a Quaker family in Co. Down. His involvement in the Gaelic League and GAA converted him to Republicanism.

Seán MacDiarmada (1884–1966): Leitrim born, MacDiarmada worked in Glasgow and Belfast where he became involved in the IRB. He worked for a time as an organiser for Sinn Féin and used this position to recruit young men into the Brotherhood.

Eoin MacNeill (1867–1945): Born in Co. Antrim, he joined the civil service but studied ancient Irish history in his spare time. This encouraged his love of Irish and he joined Douglas Hyde in setting up the Gaelic League in 1893. In 1909 he was appointed Professor of Ancient Irish History in UCD.

recruits was the schoolmaster Pádraig Pearse, who up to then had backed Redmond and Home Rule. He took the IRB oath in 1913.

The IRB's aim was an armed rebellion against British rule. But where were they to find the men and guns? The crisis over Home Rule gave them the answer.

1913: EOIN MACNEILL'S 'THE NORTH BEGAN'

In November 1913, an article appeared in the Gaelic League paper, *An Claidheamh Soluis*. Called 'The North Began', it was written by **Eoin MacNeill**, one of the founders of the Gaelic League. In it, MacNeill suggested that nationalists form their own Volunteers to put pressure on the British to keep their promise of Home Rule.

MacNeill's article was just what the IRB had been waiting for. A body of armed nationalists would provide them with the army they needed for a rebellion against British rule. Better still, the British could not stop them, since they had not stopped Carson and the UVF.

NOVEMBER 1913: SETTING UP THE IRISH VOLUNTEERS

Hobson approached MacNeill and suggested he call a meeting to discuss his idea. It was held in the Rotunda concert hall in Dublin on 25 November 1913. Thousands turned up and agreed to set up the **Irish National Volunteers**. On that first night alone over 3,000 men enrolled. They elected MacNeill as their commander and picked a Provisional Committee to run the movement. Unknown to MacNeill, who was not in the IRB, the majority of the Provisional Committee were IRB men.

FOUNDING CUMANN NA MBAN

A number of women had attended the Rotunda meeting. The Volunteers would not let them join, so in April 1914 they founded **Cumann na mBan**. Most members were wives and sisters of the Volunteers. They saw themselves as fundraisers, nurses and messengers, rather than as soldiers. This view did not suit the more militant feminists like Hanna Sheehy-Skeffington or Constance Markievicz who later became prominent in the movement.

MARCH 1914: THE CURRAGH MUTINY

By early 1914, Ireland was in crisis. Two large and growing private armies faced each other. The Home Rule Bill was due to pass its last stage in September, and if nothing was done, a civil war seemed likely.

The biggest threat was the UVF. By then it had 100,000 members. As yet they had few arms but there were rumours of plans to get more. Clearly it was time for Asquith to act. The obvious thing to do was to send the British army to disarm them. But would the army obey such an order? Some of its most senior officers were Irish unionists and many others were sympathetic to unionism.

An unwelcome answer came in March. The government decided to send some soldiers north to guard ammunition depots. Fearing that they were being sent to disarm the unionists, fifty-eight officers at the Curragh Camp offered to resign. The government hastily assured them that they would not be used against the UVF. In doing so Asquith lost his ability to use force to stop the unionist rebellion.

APRIL 1914: THE LARNE GUNRUNNING

The government's weakness became even clearer on the night of 24–25 April. The UVF had bought 25,000 rifles and three million rounds of ammunition in Germany. In a well-planned operation they landed the weapons at Larne, Bangor and Donaghadee and distributed them quickly and efficiently throughout Ulster.

The police did nothing to stop them. Either they were taken by surprise or, as nationalists suspected, they showed their unionist sympathies by not interfering. Influenced by Redmond who wanted no unionist martyrs, Asquith did not even try to punish the gun-runners.

JUNE 1914: REDMOND TAKES OVER THE IRISH NATIONAL VOLUNTEERS

MacNeill's Volunteers were also growing rapidly. By June they had about 180,000 members. This worried Redmond. As leader of the nationalist community, he could not allow a big rival organisation to emerge. He had to establish control over it.

In May he gave MacNeill an ultimatum. Either he would let Redmond nominate twenty-five Home Rulers to the Volunteer Provisional Committee or Redmond would set up a rival Volunteer movement. This demand caused a split in the Provisional Committee:

- MacNeill and Hobson argued that it was better to accept Redmond's demands than to split the movement.
- MacDiarmada and other IRB men disagreed. They saw any deal with Home Rulers as betraying the republican ideal.

When a vote was taken, they lost and Redmond's demands were accepted.

This dispute caused a rift between Hobson and the more extreme IRB men, especially Clarke and MacDiarmada. They forced Hobson to resign from the Supreme Council and later, when they planned the Easter Rising, they did not tell him what they were up to.

26 JULY: THE HOWTH GUNRUNNING

Meanwhile the Irish Volunteers were also planning to import guns. They had collected £1,500, and purchased 1,500 rifles and ammunition in Germany. Erskine Childers carried them to Ireland in his yacht, the *Asgard*. Some guns were transferred to another boat and landed quietly in Wicklow.

As a publicity stunt, Hobson arranged for the rest of the guns to land at Howth. Waiting British soldiers tried to seize them but failed. As the soldiers marched, empty-handed, back to Dublin, a crowd jeered at them. They opened fire, killing three people and wounding thirty-eight. The difference between this and the way the authorities handled the Larne gun-running increased nationalist resentment.

21–24 JULY: THE BUCKINGHAM PALACE CONFERENCE

Meanwhile the search for a compromise between unionists and nationalists continued. By now it was growing urgent, as Home Rule was due to become law in September. A worried King George V offered his residence, Buckingham Palace, as the site for an all-party conference.

It met on 21 July 1914. Asquith, Lloyd George, Redmond and Dillon faced Bonar Law, Lord Lansdowne, Carson and Craig. The Speaker (chairman) of the Commons presided. By the second day Asquith knew that no solution was going to emerge. He wrote to a friend:

> 'We sat again this morning for an hour and a half, discussing maps and figures, and always getting back to that most damnable creation of the perverted ingenuity of man – the County of Tyrone. The extraordinary feature of the discussion was the complete agreement (in principle) of Redmond and Carson. Each said 'I must have the whole of Tyrone or die; but I quite understand why you say the same!' The Speaker, who incarnates bluff English sense, of course cut in 'When each of two people say they must have the whole, why not cut it in half?' They wd. neither of them look at such a suggestion.

L G and I worked hard to get rid of the county areas altogether and to proceed on Poor Law Unions wh. afford a good basis of give and take. But again both Irish lots would have none of it. Nothing could have been more amicable in tone or more fruitless in result . . .

I have rarely felt more hopeless in any practical affair; an impasse with unspeakable consequences, upon a matter which to English eyes seems inconceivably small and to Irish eyes immeasurably big. Isn't it a real tragedy?'
(R. Jenkins: *Asquith*, Fontana 1967, pp. 358–9)

Courtesy: National Library of Ireland

Irish Volunteers on parade in Dublin.
Note the odd mixture of dress

WAR!

The Buckingham Palace Conference ended in failure on 24 July 1914. At that moment in the Balkans Austria-Hungary was about to invade Serbia. Like a flash fire, war spread across Europe, involving one country after another. German troops invaded Belgium after which Britain declared war on Germany on 3 August. The start of this much greater crisis brought the smaller crisis in Ireland to an abrupt halt.

QUESTIONS

1 What is meant by partition? Explain why partition seemed like a good solution to the crisis over Home Rule.

2 The secret talks between Carson and Redmond about partition turned on three questions. List them and in each case, explain what the leaders said about it.

3 How did most nationalists feel about (a) the unionist response to Home Rule and (b) the idea of partition?

4 Write a short paragraph on the IRB up to 1913 (include information from page 9). Why did the IRB see the crisis over Home Rule as a golden opportunity?

5 Describe the foundation of the Irish National Volunteers and Cumann na mBan.

6 Write a brief account of the 'Curragh Mutiny' and the 'Larne gunrunning'. What do these two incidents tell us about the attitudes of British officials to the unionist campaign?

7 Describe the Howth gun-running. What lessons might nationalists have drawn from that event?

8 Why and how did Redmond take over the Irish National Volunteers? What effect did that event have on the IRB?

9 Write a short account of the Buckingham Palace Conference. Read Asquith's letter. What, according to him, was the main problem? What does this letter tell us about Asquith's attitude to the crisis?

Higher Level

1 Describe the events that led to the introduction of the third Home Rule Bill in 1912 and discuss unionist reaction to it up to 1914.

2 Who were the Ulster Unionists, why did they oppose Home Rule for Ireland and how did they organise opposition to it between 1910 and 1914?

3 How successful was John Redmond as the leader of the Home Rule Party between 1900 and 1914?

Ordinary Level

"THE IRRECONCILABLE."

A 1 This cartoon appeared in October 1912. What does the cross little boy represent?
2 What does his mother want him to do?
3 Name the political party that spoke for people like him in 1912.

B Write a paragraph on the following:
1 The Ulsters Volunteers.
2 The Irish National Volunteers.

C Answer this question: How did the unionists under Carson resist Home Rule between 1912 and 1914?

③ Ireland 1914–1918: Crisis and Change

3.1

IRELAND AND THE FIRST WORLD WAR: 1914–1918

THE FIRST WORLD WAR BEGINS

On 3 August 1914, the German army entered Belgium, a small neutral country. All big countries had promised to respect Belgian neutrality, so Britain at once demanded that the Germans withdraw. When they refused, Britain declared war.

At first everyone assumed that this war, like all recent European wars, would last only a few months. The fighting would be 'over by Christmas' and then everything would return to normal. This belief influenced the actions of Carson and Redmond in August and September 1914.

CARSON AND THE WAR

In Ireland, the war brought the conflict over Home Rule to an abrupt halt. Carson reluctantly agreed to let the Home Rule Bill pass on 18 September, but only on condition that Home Rule would not begin until the war ended and the question of Ulster had been settled. He then called on the Ulster Volunteers to join the British army and defend the British Empire.

THE REASONS FOR REDMOND'S WOODENBRIDGE SPEECH

When the war started, Redmond announced that the Irish Volunteers would defend Ireland from a German attack. But after the Home Rule Bill passed, he went further. In a speech at Woodenbridge, Co. Wicklow, he called on nationalist Volunteers to resist German aggression by joining the British army.

Like most nationalists at the time, Redmond was genuinely outraged by the German attack on a small, defenceless and Catholic nation. But he had other reasons for making this speech:

- One was to prove to British unionists that Irish nationalists would stand with Britain against its Continental enemies. Fear that they might not was one reason many British people had opposed Home Rule. By calling on the Volunteers to join the war against Germany, Redmond was trying to show that this fear was unjustified.
- Redmond also assumed that in a few months he would be back again negotiating with Asquith

BROTHERS IN ARMS!

This cartoon appeared in August 1914. Explain in your own words what the cartoonist was saying.

and Carson about the fate of Tyrone and Fermanagh. Carson had shown his loyalty to the British Empire by urging the UVF to fight. Redmond knew that if he did not do the same, British politicians would be very unsympathetic to him when the talks resumed.

IRISHMEN GO TO WAR

In 1914, both nationalists and unionists supported the war. They were shocked by German behaviour in Belgium and saw Germany as an aggressor and a threat to international peace.

Unionists were eager to show their loyalty to the British Empire. Many rushed to join up and in all 30,000 Ulster Volunteers served during the war. The War Office, which was strongly unionist in sympathy, formed the 36th 'Ulster' Division to allow them to serve together. It was led by UVF officers and allowed to use Ulster unionist emblems.

In 1914, most nationalists sympathised with Belgium, a small Catholic country, and thought that Britain was right to defend it. Only MacNeill and the more extreme members of the Volunteers objected to Redmond's policy. That split the

Volunteers, but only about 7 per cent of them stayed with the extremists. The rest, who called themselves the National Volunteers, followed Redmond.

About 32,000 National Volunteers joined the British army. But when Redmond asked the War Office to form them into an 'Irish brigade' comparable to the 'Ulster' division, it refused. Most nationalists joined the 10th and 16th Divisions, but not many of their officers were Catholic or nationalist and they were not allowed to use nationalist emblems.

All three divisions suffered huge casualties. The 36th was almost destroyed at the Battle of the Somme in 1916, leaving a deep memory of loss in many unionist areas. The 10th suffered badly at Gallipoli in 1915 and the 16th in several battles in France in 1916 and 1917.

> One nationalist who joined the British army was **Thomas Kettle**. A former Home Rule MP and founding member of the Volunteers, he was in Belgium, buying arms for them when the Germans invaded and was horrified by their brutality. That convinced him that the English were fighting for a just cause. When his more extreme nationalist friends criticised him, he retorted that when England supported justice, he was not going to give up justice to annoy England. Kettle was killed in France in 1916. Some months before, his brother-in-law, Francis Sheehy-Skeffington was murdered by a British army officer during the Easter rising. In a poem to his daughter, Kettle wrote that he died *'not for flag, nor king nor emperor but for a dream born in a herdsman's hut and for the secret scripture of the poor'*.

RECRUITING MEN INTO THE ARMY

Enthusiasm for the war was greatest in the first year. Men volunteered to fight for a variety of motives – idealism, a desire for experience and adventure, unemployment. Many went because Redmond and Carson convinced them that fighting in the war was the best way to serve the cause they believed in, whether nationalism or unionism.

Courtesy: National Library of Ireland

1 This picture is a recruiting poster for the British Army. Was it aimed at unionists or nationalists? Support your answer by referring to things you can see in the picture.

Courtesy: Allen Library

2 This picture is an anti-recruiting leaflet. Who do you think might have produced it?

3 Explain in your own words the point it is making.

4 Which of these two pictures is the better production? How do you account for that?

5 Which would be more likely to influence a nationalist at the start of 1916? Explain your choice.

As word of the slaughter in the trenches reached home, the enthusiasm for fighting declined in Ireland and in Britain. In 1915 the government introduced conscription for British men, but Redmond persuaded Asquith not to extend it to Ireland. He argued that only an Irish parliament could ask such a sacrifice from its young men.

Instead there was an intensive recruitment campaign. MPs from all parties toured the country, urging men to join up and fight 'for the freedom of small nations'. The government banned emigration from Ireland, so many men who might have left to get jobs joined the army instead.

Altogether about 206,000 Irishmen fought in the first World War and about 30,000 died. The majority of recruits came from Ulster and from the towns of Leinster and Munster. Young men from rural areas or the south and west were less likely to join up. But because there was no conscription, only about 10 per cent of Irishmen of a military age went to fight, compared with about 25 per cent from Britain.

THE IMPACT OF THE WAR ON THE FARMING COMMUNITY

War brought prosperity to Irish farmers, which lasted until 1920. The German U-boat blockade cut Britain off from other food sources, and the demand for Irish beef, butter, eggs, etc. soared. Prices went up and some farmers exploited their good fortune by selling poor quality produce at the highest prices.

The smallest farmers and the landless labourers did less well. The price of their food went up but the farmers who employed them were reluctant to raise their wages. The ban on emigration also increased the number of men looking for work and this pushed wages down further.

In Britain the war opened up new areas of work for women, but that did not happen in Ireland because of the surplus of men. But in the poorest areas the wives of soldiers gained from the 'separation allowance' which the army paid them. This provided a small but steady income to many women who had had no income before.

REDMOND IN DECLINE

In September 1914, John Redmond was at the peak of his career. When the Home Rule Bill passed, he had won the prize which eluded previous Home Rule leaders. But his triumph was short-lived. From that moment on, his power and influence began to decline. There were several reasons for this:

- The Home Rule Party had only one aim – Home Rule. Now it was won, but only on paper. There was still no parliament in Dublin. Redmond was not Prime Minister of Ireland and could not decide policy or reward his followers. As the years passed nationalists came to see the passing of the Home Rule Act as a hollow victory.

- There was still the question of Ulster. Many nationalists, especially those who lived in Ulster, were appalled by the prospect of partition. But Redmond seemed unable to stop it.

- Redmond also lost his influence in London. He had been unable to get an Irish Brigade, while Carson, so recently a rebel, could get an Ulster Division. Even when fighting for the empire, it seemed, some Irishmen were more equal than others.

CARSON IN A COALITION GOVERNMENT

The greatest blow to Redmond's power came in June 1915. By then the war had lasted almost a year and there was still no sign of victory. To improve the war effort, the British Liberal, Conservative and Labour parties decided to form a coalition government.

Both Carson and Redmond were invited to join the coalition. Carson accepted and became Attorney-General. Redmond refused. His party had always rejected the idea of getting involved in a British government and his decision was popular in Ireland. But it reduced his influence in Britain. When important decisions were made, he was on the outside while his unionist opponent sat at the Cabinet table.

REDMOND AND BIRRELL

Until 1916 the growing weakness of Redmond was hidden from view. The Chief Secretary, Augustine Birrell, a convinced Home Ruler, regarded Redmond as virtually the Irish Prime Minister. He consulted him frequently and took his advice on many issues.

One piece of advice Redmond gave Birrell related to the treatment of the Volunteers who opposed Redmond's support for the war. He said they were not important and should be left alone. Birrell took this advice, a decision which proved fatal to the careers and reputations of both men.

QUESTIONS

1 What did Carson advise the Ulster Volunteers to do when the war began? Explain why he took that decision.

2 What did Redmond advise the Irish Volunteers to do when the war began? Why did he change this advice a few weeks later? How many Volunteers agreed with him?

3 Write a short account of Irishmen's involvement in the first World War. Refer to their reasons for going, the regiments involved, the numbers who fought and died and some of the battles they were involved in.

4 Discuss the economic impact of the war on (a) rural Ireland, (b) towns and cities and (c) women's work.

5 'Redmond's influence in Britain began to decline when the war started.' Set out three reasons which support this statement. Why did he lose even more influence in 1915?

PLANNING A REBELLION: 1914–1916

REDMOND'S OPPONENTS

The only opposition to Redmond's pro-war policy came from a small number of extreme nationalists and socialists. They included the IRB, James Connolly's Irish Citizen Army, Arthur Griffith's Sinn Féin party and a small section of the nationalist Volunteers. The public tended to lump them all together under the general name of 'Sinn Féiners', even though most of them had no links to Griffith's party.

> **Why Sinn Féin?** By 1914 Arthur Griffith's Sinn Féin party had few followers but his skillful propaganda made the name familiar. People called any nationalist who wanted more than Home Rule a 'Sinn Féiner'.

THE 'SINN FÉIN' VOLUNTEERS

Redmond's Woodenbridge speech had split the Volunteers. A small minority (about 10,000 out of 180,000), led by Eoin MacNeill, rejected his call to join the British army. They called themselves the Irish Volunteers but everyone else called them the 'Sinn Féin Volunteers'.

Late in 1914 they organised themselves like an army, with battalions and companies, led by elected officers. There was also a **Headquarters Staff**, with MacNeill as Chief of Staff. Unknown to him, most men on the Headquarters Staff and many Volunteer officers around the country were also members of the IRB.

The Irish Volunteers managed to hold on to most of the guns that had been smuggled into Ireland before the war. From 1914 to 1916 they drilled and held parades, armed and in uniform. Their main activity was opposing recruitment into the British army. Redmond believed they were harmless and advised the Chief Secretary, Birrell, to leave them alone.

PÁDRAIG PEARSE AND THE VOLUNTEERS

One of them was Pádraig Pearse (see page 12). Up to 1912 he supported Redmond but Ulster resistance to Home Rule convinced him that violence was inevitable. He helped to found the Irish Volunteers in November 1913. When the Volunteers reorganised, he became Director of Military Organisation, a key position that gave him influence with Volunteers around the country. About this time Bulmer Hobson swore him in to the IRB.

THE FIRST WORLD WAR DIVIDES THE IRB

The war divided the leaders of the IRB:

- MacDiarmada and Clarke saw it as the golden opportunity for a rebellion against British rule. With the Volunteers and help from Germany, they thought it could succeed.
- Hobson disagreed. He pointed to the IRB constitution which said that 'the IRB shall await the decision of the Irish nation as expressed by a majority of the Irish people as to the fit hour for a war against England'. Clearly in 1914 'the majority of the Irish people' supported Britain in the war with Germany and had no desire for a revolution.

PLOTTING A REBELLION

Clarke and MacDiarmada ignored Hobson's views. They forced him off the IRB Supreme Council, then got it to set up a Military Committee to plan a rebellion. They later included Joseph Plunkett, Éamonn Ceannt, Thomas MacDonagh and Pádraig Pearse on the Committee. At first they were doubtful about Pearse because he had only recently become a republican but his passionate commitment to the cause won them over.

Their plan for a rebellion had two parts:
- They would get military help from Germany.
- IRB men who held key positions in MacNeill's Irish Volunteers would lead them into a rebellion, whatever MacNeill thought.

Roger Casement (1864–1916): From a unionist family, Casement worked for the British diplomatic service. First from the Congo, then in South America, he published reports about the gross mistreatment of the local people. This made him famous but also led him to reject imperialism. He resigned from the service in 1912 and joined the IRB to work for Irish independence.

CASEMENT'S MISSION TO GERMANY

First the plotters sent **Roger Casement** to Germany. He was to persuade the Germans to send troops and arms to Ireland and to raise an 'Irish Brigade' from among Irish prisoners of war.

Casement's mission was a failure. The Germans knew nothing about the IRB but they did know that many Irishmen were in the British army, fighting against Germany. When only a handful of Irish prisoners of war agreed to join Casement's brigade, their scepticism grew. They would not risk German troops or guns on a hopeless cause. All they would promise was a shipload of arms, most of which had been captured from the British.

Casement felt this was not enough to guarantee a successful rebellion. He decided to return to Ireland to try to stop one breaking out. The Germans agreed to send him on one of their submarines.

PLANS FOR A RISING

Meanwhile in Ireland the planning continued. The plotters were terrified of spies and obsessed with the need for secrecy, so they told as few people as possible what their plans were. Even the President of the IRB Supreme Council was kept in the dark. For historians, this poses a problem. Since they wrote very little down and since all of them were executed in 1916, it is not always easy to be sure what they were up to.

It seems they first planned a rising for the autumn of 1915. That did not come off because of a delay in getting German arms. Next they decided on 23 April – Easter Sunday – 1916. They told the Germans to send the ship with the arms to Tralee Bay between Friday 21 and Sunday 23 April.

The arrival of the arms would be the signal for the rising to begin:
- Volunteers from the south-west were to meet the ship and distribute the guns.
- In Dublin, Volunteers would seize and hold a number of 'strongholds' around the city.

But these 'strongholds' had little military or political importance. It looks as if their main aim was to put up a good fight. Previous nationalist rebellions ended in total disaster after a few hours. The plotters were desperate to show that Irish rebels could fight bravely and hold out for a reasonable length of time.

This reflects their romantic and unrealistic ideas about soldiering. From a military point of view their plans were hopeless. Occupying and holding buildings would rob the Volunteers of the flexibility that a small, ill-equipped force needed against a much more powerful and well-equipped enemy. Only by using hit and run guerrilla tactics (such as the IRA developed in 1919–21) could they have any hope of success.

WAS THE EASTER RISING A 'BLOOD SACRIFICE'?

This raises the question: did the men who planned the Easter rising really expect or want to win? Perhaps they just intended to sacrifice their lives, hoping in that way to awaken Irish people to the shame of letting Britain rule their beloved country?

This idea is referred to as **'blood sacrifice'**. It is often linked to the date they picked for their rebellion – Easter Sunday. According to Christians, on that day Christ rose from the dead, having been sacrificed on the cross on Good Friday to save the human race from damnation. Did the rebels believe they were sacrificing themselves for the salvation and resurrection of the Irish race?

PEARSE'S MILITARISM

The writings of several of the leaders seem to support this view. Pearse is the most famous of them. In several articles and poems he exalted the use of violence. In 1913 he wrote:

'I am glad that the Orangemen have armed, for it is a goodly thing to see arms in Irish hands … I should like to see any and every body of Irish citizens armed. We must accustom ourselves to the sight of arms, to the use of arms. We may make mistakes in the beginning and shoot the wrong people; but bloodshed is a cleansing and a sanctifying thing, and the nation which regards it as the final horror has lost its manhood. There are many things more horrible than bloodshed; and slavery is one of them.' (R.D. Edwards, *Patrick Pearse, the Triumph of Failure*, London 1977, p. 179)

In 1915, he wrote of the European war: *'It is good for the world that such things should be done. The old heart of the earth needed to be warmed by the red wine of the battlefields'* (P.H. Pearse, *Political Writings*, Dublin, p. 215). In a famous speech he gave in 1915 at the grave of the old Fenian, O'Donovan Rossa, he expressed clearly the idea that the death of patriots can revive the spirit of nations. *'Life springs from death, and from the graves of patriot men and women spring living nations.'*

And in some poems, especially in *The Mother* and *The Fool*, Pearse seemed to say that he was prepared to sacrifice his own life in pursuit of this ideal. Similar sentiments can be found in the writings of Joseph Plunkett, Thomas MacDonagh and James Connolly.

But Irishmen were not the only ones to use language like this in 1914. Extravagant praise of warfare and bloodshed could be heard in many countries. It shocks us in the 21st century because we look back at the millions who died in years that followed. But up to 1914 people only knew the peaceful 19th century that lay behind them. It was easy for them to think of war as something glamorous, romantic and detached from human suffering. Experience was to teach them otherwise.

But even if Pearse and one or two others were thinking of a blood sacrifice, more hard-headed conspirators like Clarke, MacDiarmada and others probably hoped to win. And the choice of Easter Sunday is easy to explain. What better time than the middle of a holiday to catch the enemy off its guard?

JAMES CONNOLLY AND THE IRISH CITIZEN ARMY JOIN THE PLOT

Early in 1916, the Military Committee's plans were threatened by the socialist leader James Connolly. A Marxist, Connolly wanted an international workers' revolution to overthrow the capitalist system. The British Empire, he believed, was the main supporter of capitalism. A good way to start a workers' revolution would be to attack that empire in Ireland.

Connolly was the leader of the Irish Citizen Army which had been set up during the big Dublin strike of 1913 to protect workers from police brutality. Once war started in 1914, he began to consider using it to attack British rule in Ireland, hoping to spark off the worldwide workers' revolution. But with only 200 members, the Irish Citizen Army was too small to act alone.

Connolly let the IRB know that he would join them if they started a rebellion but they did not tell him their plans. When 1915 passed without them doing anything, Connolly threatened to lead his men out to fight alone. This would have endangered the IRB's plans, so in January 1916 they took him into their confidence.

MACNEILL'S VIEWS ABOUT A RISING

The IRB plan for a rebellion depended on the Volunteers. But most Volunteers were not in the IRB. They gave their loyalty to their Chief of Staff, Eoin MacNeill and would only fight if he told them to.

MacNeill, however, disapproved of the idea of a rising. Irish people, he argued, did not want one. It would cause unnecessary suffering to innocent civilians and would have no hope of success. But MacNeill also warned that the Volunteers would fight if the British tried to disarm them, if they tried to impose conscription or if they went back on their promise of Home Rule after the war.

Most Volunteers, and some IRB men like Hobson, shared MacNeill's views. Redmond knew that and so did Birrell. This explains the extraordinary tolerance the British government showed towards the Irish Volunteers before 1916. To the fury of unionists, it allowed them to recruit men and to hold parades and mock battles without any interference from the police or the military.

THE FATE OF THE *AUD*

By February 1916, all the plans for a rising were in place. The conspirators then sent word to the Germans that they were ready. The arms ship, the *Aud*, left for Ireland on 9 April with 20,000 rifles and ten machine guns. Its orders were to arrive off Tralee between Friday 21 and Sunday 23 April. Then the conspirators changed their minds. They sent another message that the ship should only arrive on Sunday.

The *Aud* had no radio, so its captain never got this message. It reached Tralee Bay on Friday morning but there was no one there to meet it. It cruised around for some hours until it was captured by the British navy, which escorted it to Cork. As it entered the harbour, the captain ordered his men off the ship and sank it with its cargo of arms.

DECEIVING MACNEILL WITH THE 'CASTLE DOCUMENT'

The conspirators also had to persuade MacNeill to order the Volunteers to fight on Easter Sunday.

While he had made it clear that he opposed a rebellion, he also said that if the British tried to disarm the Volunteers, they would fight. This gave the conspirators the opening they needed.

On Wednesday, 19 April, a strange document appeared in the newspapers. Written on Dublin Castle notepaper, it contained a list of people, including leading Volunteers, who were to be rounded up by the authorities. Called the 'Castle Document', it was almost certainly forged by MacDiarmada and Plunkett, but at first MacNeill thought it was genuine. To resist the arrests he believed were coming, he ordered the Volunteers to rise on Easter Sunday.

THURSDAY, 20 APRIL: THE PLOT UNRAVELS

On Thursday evening MacNeill discovered he had been tricked. With Hobson, he went to St Enda's to confront Pearse, who admitted that the IRB had planned a rising. An angry MacNeill cancelled his previous order.

FRIDAY, 21 APRIL: A DISASTROUS DAY

On Friday morning Pearse, MacDiarmada and MacDonagh went to see MacNeill. They told him a German arms ship was coming. MacNeill realised that once it arrived, the British would arrest Volunteer leaders anyway and that the arms gave them a slightly better chance of success. He changed his mind and wrote a circular to Volunteers repeating his orders of Wednesday.

What no one in Dublin yet knew, of course, was that a few hours earlier the Royal Navy had captured the *Aud*. At about the same time, Roger Casement landed from a German submarine near Tralee. Almost at once, the police arrested him. When they realised who he was, they rushed him to London. But as the British authorities knew nothing of the conspiracy, they believed he had come back to lead a rising and that they had captured its leader.

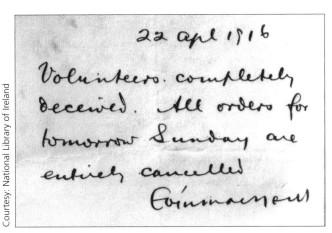

MacNeill's cancellation

SATURDAY, 22 APRIL: MACNEILL'S CANCELLATION

On Saturday rumours about these developments reached Dublin. By evening MacNeill knew the arms were gone and that a rising no longer had any hope of success. He issued orders cancelling the 'manoeuvres' planned for Sunday. Messengers were sent around the country and, as an added precaution, a notice was published in the *Sunday Independent*.

SUNDAY, 23 APRIL: TWO DECISIONS

On Sunday two important meetings were held in Dublin.

In the Castle, the head of the civil service, Sir Mathew Nathan and the Lord Lieutenant met with the military and police chiefs to consider what to do. They now had clear proof that the Volunteers were in contact with the Germans. The Lord Lieutenant wanted to round them up immediately. Nathan insisted that they must wait to consult Birrell, who was on holiday. He pointed out that there was no hurry. The German arms were gone, Casement was under arrest, and there was MacNeill's cancellation notice in the paper. Reluctantly the others agreed to wait a few days.

Meanwhile, in Connolly's headquarters at Liberty Hall, the conspirators met to consider the ruin of their plan. Rather than lose everything, they decided

to rally as many men as possible and go out to fight on Monday. After the confusion of the previous days they knew they had no hope of success. But they were determined to make a gesture, knowing that it could cost them their lives. If they intended a blood sacrifice, this is when it became obvious, not earlier.

QUESTIONS

1 List the groups who opposed Redmond's policy on the war.

2 Explain the phrase 'England's difficulty is Ireland's opportunity'. Which members of the IRB thought they should seize the opportunity and what did they do about it?

3 Name the men who planned the Easter rising. Explain what their plans were and discuss their strengths and weaknesses.

4 Write a paragraph about James Connolly and the Irish Citizen Army and explain how they became involved in the 1916 rising.

5 What did Eoin MacNeill consider was the purpose of the Volunteers and how did the plotters persuade him to order the Volunteers to fight?

6 Write a short paragraph on each of the following: (a) Eoin MacNeill and the aims of the Irish Volunteers; (b) The British government's attitude to the volunteers.

7 Write a paragraph on Roger Casement and his part in the Easter rising.

8 Do you think the conspirators planned the rising as a 'blood sacrifice'? Give reasons for your answer.

9 Make a timetable showing how the conspiracy fell apart between Wednesday 19 and Sunday 23 April.

THE EASTER RISING AND ITS AFTERMATH: 1916

MONDAY, 24 APRIL: THE RISING BEGINS

Easter Monday was fine and sunny. Dubliners were in a relaxed mood as they strolled about enjoying the Bank Holiday. Few paid any attention as hundreds of Volunteers and the men and women of the Citizen Army assembled at Liberty Hall. Since 1913 the sight of armed men marching around the city playing soldiers had become commonplace.

But this time the Volunteers were in earnest. They marched to various points around the city and at noon they took over several buildings. In O'Connell Street, Volunteers and the Citizen Army occupied the General Post Office (GPO), which they had chosen as their headquarters. Pearse, pale and tense, came to the street and read, to a puzzled and indifferent crowd, the proclamation of the Irish republic.

It was signed by all seven members of the IRB's Military Committee. They called themselves 'the Provisional Government of the Irish Republic' and had chosen Pearse to be 'President of the Republic'. That was not because he was their leader but because their choice was limited. Clarke and MacDiarmada, used to the secrecy of the IRB, did not want so prominent a position, Plunkett was dying of TB, and Connolly was unacceptable as a socialist.

In any case, Pearse, tall, handsome and respected for his work in the Gaelic League and St Enda's, made the ideal front-man. As President, he was also officially Commander in Chief of the Volunteers but in fact Connolly, who had once served in the British army, was in charge of military operations.

THE RISING OUTSIDE DUBLIN

The original plan was for a countrywide rising, but the confusion of the previous days meant little happened outside Dublin:

- In Wexford and in Galway, some Volunteers mobilised but were not involved in fighting.

- In Ashbourne, Co. Meath, Thomas Ashe seized arms and ammunition when he captured four police barracks. This was the most effective military action of the rising and his tactics foreshadowed the guerrilla tactics used after 1919.

- Elsewhere Volunteers, confused by a series of contradictory orders and unable to find out what was happening, waited for instructions that never came.

REBEL POSITIONS IN DUBLIN

In Dublin about 1,500 Volunteers and members of the Irish Citizen Army responded to the call. They seized strong positions around the city centre (see map). Two of these, the GPO and the Four Courts, were on the north of the Liffey, and four, Boland's Mills, Stephen's Green, Jacob's Factory and the South Dublin Union, were on the south.

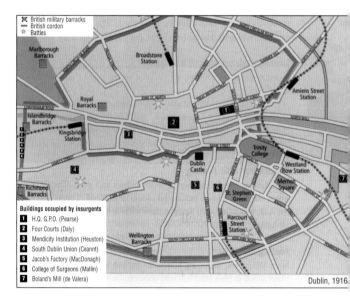

Dublin, 1916

A small group tried to take Dublin Castle. It had only a handful of policemen to defend it, but the attackers did not know that. When the police opened fire, the Volunteers retreated.

WOMEN IN THE RISING

In the confusion before the rising began, Cumann na mBan had been given no instructions but about ninety women offered their services to the various garrisons. Only de Valera in Boland's Mills refused to admit them. Mostly they acted as nurses, secretaries and couriers who carried messages from one post to another. But women and men were equal in the Citizen Army. In Stephen's Green **Countess Markievicz**, in a green tweed uniform, was second in command to Michael Mallin and, on the first day deliberately shot a policeman.

THE BRITISH REACTION

The rising took the British by surprise. That should not have happened. British Intelligence monitored communications between the American-Irish and the Germans, and had learnt that a rebellion was planned for Easter. But to maintain secrecy, they did not tell Dublin Castle where the information came from and the Castle authorities dismissed it as a mere rumour.

When fighting began, there were only about 1,500 armed police and 2,500 soldiers in Dublin. Reinforcements were rushed in from around the country. On Tuesday 25 April martial law was declared and **General Sir John Maxwell** was put in charge.

24–28 APRIL: THE SIEGE OF THE GPO

Maxwell ordered his troops to surround the city centre. This cut off the Volunteers south of the Liffey from those on the north. The British then concentrated most of their attack on the GPO, leaving the other Volunteer garrisons alone. A gunboat, the *Helga*, was brought into Dublin bay and it shelled O'Connell Street and the GPO.

FRIDAY, 28 APRIL: WITHDRAWAL FROM THE GPO

By Friday the GPO was on fire and half of O'Connell Street was in ruins. Inside the GPO, Connolly was badly wounded and it was clear the Volunteers had to get out. They broke through the walls and withdrew into nearby Moore Street.

SATURDAY, 29 APRIL: SURRENDER

Some wanted to surrender but Pearse refused until he saw a civilian, his wife and daughter killed in the crossfire. That seems to have brought home to him that they were endangering the lives of the people living in this densely crowded slum area. Reluctantly he agreed to talks.

Pearse surrenders. This picture has clearly been doctored. Elizabeth O'Farrell who was beside him has been airbrushed out, but you can still see her feet

Courtesy: National Library of Ireland

Elizabeth O'Farrell of Cumann na mBan was sent with a white flag to seek terms from the British. They insisted on unconditional surrender, to which Pearse reluctantly agreed. O'Farrell then carried the order to surrender to the other posts, some of which had seen no fighting. Reluctantly, they obeyed Pearse.

SUNDAY, 30 APRIL: PEACE RETURNS

By Sunday Dublin was almost quiet. 450 people, about 300 of them innocent civilians, were dead and 2,614 were wounded. Damage estimated at £2 million had been done to property and the centre of the city was a smoking ruin.

WHAT HAD HAPPENED IN DUBLIN?

When word of the rising in Dublin first reached them, most Irish people were bewildered. What was going on? In Dublin people gathered to watch the fighting and swap wild rumours. Outside Dublin, information was even scarcer. Trains stopped running and post could not be delivered. The offices of the *Irish Independent*, the country's biggest newspaper, were destroyed in the fighting. Only the unionist *Irish Times* was published during the week and military censorship prevented it from saying very much.

Abbey Street and O'Connell Street after the Rising

With no certain news, the country buzzed with rumours:

- It was a German invasion!
- It was a socialist revolution led by Larkin!
- It was the 'Sinn Féiners'.

But no one knew for certain. Even when the fighting ended, hard information remained scarce.

THE FIRST REACTIONS

It took a week or two for a clearer picture to emerge. Then the response varied:

- Unionists, of course, saw the rising as a treacherous attack on the empire in its hour of need.
- Among nationalists feelings were mixed. Some were angry at the death and destruction. As Volunteer prisoners were being marched through Dublin, people threw mud on them.
- Others were more ambivalent. They disliked the violence, but were proud that at least the rebels had held out for a week. Perhaps they had been foolish but they were also brave.

REDMOND AND DILLON ON THE RISING

The rising was a bitter blow to Redmond, Dillon and the Home Rule Party. It seemed to undo everything they had worked for. When it began, Redmond was in London. On the Tuesday of Easter week he rose in parliament to denounce the rising as a German plot.

But Dillon was in Dublin all through the rising and more in touch with nationalist feeling. On Sunday, as the last of the rebels surrendered, he wrote to Redmond, warning:

'You should urge strongly on the government the extreme unwisdom of a wholesale shooting of prisoners. The wisest course is to execute no one for the present ... So far the feeling of the population of Dublin is against the Sinn Féiners. But a reaction might very easily be created.' (F.S.L. Lyons: John Dillon, p. 373)

DEALING WITH THE REBELS

Redmond gave this message to Asquith, but it was not well received. Deeply involved in a dangerous war, the British saw the rising as a German-inspired 'stab in the back'. They were in no mood to consider Irish feelings. General Maxwell was given a free hand to do what he felt was necessary.

In Dublin, the British army rounded up hundreds of men and women. Around the country they launched intensive arms searches and arrested thousands of 'Sinn Féin sympathisers', many of whom knew nothing of the rising. In all about 3,000 people were arrested.

From the prisoners, the police picked out 'ringleaders' who were to be tried by courts-martial. Some were easy to identify, such as the seven men who signed the Proclamation or the commanders of garrisons like Thomas MacDonagh and Éamon de Valera, but a few were minor figures like Pearse's brother, Willie. In all 186 men and one woman were tried and 88 were sentenced to death.

MARKIEVICZ'S FATE

Constance Markievicz was one of them. Before the rising she had become notorious, partly because of her aristocratic background and title, partly from her habit of dressing like a man in a military uniform and carrying a gun. During Easter week, rumours gathered around her. The British officer whom Pearse surrendered to wanted to know where she was and would not believe Pearse when he said she was not in the GPO. In Stephen's Green, the man whom Constance Markievicz surrendered to spread the rumour that she kissed

Constance Markievicz (1868–1927): Constance Gore Booth was born in 1868 into a landlord family in Co. Sligo. She studied art in London where she met Count Casimir Markievicz whom she married in 1901. In 1903, they returned to live in Dublin where she became involved in Sinn Féin and other nationalist movements. In 1909, she helped to found Na Fianna, a boy-scout type movement affiliated to the IRB. She admired Connolly and supported the strikers during the 1913 lock-out. This led to her involvement in the Irish Citizen Army.

her gun before handing it over. She later denied this.

Like all the others, her court-martial was held in secret. W.E. Wylie, who acted as prosecutor, wrote years later: *'she curled up completely: "I am only a woman", she cried, "and you cannot shoot a woman. You must not shoot a woman". She never stopped wailing the whole time she was in the court room'* (Leon Ó Broin, *W.E. Wylie and the Irish revolution*, Dublin 1989, p. 27). But when the court-martial records were finally released in 2002, they show that what she actually said was: *'I went out to fight for Ireland's freedom and it doesn't matter what happens to me. I did what I thought was right and I stand by it.'* (Brian Barton, *From Behind Closed Doors*, Belfast 2002, p. 80)

The court-martial sentenced her to death, but also recommended mercy *'solely and only on account of her sex'*. Asquith had already ordered Maxwell not to execute her because it would be bad for Britain's image to shoot a woman. Her sentence was reduced to life imprisonment.

THE IMPACT OF THE EXECUTIONS

The other ringleaders were shot in batches of two or three. First to die on 3 May were Pearse, Clarke and MacDonagh. More executions followed on 4, 5, 8 and 9 May. Often the announcement of an execution was the first firm news people had but, since the trials were in secret, no one could judge whether those executed were guilty or innocent.

Tension rose as, day by day, more executions were announced. No one knew how many were to die or who would be next. People grew fearful for their loved ones and nationalist opinion began to swing round to support the rebels.

John Dillon realised what was happening. He rushed to London where he shocked the House of Commons by praising the bravery of the rebels. In a passionate speech he called on the government to stop the executions, warning: *'You are washing out our whole life's work in a sea of blood.'* (F.S.L. Lyons: *John Dillon*, p. 381)

On the day after Dillon spoke, Seán MacDiarmada and James Connolly were shot. Connolly was so badly wounded that he had to be tied to a chair. But they were the last to die. Convinced by Dillon, Asquith went to Dublin and ordered an end to the executions.

The rest of those sentenced to death were given life sentences. Besides Markievicz, they included de Valera and William T. Cosgrave. They probably escaped because they were still minor figures, almost unknown to the authorities. The rest of those arrested were either freed or interned without trial in Britain.

TRYING FOR HOME RULE AGAIN

Dillon and Redmond also persuaded Asquith that only immediate Home Rule would undo the damage done by the executions. Of course the unionists still opposed it, so Asquith sent his most able minister, David Lloyd George, to try once more to solve the problem left to one side when war began in 1914.

Lloyd George went from Redmond to Carson, arguing and persuading. After two months he announced they had made an agreement:

- He had persuaded Redmond to accept Home Rule for twenty-six counties and to leave six counties (including the disputed Tyrone and Fermanagh) to the unionists. Redmond only accepted this because Lloyd George assured him partition was **temporary**.
- He had persuaded Carson to agree publicly to give up Donegal, Cavan and Monaghan. But Carson also got a written promise from Lloyd George that the exclusion of the remaining six counties from Home Rule was to be **permanent**.

PARTITION DISCUSSED AGAIN

The deception was soon exposed by southern unionists who feared partition. Realising he had been tricked, Redmond renounced the deal. But the whole episode was a bad blow for the Home Rule Party. For the first time, Redmond had agreed to give up parts of Ulster where there was a nationalist majority. Nationalists from these areas were appalled. Some of them left the Home Rule Party and formed the **Irish Nation League** to campaign against partition.

THE HOME RULE PARTY UNDERMINED

By the end of 1916, the Home Rule Party was losing popularity fast. There were several reasons for this:

- Home Rule, although passed in 1914, had not come into force. That left Home Rulers with nothing to aim for.
- The rising won sympathy for more extreme nationalists and undermined support for moderates.
- Redmond's apparent acceptance of partition.

But as yet extreme nationalists had no alternative party. The Home Rule Party was safe as long as its opponents were unable to form a united party to challenge it.

QUESTIONS

1 Find and read a copy of the Proclamation the rebels issued in 1916. To whom is it addressed? Do you see anything interesting in those words?

2 List three of the aims they outlined and say how they hoped to win them.

3 Where did most of the fighting take place during Easter week 1916? Describe the main events of the week.

4 Describe the reactions of the British authorities during and after the rising. Do you think the executions were justified?

5 What did nationalists think of the rising at first and why did those views change over the months which followed?

6 Why did the issue of Home Rule come up again in the summer of 1916? Explain what happened and its impact on the Home Rule Party.

3.4

THE VICTORY OF SINN FÉIN: 1917–1918

DIFFICULTY OF ORGANISING OPPOSITION TO HOME RULE

In the second half of 1916, opposition to the Home Rule Party was growing. The most prominent organisations opposing it were:

- The **Irish Nation League**, which consisted mainly of Ulster nationalists, wanted a Home Rule parliament with more power and no partition.
- The **Irish National Aid Society** was more republican. Founded by Kathleen Clarke, whose husband and brother had been executed, it organised commemorations for the executed men and collected money to help families whose breadwinners were dead or in prison.

But these movements were weak. The idea of 'Sinn Féin' – meaning nationalists who supported the rebels or wanted more than the traditional Home Rule – existed but there was no Sinn Féin party for voters to support. Strangely enough it was Lloyd George who helped it to emerge.

DECEMBER 1916: LLOYD GEORGE FREES THE UNTRIED PRISONERS

At the end of 1916, Lloyd George became Prime Minister of Britain. By then the war with Germany had lasted over two years and victory seemed as far away as ever. British MPs blamed Asquith, so they replaced him with the more energetic Lloyd George. His top priority was to win the war and to do what he thought was necessary to persuade the Americans to join in. But Irish-Americans opposed that because of Britain's record in Ireland. To win them over, Lloyd George let the interned prisoners out for Christmas.

He also hoped this would win over Irish nationalists but he was wrong. The people he freed had spent nine months in prison camps that were known as 'universities of republicanism'. They returned home as committed republicans, determined to complete the unfinished business of the Easter Rising and to end British rule in Ireland.

ARTHUR GRIFFITH REBUILDS SINN FÉIN

One of those freed was Arthur Griffith. He was the accidental beneficiary of the Easter Rising. The IRB men who planned it had no time for his dual monarchist idea and his (relative) pacifism. They did not take him into their confidence and when the fighting began he was as surprised as everyone else. He went to the GPO to offer his services but Pearse sent him home to continue his work of propaganda. The British arrested him, but quickly realised that he had not been involved. He was not tried by court-martial but was kept in prison with the rest of the untried prisoners.

When Griffith came out of prison at the end of 1916 he found the world had changed dramatically. The name of 'Sinn Féin' was now indelibly connected to the Rising and all nationalists who rejected Home Rule were called 'Sinn Féiners' whatever party they belonged to.

Griffith set to work to rebuild the Sinn Féin party. He put forward his old programme again:
- Withdraw all MPs from Westminster.
- Set up a parliament in Ireland.
- Form an Irish government and run the country.

In 1917, Griffith added something new. When the United States entered the war in April, one of the war aims that President Woodrow Wilson stated was 'self-determination for small nations'. Griffith proposed that Sinn Féin would appeal to the post-war peace conference to recognise Ireland's right to self-determination.

Michael Collins (1890–1922): Born in Cork, Collins spent ten years in London, working as an accountant. He joined the IRB and returned to Dublin early in 1916 to avoid conscription and take part in the Rising. He fought in the GPO and afterwards was interned in Frongach prison camp (Wales).

MICHAEL COLLINS AND THE IRB

Another man Lloyd George freed was **Michael Collins**. After his release, the Irish National Aid Society employed him as an organiser. He did the job with great efficiency, but at the same time he was busy rebuilding the IRB. In 1917, after the death of Thomas Ashe on hunger strike, Collins became President of the IRB. It and the contacts he made at this time were to become the basis of the spy network he later used against the British.

CATHAL BRUGHA AND THE VOLUNTEERS

Collins worked closely with **Cathal Brugha**. He had been badly wounded during Easter week and as a result escaped imprisonment. When his health recovered late in 1916 he began to rebuild the Volunteers.

Like Collins, Brugha was a dedicated revolutionary, prepared to fight for a completely independent Irish republic. But unlike Collins, he blamed the IRB for the failure of the Rising, so he wanted no more secret societies. He concentrated on the Volunteers because he believed that only a completely open army could defeat the British.

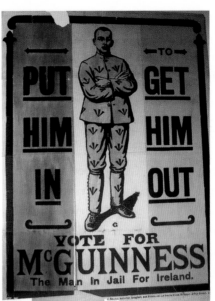

Sinn Féin's poster for the south Longford election

Courtesy: Allen Library

'SINN FÉIN' WINS A BY-ELECTION IN ROSCOMMON

The public called all these groups 'Sinn Féiners' but at first they were quite disunited. It was a by-election in February 1917 that first drew them together.

When the Home Rule MP for North Roscommon died, local people invited **Count Plunkett** to stand as a 'Sinn Féin' candidate. One of his sons, Joseph Plunkett, had been executed in 1916 and two more were still in prison, so he was clearly identified with the Rising.

Brugha, Griffith, the Volunteers, the IRB and the Irish Nation League all braved the winter snows to go to Roscommon to campaign for him. He won easily, then promised not to take his seat at Westminster. This was Griffith's policy, but Plunkett would not join Griffith's party. Instead he added to the confusion by starting his own party, which he called the Liberty League.

THE IMPORTANCE OF BY-ELECTIONS

The North Roscommon by-election was very important. Until then, republicans like Brugha and Collins despised political parties and politicians, even Griffith. The by-election showed them that united political action could win popular support for their cause. When another by-election occurred in South Longford, they nominated one of the men in prison as a candidate and won again.

But their victories also showed up the divisions among those who worked under the banner of 'Sinn Féin':

- They were divided on aims – did they want a republic, dual monarchy, or some form of Home Rule?
- They were divided on methods – would they resist British rule by force or by political means?
- And above all, they were divided on leadership – Griffith, Plunkett and several others had a good claim to lead the new movement.

EMERGING UNITY

In the matter of leadership, Griffith had the great advantage of the Sinn Féin name. When new clubs sprang up around the country after the by-elections, they always called themselves 'Sinn Féin' clubs, whether they followed his ideas or not. As a result, by the summer of 1917 the movement was uniting behind him. But then a more charismatic leader appeared on the scene.

THE EMERGENCE OF ÉAMON DE VALERA

In June, there was a by-election in East Clare. Republicans nominated another prisoner, Éamon de Valera, as their candidate. Before the by-election was held, Lloyd George, still trying to please the Americans, set de Valera and the other life prisoners free. He returned to Ireland in time to be elected.

Éamon de Valera (1882–1975): Born in New York to an Irish mother and a Spanish father, de Valera was reared by his grandparents in Limerick. A bright student he got the chance to go to university and became a maths teacher. Membership of the Gaelic League drew him towards republicanism. He joined the Volunteers in 1913 and in the rising was given command of the garrison in Bolands Mills. Sentenced to death, his sentence was commuted to life imprisonment.

JUNE TO OCTOBER 1917: UNITING BEHIND DE VALERA

De Valera was a man the pro-rising groups could unite around. He had the status of being the senior surviving commandant from Easter week and in jail he had won respect for his leadership qualities. Once elected an MP, he began talks aimed at uniting the various factions.

Griffith was willing to step aside in favour of de Valera, so the question of leadership was easily solved. It was harder to get agreement on aims. Hard-line republicans like Brugha and Collins wanted nothing less than a republic. Moderates like Griffith were sure the British would never agree to that and wanted to keep the idea of a dual monarchy as a bargaining counter.

Finally, they all accepted a form of words which de Valera suggested:

'*Sinn Féin aims at securing the international recognition of Ireland as an independent Irish Republic. Having achieved that status, the Irish people may, by referendum, freely choose their own form of government.*' (Brian Farrell: *The Founding of Dáil Éireann*, Dublin 1969, p. 20)

OCTOBER 1917: FOUNDING THE 'SECOND' SINN FÉIN PARTY

The Sinn Féin Ard Fheis met in October 1917. From every county in Ireland 1,700 delegates turned up. Most of them were young, energetic and idealistic. They elected de Valera as President, Griffith as Vice-President and an Executive Committee that contained both men and women. They also adopted Griffith's policies of:

- Abstention from Westminster.
- Formation of an Irish government to resist British rule.
- An appeal to the peace conference as the means of achieving the republic.

Historians call this the 'second' Sinn Féin party to distinguish it from Griffith's original (or 'first') Sinn Féin. It was different from the first because it was led by de Valera, not Griffith, it aimed at a republic, not dual monarchy and it was much more successful in winning support.

The Home Rule Party used a green flag with a gold harp as the Irish flag. Sinn Féin preferred the green, white and orange tricolour. After they won independence, their flag became the flag of the new Irish State

LINKING THE VOLUNTEERS WITH SINN FÉIN

Sinn Féin also had a more ambivalent attitude towards violence. Knowing that most nationalists disliked violence, it did not say it would use force to achieve its aims. But from the start it had close ties with the Volunteers, who were an army and clearly intended to fight.

On the day after the Sinn Féin Ard Fheis, the Volunteers held their annual convention. They elected de Valera as President and chose a twenty-member Executive Committee. Six members, including Brugha, Collins and Mulcahy, were also on the Sinn Féin Executive. Thus the two movements, the political party and the army, formed a common front. Together, they were now able to take on Redmond's Home Rule Party.

THE IRISH CONVENTION, JULY 1917 – APRIL 1918

Meanwhile Lloyd George, still wooing American opinion, continued his conciliatory approach to Ireland. In July 1917 he set up an **Irish Convention**, chaired by Sir Horace Plunkett, the widely respected founder of the Irish co-operative movement. He invited all Irish parties to attend and try to work out a compromise between unionists and nationalists. He promised that Britain would accept anything the members agreed on.

The convention was doomed from the start. Sinn Féin and the trade unions refused to attend. The Ulster Unionists were present, but Carson would only consider the permanent exclusion of six Ulster counties, which he was offered in 1916. By then Redmond was a dying man. In a last desperate attempt to save his life's work, he tried to make a deal with the Southern unionists. But no one wanted it, and when Redmond died in March 1918 his successor, **John Dillon**, pulled the Home Rule Party out of the Convention.

1918: LLOYD GEORGE PROPOSES CONSCRIPTION

Conscription was introduced in Britain in 1915. Redmond had insisted that only an Irish parliament could force young Irishmen to fight, so it was not extended to Ireland. This was never popular in Britain, especially after the Easter Rising.

Early in 1918, following the Russian Revolution, Lenin took Russia out of the war. That freed a large part of the German army, which launched a fierce attack along the Western Front. To resist them, Britain desperately needed more men.

Against the advice of his Irish experts, Lloyd George decided to extend conscription to Ireland.

COMBINED RESISTANCE

The threat of conscription united all Irish nationalists:

- In the Commons, Dillon objected vehemently but Lloyd George ignored him. When the Conscription Bill passed, he led his party home to Ireland where he joined with Sinn Féin to resist it.
- The Volunteers announced that they would resist by force, and thousands of men flocked to join their ranks. By the autumn of 1918 they had about 100,000 members.
- Trade unions organised a one-day general strike in protest.
- Catholic bishops denounced conscription. They allowed signatures to a national pledge against it to be collected at church gates after Mass.

MAY 1918: THE 'GERMAN PLOT'

When the crisis was at its height the government suddenly arrested seventy-three prominent Sinn Féiners including de Valera, Griffith, Kathleen Clarke and Countess Markievicz. The British claimed they had discovered a 'German plot' to import arms for Sinn Féin but no one in Ireland believed them. To many people the arrests seemed to prove that the government feared Sinn Féin more than the Home Rulers. This increased support for Sinn Féin.

In the end, conscription was never imposed. In June 1918 the German offensive collapsed, so extra soldiers were not needed. And Lloyd George finally realised how impossible it would be to impose conscription on a hostile population.

THE IMPACT OF THE CONSCRIPTION CRISIS AND THE 'GERMAN PLOT'

The conscription crisis and the 'German plot' arrests had a profound effect on Ireland:

- They discredited the moderate nationalists of the Home Rule Party. They had argued that the best way to look after Ireland's interests was to take their seats in the Commons. Yet on this vital matter, the British government would not listen to them.

- That seemed to prove that Sinn Féin was right. They said that going to Westminster was a waste of time because the British paid no attention to Irish opinions.
- Within Sinn Féin the arrests left militant republicans like Collins, Brugha, Richard Mulcahy and Rory O'Connor in control. They were more committed to violence than to politics and from then on the Volunteers, with their militant aims, began to overshadow the political Sinn Féin.
- The Volunteers had threatened to resist conscription by force. Many nationalists believed that was why Lloyd George had dropped the idea. They drew the natural conclusion – as the British had shown over Carson and the UVF, the only thing they would listen to was the threat of force.

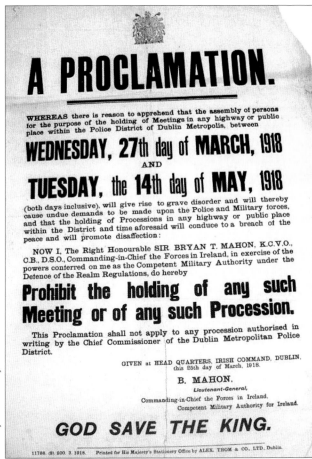

The British government took extensive powers to limit civil rights during the war. In Ireland these powers were mainly used to limit Sinn Féin demonstrations

1 Do you think it was justified in doing so?
2 Do you think proclamations like this would help or hinder Sinn Féin? Explain your answer.

Table A

Results of the 1918 election in Britain			
Parties in coalition government		Opposition parties	
Lloyd George's Liberals	Conservatives	Asquith's Liberals	Labour
136	338	18	59

DECEMBER 1918: THE GENERAL ELECTION IN BRITAIN

On 11 November 1918, the first World War came to an end. At once Lloyd George called a general election for December.

In Britain, the main issue was war. Lloyd George, the leader of the Liberal Party, decided to continue his wartime coalition with the Conservatives, hoping that would give him victory. Asquith and other Liberals disagreed, and that split the Liberal Party.

Grateful British voters gave Lloyd George and his coalition partners a massive victory (see Table A). They won 474 seats compared with 77 for the opposition. But for Lloyd George this result was less satisfactory than it looked. He had to depend on the votes of the Conservatives to stay in power, whereas they had enough votes to rule without him. If he went against their wishes they could easily remove him as Prime Minister. This affected his policies, especially towards Ireland, and led to his fall from power at the end of 1922.

THE 1918 ELECTION IN IRELAND

The election in Ireland was more complicated than the election in Britain:
- Nationalists and unionists faced each other again, picking up where they had left off in 1914.
- On the nationalist side the once mighty Home Rule Party now faced a dangerous challenge from the young and energetic men and women of Sinn Féin.

UNIONISTS VERSUS NATIONALISTS

In the south, unionists had little chance of winning seats outside the Dublin area and Trinity College, so the contest between unionists and nationalists was mainly confined to Ulster. **Sir Edward Carson**, who had been a minister in the wartime coalition, still led the Unionist Party, with **Sir James Craig** as his second-in-command. Carson firmly restated the unionist aim of remaining within the United Kingdom and appealed to voters to support him.

Facing him were two nationalist parties, the Home Rulers, now led by John Dillon and the Sinn Féiners, whose leaders were still in jail. They realised that if they fought each other in Ulster, the nationalist vote would be split and unionists would win more seats. To avoid that, they made a deal to divide eight Ulster seats between them.

HOME RULE VERSUS SINN FÉIN

In the south the Labour Party, founded by James Connolly in 1912, had considered running candidates, but bowed to Sinn Féin pressure to stand aside. That left nationalist voters with a clear choice between two nationalist parties. They could either vote for:

- Éamon de Valera's new Sinn Féin and its demand for an Irish republic. It promised to abstain from Westminster and it had links to the men of violence in the Volunteers.
- Or they could vote for John Dillon's familiar Home Rule Party whose MPs would go back to Westminster and ask again for Home Rule for Ireland.

THE TWO PARTIES

The Sinn Féin Party was in a strong position:

- It was well organised with about 1,200 branches and 100,000 members, both men and women. Most were young and eager to work for the cause.
- It was supported by the Volunteers, the Gaelic League Cumann na mBan and other nationalist movements.
- People believed it had defeated conscription.
- A string of by-election victories had taught Sinn Féiners a great deal about electioneering.
- They had an attractive policy, which seemed to promise independence for Ireland without the need to fight for it.

- During the campaign Sinn Féin had the great advantage of being harassed by the British authorities. Many of its candidates were in jail, its meetings banned, its newspapers censored. Far from hampering it, the harassment earned it sympathy and support.

By contrast, the Home Rule Party was in poor shape:

- Although Dillon was more vigorous than Redmond, he was almost seventy, and other leading members of the party were also elderly.
- For many years the Home Rule Party had not faced any competition in nationalist areas. Some of its MPs never had to fight an election before. Local party branches, having no work to do, had declined or vanished completely. As a result, in twenty-five constituencies, the Home Rule Party did not even put up a candidate to stand against Sinn Féin.

A MORE DEMOCRATIC ELECTION

The 1918 election was more democratic than any previous election. Some months earlier, parliament had extended the right to vote to all men over twenty-one and to women over thirty who paid local taxes or were married to a man who did. That increased the number of voters from 30 per cent to 75 per cent of all adults.

A Sinn Féin comment on its contest with the Home Rule Party

For the first time too, women could be candidates. Sinn Féin nominated two. One, Winifred Carney, was defeated in Belfast; the other, Constance Markievicz, was elected in Dublin. Markievicz, who was in prison throughout the campaign, won by 7,835 votes to 3,742. She was the first woman ever elected to the British House of Commons, though as a Sinn Féiner, she did not take her seat there.

The Act that gave women the vote also rearranged constituencies to take account of changes in population since the 1880s. This mainly affected Ulster, where Belfast and other towns had grown rapidly. The new arrangement was fairer to unionists, since more unionists than nationalists lived in towns and it helped them to win more seats.

Table B

Irish election results, 1910 and 1918, compared			
	Unionists	Sinn Féin	Home Rulers
Dec. 1910	19	No candidates	84
1918	26	73	6

THE ELECTION RESULTS

- When the votes were counted, the Unionist Party did well. It increased to twenty-six MPs from the nineteen it had after the last election in 1910. It won three seats in the south, two seats for Trinity College and one from Dublin. The rest were in north-east Ulster.
- On the nationalist side the results were dramatic. Home Rule MPs fell from eighty-four in 1910 to six. Of these seats, four were won in Ulster as a result of the deal with Sinn Féin.
- Sinn Féin, which did not contest a single seat in 1910, now won seventy-three. But this was not quite as impressive as it looks. The election was held under the British 'first past the post' voting system, not Proportional Representation. As Table C shows, the Home Rule Party won a large number of votes. They just did not win a fair share of seats.

Table C

Nationalist votes cast in 1918	
Votes for Sinn Féin	Votes for Home Rule
485,105	237,393

THE IMPORTANCE OF THE 1918 ELECTION

The 1918 election was one of the most important in Irish history:

- It was the last general election held on a 32-county basis.
- Ulster unionists, seeing Sinn Féin with its demand for a republic winning so much support, became more determined than ever to keep the areas they controlled within the United Kingdom.
- Nationalists showed they would no longer be content with the limited independence offered by Home Rule. In supporting Sinn Féin they had voted for a 'republic' though it was far from clear what they meant by that or if they could get it.

QUESTIONS

1 Who was David Lloyd George and how did he help the emergence of a Sinn Féin party in 1917?

2 Write a short note on each of the following: (a) Arthur Griffith after 1916; (b) Michael Collins and the revival of the IRB; (c) Cathal Brugha and the rebuilding the Volunteers; and (c) the importance of the Roscommon election.

3 Who was Éamon de Valera and how did he unite the Sinn Féin Party in 1917?

4 What was the 'conscription crisis' and why was it so important?

5 How was the 1918 election different from previous elections? What was the result of the election in Britain?

6 In Ireland three parties contested the election. Name them and in each case say what the party promised to do if elected.

7 Compare the Home Rule Party with the Sinn Féin Party. How do you explain Sinn Féin's victory?

8 Why is the 1918 election considered one of the most important elections in Irish history?

LEAVING CERTIFICATE QUESTIONS

Higher Level

1 How did the First World War affect Ireland?

2 Outline the plans made for the Easter Rising in 1916 and describe the main events of Easter week.

3 'All changed, changed utterly.' Do you think W.B. Yeats' assessment of the impact of the Easter rising is valid? Explain your opinion.

4 Why did the Nationalist (Home Rule) Party decline after 1916? How do you explain the victory of Sinn Féin in the 1918 election?

Ordinary Level

A Look at the cartoon on page 50.

  1 At the beginning of 1918 who led the party represented by the candle?

  2 What did the artist think would happen to that party?

  3 Was this proved correct at the end of 1918? Explain your answer.

  4 Give three reasons for Sinn Féin's victory in 1918.

B Write a paragraph on **one** of the following:

  1 Constance Markievicz's part in the 1916 Rising.

  2 The foundation of the Second Sinn Féin Party in October 1917.

C Answer **one** of the following questions:

  1 What part did Irishmen play in World War I?

  2 Why did Sinn Féin win the 1918 election?

4 Revolution and Partition 1919–1921

THE GOVERNMENT OF DÁIL ÉIREANN

21 JANUARY 1919: THE FIRST DÁIL MEETS

During the 1918 election Sinn Féin had promised that its MPs would:

- Abstain from Westminster and stay in Ireland.
- Form an Irish parliament and government.
- Appeal to the Peace Conference in Paris to recognise the right of Irish people to self-determination.

As soon as the election was over, they set about fulfilling those promises. The Peace Conference was due to meet in Paris at the end of January 1919, so they had to act quickly.

They invited all 105 Irish MPs to meet in the Mansion House in Dublin on 21 January 1919. Naturally none of the six Home Rule MPs or the twenty-six Unionist MPs accepted the invitation. But of the seventy-three Sinn Féin MPs elected, only twenty-seven turned up. Most of the rest were still in prison after the 'German plot' arrests, and

two, Michael Collins and Harry Boland, were in England trying to get de Valera out of Lincoln jail.

Those twenty-seven men formed the first independent Irish parliament, **Dáil Éireann**. The present Irish state dates its existence from that meeting, which lasted two hours. Working completely in Irish the Dáil made three important decisions:

- It repeated the **Declaration of the Republic**, made in 1916.
- It issued a '*Message to the Free Nations of the World*', asking them to support the Irish Republic's claim for self-determination. **Seán T. O'Kelly** was chosen to lead a delegation to present Ireland's case for self-determination at the Peace Conference in Paris.
- It passed the **Democratic Programme**, which promised a new education system, reform of the Poor Law and other social reforms. Sinn Féin did this in return for the Labour Party's agreeing not to contest the general election. The Democratic Programme was a watered-down version of the demands put forward by the Labour Party leader Thomas Johnson, which were too socialist for Sinn Féin leaders like Collins.

DE VALERA FREED

Collins got de Valera out of Lincoln Jail early in February. By then it was clear that the Peace Conference would not recognise Irish independence. The American President, Woodrow Wilson, would not even meet the Irish delegates, because he regarded Sinn Féin as allies of Germany and did not want to annoy his British friends.

As soon as he was free, de Valera decided to go to America. He believed that he could get Irish-Americans to put pressure on Wilson to change his mind. But Collins persuaded him that he must first return to Dublin to meet the Dáil.

1 APRIL: THE DÁIL GOVERNMENT FORMED

On 1 April the Dáil elected de Valera as **President**. He appointed his followers as Cabinet ministers:

- **Griffith** became Vice-President and Minister for Home Affairs.
- **Brugha** was Minister for Defence.
- **Collins** was Minister for Finance.
- **William T. Cosgrave** was Minister for Local Government.
- **Count Plunkett** was Minister for Foreign Affairs.
- **Robert Barton** was Minister for Agriculture.
- **Constance Markievicz** was Minister for Labour. (She was the second woman to be appointed a Cabinet minister in European history. De Valera probably appointed her to please the labour movement.)

These people planned to take over the country. On the face of it, they seemed unlikely to succeed:

- They were young and lacked experience. Only two had been elected to parliament before; only five had even served on a local council.
- They had no civil service to help them and they lacked offices in which to keep files or to meet people.
- Above all, they were opposing the established government of the country that could use its police and army to arrest and imprison them.

It is not surprising that at first, few people took them seriously.

JUNE 1919 – DECEMBER 1920: DE VALERA IN AMERICA

De Valera left for America in June. He only planned to stay a short time but he stayed away for eighteen months, not returning until December 1920. At first Irish-Americans welcomed him warmly. He spoke to large and enthusiastic audiences right across the States and raised substantial sums of money. But Irish-Americans were divided among themselves, and de Valera, who at this stage lacked political experience, soon got caught up in their quarrels.

De Valera also failed to persuade either of the American parties, the Republicans and the Democrats, to support Irish demands for self-determination during the 1920 presidential election. In December 1920 he finally returned

Sinn Féin leaders at the first Dáil Éireann

home. He had failed in his main aim but he brought the Irish struggle to the attention of Americans and collected money that helped to pay for the Dáil government and the War of Independence.

THE DÁIL GOVERNMENT

During de Valera's absence, Arthur Griffith presided over the Dáil as 'acting-President'. He had always claimed that the Irish could take control of their country by setting up their own government and ignoring the British. Now he had a chance to put that idea into action.

Slowly through 1919 and 1920 a Dáil government began to take shape. Its more successful departments included Finance, Local Government, and Justice.

MICHAEL COLLINS AND THE DEPARTMENT OF FINANCE

Collins was Minister for Finance. His job was to raise money to pay for the activities of the Dáil and its army. At first he hoped to collect the taxes people owed to the British, but this proved impossible. As a result, his main income came from the sale of Dáil Bonds to the public, both in Ireland and abroad. In Ireland the Bonds raised £358,000, while de Valera sent substantial sums from America.

A poster advertising Dáil Bonds. List the things it says the money will be used for. What is not mentioned?

Collins spent this money on offices and salaries for the Dáil and its civil servants, on propaganda to tell the world about Ireland's struggle and on guns for the Volunteers. Although he was the most wanted man in Ireland, whose offices were often raided by the Black and Tans, he kept careful records of both income and expenditure. He also insisted that other ministers keep receipts and account for the money they spent.

ARTHUR GRIFFITH AND THE SINN FÉIN COURTS

One of the greatest successes of the Dáil government was the court system it established. This began by accident. Before the 1918 election some people in Clare decided not to go to the British courts when they had a dispute with a neighbour. Instead they agreed to accept the arbitration of some respected local person (priest, school-teacher, doctor, etc). From 1919 similar courts were set up in other areas.

In June 1920, Griffith's Department of Home Affairs began to organise Sinn Féin courts systematically. As well as local parish courts, they set up District Courts and Circuit Courts to try more serious cases and a Supreme Court to which people could appeal against the decisions of the lower courts. They sent organisers to spread this legal system to new areas. After Griffith was arrested in November 1920, Austin Stack continued the work and by July 1921 there were over 900 Parish Courts and over seventy District Courts in operation.

As the power of the RIC declined (see page 58), the IRA began to act as a police force. They arrested criminals and took them before the Sinn Féin courts. Then they inflicted the punishments which the courts decided. These included beatings, exiling from the area and in some cases the death penalty. Their success in maintaining law and order helped to win public support for the Dáil government.

WILLIAM T. COSGRAVE AND THE DEPARTMENT OF LOCAL GOVERNMENT

Another successful department was Local Government. Elections to local councils were held in 1920. To stop Sinn Féin winning every seat, the British introduced the **Proportional Representation** (PR) system of voting.

Despite this Sinn Féin gained control of twenty-eight of the thirty-three county councils (including Tyrone and Fermanagh) and of seventy-two corporations and town councils (including Derry city). All Sinn Féin controlled councils then cut their links with the British Local Government Board and affiliated with the Dáil Department, even though this meant losing grants which amounted to 15 per cent of their income.

Before 1920, many local councils had been notorious for bribery and corruption. The Dáil Department took this very seriously, and even before the truce it made strenuous efforts to clean them up. These efforts continued under the Free State government after the Treaty.

FOREIGN AFFAIRS AND PROPAGANDA

The Dáil hoped that foreign governments would recognise Irish independence. To put the Irish case to an international audience they formed a Department of Foreign Affairs. The work of this department often overlapped with the propaganda department.

The delegates to the Paris Peace Conference were the first Irish diplomats. After the Conference refused to admit them, O'Kelly remained on in Paris. Later Irish people living in Rome, Berlin and other capitals were appointed to represent the Dáil government. No foreign government would receive them officially, because they did not want to offend the British. But behind the scenes, these people talked to officials, politicians and the press, countering British propaganda and putting over the Irish case.

In Dublin, the Dáil's propaganda department was headed by Desmond FitzGerald and, after his arrest, by Erskine Childers. Their aim was to present the Irish side of the story and make it difficult for the British to hide what was really going on in Ireland.

Each week from November 1919 to July 1921, they issued the *Irish Bulletin*. It contained reports of the atrocities committed by the Black and Tans (and may even have invented a few). Sympathetic newspapers and individuals in Britain and other countries received copies. When foreign visitors or newspaper reporters came to Ireland to see for themselves, they were taken to secret meetings with leading members of the Dáil.

MARKIEVICZ AS MINISTER FOR LABOUR

Markievicz set up a labour court and tried to negotiate in trade disputes. But her early arrest and imprisonment limited the work she could do.

GOVERNING 'ON THE RUN'

All these departments worked under the greatest difficulty. The British refused to recognise the Dáil's claim to be a parliament and outlawed it in 1919. As the IRA's war with the British forces escalated, members of the Dáil government had to 'go on the run' and some were arrested. The RIC and the Black and Tans frequently raided their offices, making it difficult to keep records.

Yet in spite of all these difficulties, the Dáil government managed to survive. Its ambitious aim of replacing the British administration in Ireland had a limited success, but given the circumstances in which it operated, it is remarkable that it had any success at all.

British soldiers search a car at Doyle's Corner, Phibsboro, Dublin in 1921

Courtesy: RTÉ Stills Library

Q U E S T I O N S

1 When did Dáil Éireann first meet? Why did so few TDs attend? Write a sentence on each of the decisions it made.

2 Where was Éamon de Valera between June 1919 and December 1920, and what was he doing there?

3 Name four of the departments set up by the Dáil government. Select two of them and write a short paragraph about each of them.

4 Griffith had always claimed that Irish people could take over the government of the country from the British. Do you think the Dáil government proves or disproves his claim? Set out clearly the facts which support your answer.

4.2

THE IRA AND THE WAR OF INDEPENDENCE

PLANNING VIOLENCE

Griffith and some Sinn Féin leaders may have genuinely believed that they could win Irish independence by appealing to the Peace Conference and by passive resistance to British rule. This belief may also have convinced many voters to back them.

But even before the 1918 election some leaders of Sinn Féin had very different plans. Since they came out of prison in 1917, Collins, Richard Mulcahy, Cathal Brugha and many local Volunteer commanders, like Seán Treacy in Tipperary, had been preparing to fight again.

THE VOLUNTEERS

These men were active in the Volunteers, which had been reorganised in 1917. They were led by an **Executive Committee** and at the Volunteer

Convention in October chose de Valera as President and Cathal Brugha as Chairman. They also set up a **General Headquarters** (**GHQ**) with Richard Mulcahy as Chief of Staff and Michael Collins as Director of Organisation and Intelligence. Around the country Volunteers were divided into brigades and battalions, each with its own officers, elected by the men.

GETTING ARMS

Long before the Dáil was elected, Volunteer leaders were planning a war against British rule. Their numbers grew during the conscription crisis, reaching about 100,000 by the end of 1918. Of those, about 15,000 would be willing to fight but they had a problem getting arms. They smuggled some into the country, bought more from British soldiers and on several occasions in 1918 stole them from private houses and gun shops.

21 JANUARY 1919: SOLOHEADBEG

The armed policemen of the RIC were an obvious source of arms. On 21 January 1919 a group of Tipperary Volunteers led by Seán Treacy ambushed two policemen in Soloheadbeg. They shot them and took their guns and the dynamite they had been escorting.

Soloheadbeg is often seen as the first blow in the War of Independence. It happened on the day that Dáil Éireann met for the first time but the Dáil did not know or approve of what Treacy and his men did. Neither did the Volunteers' own GHQ. This set the pattern for the war that followed. The Volunteers (or the IRA as they took to calling themselves after the Dáil declared a republic), fought their war in their own way. They paid little attention to the Dáil and its government, which were supposed to be their political masters.

MICHAEL COLLINS'S SPY NETWORK

The Volunteer GHQ was in Dublin. Richard Mulcahy, the Chief of Staff, worked closely with Michael Collins, the Director of Intelligence. They tended to ignore Cathal Brugha who, as Minister for Defence in the Dáil government, was officially their superior.

Collins believed that earlier rebellions failed because the British government knew more about the rebels than they knew about it. He set out to reverse that situation. After he was freed in 1916, he built up a network of contacts around the country. They included maids, typists, railwaymen, hotel porters, civil servants working for the government, policemen and even detectives.

RIC and British army patrol armoured cars leaving Limerick on a scouting expedition

Any scrap of information they came across – bits of gossip, copies of government letters, word of troop movements, rumours about raids – they passed on to Collins. He used the information to outwit the British. Advance warning about troop movements was sent to local Volunteer commanders to help them plan ambushes. Knowledge about planned raids enabled Dáil ministers to move their offices before the RIC arrived.

THE 'SQUAD'

But Collins was also determined to stop the British government finding out about the Volunteers and Sinn Féin. In Dublin Castle, a small group of detectives, known as G-men, had for years spied on nationalist organisations. Early in 1919, Collins warned them to stop their work. Some obeyed, others did not. In July 1919, he formed a handpicked 'Squad' of twelve Volunteers and told them to kill one of the detectives who had disobeyed. The rest lost their enthusiasm for the job.

Collins ruthlessly used the Squad to kill anyone who he thought was a threat to the movement.

One victim was an elderly accountant called Alan Bell. The British government had employed him to trace the bank accounts in which Collins was keeping money gathered in the Dáil loan (see page 55). One day on his way home, Bell was taken from a tram and shot, and his killers walked quietly away. The cold-blooded killings shocked moderate Sinn Féiners like Griffith, but Collins ignored their protests. His ruthless use of terror achieved its aims, and the government's sources of information dried up.

THE IRA CAMPAIGN AROUND THE COUNTRY

Outside Dublin the level of IRA violence varied from place to place. Each local commandant controlled his own area. GHQ sent him guns and information but in the end, only the local man knew how many weapons and men he had and what the local possibilities were. IRA commandants such as **Tom Barry** in Cork, **Michael Brennan** in Clare, **Seán Treacy** in Tipperary and **Seán MacEoin** in Longford made frequent attacks on British forces. Other parts of the country were much quieter.

Violence began slowly. In 1919 it mainly consisted of arms raids on RIC barracks, where a total of nineteen policemen were killed. The Dáil did not authorise this campaign but in April 1919 it had called for a boycott of the RIC. Volunteers may have regarded this as justifying them in killing policemen.

Late in 1919, the RIC closed small police stations and concentrated their men in heavily fortified barracks in the larger towns. In 1920 the Volunteer GHQ encouraged local commandants to begin systematic attacks on the fortified barracks. Between January and June 1920, sixteen were destroyed and twenty-nine damaged. By then the RIC had lost control of much of the country. This was an important reason for the success of the Dáil courts.

THE DECLINE OF THE RIC

Sinn Féin propaganda tried to demonise RIC men as British agents, but in fact most of them were ordinary Irish Catholics, very like today's Garda. Before 1919 their main victims had been local criminals. The rise of IRA violence presented them with a terrible dilemma. As ordinary Irishmen where did their loyalty now lie: with the British government which paid their wages or with their fellow countrymen who were shooting at them?

A few gave information to the IRA. Many turned a blind eye to Volunteer activity, or resigned. Some continued to serve the Crown as loyally as they had always done. But in these circumstances not many young men wanted a career in the RIC and it became almost impossible to recruit new members.

LLOYD GEORGE AND THE VIEWS OF THE CONSERVATIVES

The growing disorder in Ireland was a problem for the Prime Minister, David Lloyd George. He was a Liberal but since 1918 he had led a coalition government in which the Conservatives were the bigger party (see page 49). That meant he had to keep their views in mind when dealing with Ireland.

Before the First World War, Conservatives were totally opposed to Home Rule and had given unreserved support to Carson and the Irish unionists. But during the war Conservative views changed:

- They realised that some kind of Home Rule was inevitable, but they wanted it to be as limited as possible.
- They also wanted to protect their unionist allies by giving them their own state in Ulster.

LLOYD GEORGE DECIDES HIS POLICIES

Lloyd George had to keep these Conservative views in mind when dealing with Ireland. In the first half of 1919 he had been busy with the Peace Conference in Paris but by September it was finished. By then IRA violence was increasing. Another problem was the Home Rule Act. It had been passed in 1914 and suspended until the World War was over. Therefore, it was now due to come into operation.

These things forced Lloyd George to focus on Ireland. He decided that it was impossible to deal with both nationalists and unionists at once. Instead he would divide the problem into two parts:

- First he must defeat the IRA. When that was done he would be free to negotiate with Sinn Féin on his own terms.
- Meanwhile he would protect the unionists by giving them control of 'Ulster' (see section 4.3).

THE 'BLACK AND TANS' AND THE AUXILIARIES

Lloyd George would not admit that Dáil Éireann was a real parliament or the IRA a real army. He called them 'a murder gang'. The proper way to fight a murder gang, he argued, was with police, not soldiers, and he wanted to use the RIC against them rather than the British army. Since not many Irishmen wanted to join the RIC, Lloyd George decided to recruit policemen in Britain. Unemployment was high there after the war and many young men were glad to get a job policing Ireland.

Sinn Féin propaganda tried to suggest that the new recruits were criminals. They were not, but they were tough ex-soldiers, recently back from the trenches.

In March 1920 they began to arrive in Ireland. Due to a shortage of police uniforms, they were dressed in a mixture of army khaki and the RIC's dark-green. This won them their nickname, the '**Black and Tans**'. Later, ex-army officers were recruited to form an **Auxiliary Division of the RIC**. It was led by Brigadier Crozier, formerly an officer in the Ulster Volunteers. Both Black and Tans and Auxiliaries soon earned a reputation for ruthless and undisciplined behaviour.

FLYING COLUMNS AND AMBUSHES

After the Black and Tans arrived, violence increased. They patrolled the countryside in convoys of lorries and raided houses, searching for Sinn Féiners. This forced the IRA to change its tactics. It was no longer safe for active Volunteers to live at home. Many went 'on the run'. They formed **flying columns** of twenty or thirty men. Paid as full-time soldiers and better trained and armed than the average Volunteer, men of the flying columns moved from place to place, living

A group of British soldiers passing through a town

Members of a flying column. This picture was taken during the truce and was probably staged for the camera

rough in the countryside or getting shelter from sympathetic or intimidated families.

Usually flying columns worked with local IRA brigades to stage ambushes. When they heard that a convoy of soldiers or Black and Tans was on its way, they felled trees to block it and opened fire on it from nearby ditches. When the fighting ended, the IRA men slipped away, disappearing among the usually sympathetic local people.

REPRISALS FROM THE BLACK AND TANS

IRA ambushes provoked reprisals from the Black and Tans. Being strangers to a district, they could not tell friend from foe. When the IRA killed some of them, they hit back blindly at everyone, Home Ruler and Unionist as well as Sinn Féiner. Lorry loads of drunken Black and Tans descended on Balbriggan, Tobercurry, Tuam, Mallow, Ennistimon and other towns, burning houses, looting shops, beating up or murdering prisoners. Convoys of lorries careered through the country, shooting at innocent bystanders. The British government turned a blind eye to reprisals, hoping they would discourage people from supporting the IRA.

But the reprisal policy backfired. Moderate Sinn Féiners who had disapproved of IRA violence, now swung in behind the IRA. Reprisals were also good propaganda for Sinn Féin. British and other foreign journalists wrote about them and many people in Britain, who were proud of their country's democratic record, were outraged. They felt ashamed that their government, which was

supposed to be upholding law and order, should allow this kind of behaviour.

1920: INCREASING VIOLENCE

A number of events in 1920 show how the violence escalated:

- In March, men with their faces blackened murdered Tomás MacCurtain, the Lord Mayor of Cork and the local IRA commander. The British government claimed he was killed as part of an internal IRA feud but an inquest jury in Cork brought in a verdict of wilful murder against Lloyd George.

- MacCurtain's successor, Terence MacSwiney, was arrested soon after. He demanded to be treated as a prisoner of war and not a common criminal. When this was refused, he went on hunger strike. After seventy-three days without food, he died in Brixton prison near London on 25 September. His death attracted worldwide attention.

- Kevin Barry was arrested after an ambush in Dublin in which a seventeen-year-old British soldier was killed. He was found guilty of murder and sentenced to death. There were many pleas for mercy because he was only eighteen, but they were ignored and he was hanged on 1 November.

21 NOVEMBER: BLOODY SUNDAY

Over the summer of 1920 Dublin Castle also began to rebuild the spy network that Collins had destroyed. They brought in a group of agents, known

No. 20.

BRIGADE PROCLAMATION

**By Colonel Commandant N. J. G. CAMERON, C.B., C.M.G., A.D.C.,
Commanding 16th Infantry Brigade, and Military Governor.**

On various occasions when members of the Royal Irish Constabulary or Loyalist Civilians have been brutally murdered by rebels or when the houses of Loyalist Civilians have been destroyed by rebels, it has been necessary as a punishment to destroy the houses of rebels or of persons who are known to be in active sympathy with the rebels who commit these outrages.

It has come to notice that in some cases the rebels have as a reprisal destroyed the houses of Loyalists.

Be it known that in such a case, for ever Loyalist's house destroyed by rebels TWO houses of rebels or sympathisers with rebels will be destroyed.

If the rebels repeat their action this proportion of TWO for ONE will be increased.

Signed at Fermoy this 23rd day of May, 1921.

N. J. G. CAMERON, Colonel Commandant,
Commanding 16th Infantry Brigade, and Military Governor.

Courtesy: Allen Library

Read this proclamation.

1 *Who issued it?*
2 *Explain in your own words what it says.*
3 *If you were living in the area affected how would you react to the proclamation?*

as the 'Cairo gang'. One by one they moved to Dublin, some with their families, posing as innocent civilians. Collins soon heard about them through his sources in the police. He summoned Volunteers to Dublin to supplement the Squad and on Sunday, 21 November sent them out in pairs to kill the men. Fourteen were shot, some in front of their families. Most, though not all, of the men killed were agents.

Collins had chosen that Sunday because there was a big GAA match in Croke Park. The crowds coming to Dublin provided cover for the Volunteers who came to take part in the shooting. The authorities guessed this. In the afternoon heavily armed troops surrounded Croke Park. Exactly who shot first is not clear, but the police certainly fired into the crowd, killing twelve people.

Later that night, three men, who had been captured in Dublin the day before, were shot in Dublin Castle. Two were prominent members of the IRA, the third was an innocent civilian. According to the official report they had been trying to escape, but few nationalists believed that.

28 NOVEMBER: THE KILMICHAEL AMBUSH

A week after Bloody Sunday, Cork Volunteers ambushed an Auxiliary patrol at **Kilmichael** near Macroom. The Volunteer leader was Tom Barry, a former British soldier. The Auxiliaries surrendered, then Barry's men shot all but one of them. This has aroused a great deal of controversy. In his memoirs, Barry claimed that the Auxiliaries first surrendered, then opened fire on his men, which justified the killing. But evidence from the time suggests that he may just have let his men kill them after they surrendered.

11 DECEMBER: THE BURNING OF CORK

On 11 December, there was an IRA ambush near Cork. That night Black and Tans and Auxiliaries poured into the city and set fire to parts of it. This was the most spectacular of the reprisals. At Westminster the Chief Secretary, Hammar Greenwood, denied that the Crown forces were to blame and suggested that Cork people had fired their own city.

THE IRA UNDER PRESSURE

After these events the British army became more involved in the war with the IRA. At the end of 1920 martial law was declared in Cork, Kerry, Tipperary and Limerick; later it was extended to Clare, Kilkenny, Wexford and Waterford. It allowed the army to search houses, to impose curfews, to try people in army rather than civil courts and to intern suspects without trial.

Martial law put increased pressure on the IRA and Sinn Féin:

- At the end of 1920 Griffith and several leading members of the Dáil were arrested and imprisoned.
- Army sweeps followed and by July 1921, 4,500 Volunteers were being held in prison camps.
- It became much harder to get arms.
- It became more difficult to stage big attacks. There were only two successful attacks on police barracks in 1921.

The ruins of Cork after it was burned by the Black and Tans, December 1921

VIOLENCE GROWS WORSE

The authorities also uncovered many of Collins' spies, so that the IRA was getting less information. On the other hand, more people were passing information to the British. The IRA responded by shooting people they suspected of spying and dumping their bodies with the word 'spies' tied around their necks.

Some IRA men used this brutal policy as an excuse to murder people they disliked for one reason or another. In some cases, especially in Cork and in Cavan and Monaghan, the victims were Protestants. This brought a sectarian element into the IRA campaign and worried the GHQ. They feared it would alienate public opinion in Ireland and abroad. They tried to stop it, but their control over local IRA commanders was very limited.

By 1921 reprisal and counter-reprisal made life miserable for ordinary people. In Dublin, street battles became more common, killing innocent passers-by. Between January and July about 300 of the Crown forces and over 700 civilians (who included IRA men) were killed.

FRICTION AMONG THE LEADERS

In 1921 divisions emerged among the leaders of Sinn Féin and the IRA. At their core was the tension between Cathal Brugha as Minister for Defence and the men in the IRA Headquarters, especially Collins and Mulcahy.

As minister, Brugha felt he ought to control the army. He intervened in the work of the GHQ, giving orders to Mulcahy, the Chief of Staff. But he was not directly involved in the fighting, since he was also working in his family business. That made the fighting men despise him, and they thought his ideas were impractical. For example, Brugha disapproved of ambushes and wanted the Volunteers to be involved in direct battles with the Crown forces. But active Volunteer commandants, aware of how few men and guns they had, believed this was unrealistic.

Brugha also objected to the IRB, the secret society which was the basis of Collins's power. Many Volunteer officers were also in the IRB. Who, Brugha wondered, would these men obey: their leaders in the IRB or those in the Volunteers?

Part of the problem was Brugha's jealousy of Collins. Newspapers presented Collins as the glamorous hero, while they ignored Brugha who, as minister, was supposed to be the boss of Collins. Collins did not help the situation by showing contempt for Brugha, whom he regarded as an inefficient part-timer.

DE VALERA TAKES SIDES

In December 1920, de Valera finally returned from America. The country had changed greatly since he left. War and terror, reprisal and counter-reprisal were now commonplace. Like many in Sinn Féin, de Valera was uneasy at the kind of war the IRA was fighting. He also shared Brugha's jealousy of Collins's reputation. When he left in 1918 he was the best-known figure in Sinn Féin; when he returned he found Collins had replaced him as the popular hero.

De Valera backed Brugha's demand for more open battles. In May 1921, they persuaded GHQ to launch a frontal attack on the Customs House in Dublin, where the British local government records were stored. The attack was a success and the Customs House was burned. But the IRA lost over eighty men, dead or captured, and their arms. Given the pressure it was under, that was too high a price to pay for victory.

LLOYD GEORGE GETTING READY FOR PEACE

By the middle of 1921, Lloyd George was waiting for an opportunity to make peace. By then he had protected the unionists by giving them their own state (see section 4.3) and that opened the way for a deal with Sinn Féin. Through the winter of 1920–21 he asked journalists, politicians and priests who visited Dublin to try to find out what they wanted. When he heard that de Valera had returned, he gave orders that he was not to be arrested. De Valera had not been involved in events like Bloody Sunday, and that made him more acceptable to British people than leaders like Collins. All Lloyd George needed was an excuse to call for talks.

QUESTIONS

1 Describe how the Volunteers reorganised after 1917 and prepared for war.

2 What was the relationship between the Sinn Féin Party and the Volunteers between 1917 and 1921? Do you think that had any implications for democracy in Ireland? Explain your answer.

3 Write a short account of Michael Collins as a military leader. How did that affect his relationship with Griffith, Brugha and de Valera?

4 Who was the British Prime Minister in 1919–21? What were his priorities in Ireland? Describe some of the steps he took against the IRA.

5 'The reprisal policy backfired on the government.' (a) What were reprisals? (b) How did they 'backfire on the government'?

6 Select three episodes in the War of Independence and describe them. Which of them do you think would have had most impact on (a) moderate nationalists and (b) people in Britain? Explain your choice.

7 What did the British do in 1921 to put the IRA under pressure?

8 Late in 1920 de Valera returned to Ireland. What was the result of that for (a) other leaders and (b) Lloyd George?

4.3

PARTITIONING IRELAND

THE UNIONISTS AND SINN FÉIN

Irish nationalists changed greatly between 1914 and 1918 but Irish unionists did not. Events after 1916 simply reinforced their fear of being ruled by a Dublin government and their determination to stay inside the United Kingdom:

- Sinn Féin's victory in 1918 horrified them. They were loyal to the king and felt at home in the United Kingdom, so they had no sympathy for Sinn Féin's ideal of an independent republic, fully separate from Britain.

- The IRA campaign in the south reinforced unionist fears. Inevitably, many of the IRA's victims were people of unionist sympathies and in some places the IRA campaign had a sectarian tone. To unionists this confirmed the danger for Protestants of a Catholic-dominated state.

UNIONISTS STRONGER AFTER 1918

The 1918 election put the Unionist Party, still led by Sir Edward Carson and Sir James Craig, in a stronger position than it had in 1914. They won twenty-six seats and their allies, the Conservatives, dominated Lloyd George's coalition government. Sinn Féin's decision to abstain from Westminster also strengthened them. When Lloyd George came to deal with Ireland in 1919 there were twenty-six MPs to represent the unionist point of view, compared with only six nationalists. That made it easier for Carson and Craig to get what they wanted.

SINN FÉIN'S ATTITUDE TO THE UNIONISTS

De Valera and other Sinn Féin leaders gave little thought to the unionists. They knew very little about them, seldom visited Belfast and were unsympathetic to its industrial culture. They thought that the unionists were bluffing or else that the British were manipulating them to stop nationalists getting independence. Once the British agreed to give the nationalists what they wanted, the unionists would fall into line.

This attitude can be seen in a dismissive comment from de Valera after he met Craig secretly in Dublin on 5 May 1921:

> 'I do not see any hope of ending the struggle with England through a prior agreement with the unionist minority. At bottom the question is an Irish/English one and the solution must be sought in the larger general play of English interest.' (Longford and O'Neill, *Eamon de Valera*, p. 123)

This was completely unrealistic:

- It took no account of the very real fears that unionists had about being ruled by a Catholic-dominated, rurally-biased Dublin government and of their willingness to fight to stop it.
- It also ignored the sense of obligation British politicians, especially Conservatives, felt towards the only group in Ireland who were loyal to Britain. No British government could possibly push reluctant unionists out of the United Kingdom and under a Sinn Féin controlled government against their will.

1920: THE START OF VIOLENCE IN THE NORTH

The IRA was not as strong in Ulster as in other parts of the country. It was only in 1920 that it began to attack the RIC there. This provoked the unionists to revive the Ulster Volunteer Force (UVF) which had been inactive since 1914. The result was a flare up in sectarian violence.

Rioting began in Derry in June 1920. In July mobs in Belfast expelled 5,500 Catholics and 1,900 Protestants who were not considered sufficiently loyal, from the shipyards. Although it was claimed that the people expelled were Sinn Féiners, an important underlying reason was the economic situation. Demand for ships fell after the war and some people were going to lose their jobs. Traditionally in Belfast it was Catholics who suffered in these circumstances.

From Belfast, rioting spread to nearby towns like Banbridge and Lisburn. Reports of IRA attacks on policemen and Protestants in the south fuelled the anger of unionist mobs. Over the next year, about 11,000 Catholics were driven from their jobs, many Catholic houses and shops were burned and over 500 people killed.

ESTABLISHING THE 'SPECIAL CONSTABLES'

In September 1920, in an attempt to control the violence, the government established a new force of 'Special Constables'. Although in theory Catholics as well as Protestants could join, almost all the 'Specials' came from the UVF. The British army commander, General Macready, described their formation was 'raising Carson's army from the grave'. The 'Specials' patrolled their local areas and had a free hand to put down disorder. They used this power with great brutality and little impartiality, often settling personal scores against Catholic neighbours.

THE BELFAST BOYCOTT

In the south, these developments caused anger and dismay. In places, shopkeepers began to boycott goods from Belfast and in August the Dáil adopted the 'Belfast boycott' as its official policy. This ill-thought-out tactic damaged some northern businesses, even some owned by Catholics, but did little to protect northern nationalists. But the boycott confirmed the unionist belief that southern politicians wanted to undermine their economy. Instead of encouraging unity, the Dáil's boycott seemed to support the partition of the country that the London parliament was trying to introduce.

LLOYD GEORGE'S PLAN FOR 'HOME RULE ALL ROUND'

In September 1919 Lloyd George again turned his attention to Ireland (see page 59). As well as suppressing the IRA, he planned to solve the issue of partition that had stopped Home Rule in 1914. He decided on a plan that became known as 'Home Rule all round'.

It proposed dividing Ireland into two states, 'Northern Ireland' and 'Southern Ireland'. Each state would have a Home Rule parliament with limited powers. Lloyd George wanted 'Northern Ireland' to contain all nine Ulster counties. In those counties Catholics and Protestants were roughly equal in number and he reckoned that this would prevent one from bullying the other.

At first Carson and Craig were doubtful about Lloyd George's plan. They had campaigned to stay in the United Kingdom, not to have Home Rule. But soon they saw advantages in his proposals. With their own elected parliament they would be secure. No future British government could ever force them under a Dublin government.

But they did not want a nine-county Northern Ireland. With the two communities so nearly equal, they feared that a small change in population might produce a nationalist majority and force them under Dublin control. Instead they demanded six counties, Antrim, Armagh, Down, Derry, Fermanagh and Tyrone (see map page 25). In that area the unionists were 65 per cent of the population and the nationalists 35 per cent. This, they felt, would give them a permanent majority and keep them safe.

THE GOVERNMENT OF IRELAND ACT, DECEMBER 1920

The result of these negotiations was the **Government of Ireland Act**, which passed in December 1920. Its main terms were:

David Lloyd George at a political rally

Courtesy: Corbis

- The island of Ireland was to be divided into two states – 'Southern Ireland', with twenty-six counties and 'Northern Ireland', with six counties.
- Each state was to have its own parliament, containing a Commons and a Senate. To give the minorities a fair share of seats, elections would be by Proportional Representation (PR). The unionists had opposed this but they were overruled.
- Each parliament was to elect a government, headed by a Prime Minister. The government was to be responsible for governing its area but certain powers were reserved for the Westminster parliament. The reserved powers included the monarchy, peace and war, control of the armed forces, coinage, post, income tax and excise duties.
- Each area would elect MPs to the Westminster parliament.
- Knowing that nationalists wanted to keep Ireland united, the British left links between the two states, hoping this would induce Sinn Féin to talk later. North and South would share one Viceroy (representing the king) and a Council of Ireland to which the two parliaments would send MPs. The Council would oversee areas of common interest like trade and fisheries. If both parliaments agreed, they could transfer more powers to the Council and so bring about a reunification by agreement.

SETTING UP NORTHERN IRELAND

Because of the growing violence in the north, Lloyd George wanted Northern Ireland to be set up as soon as possible.

Even before the Government of Ireland Act was passed, he sent an official to Belfast to prepare for the unionist take-over (see page 160). Elections for the two new parliaments were scheduled for May 1921.

In Northern Ireland, the elections went ahead as planned. Three parties fought for the fifty-two seats:

- The **Unionist Party**, which was now led by Craig, since Carson had decided to retire.
- The **Nationalist (Home Rule) Party** had remained stronger in Ulster than elsewhere in Ireland. Led by Joseph Devlin, it represented a more moderate nationalist point of view.
- **Sinn Féin** was less strong in Ulster than elsewhere. It demanded a republic and refused to recognise partition.
- The two nationalists parties knew that if they fought each other, the Unionists would win more seats. For that reason they agreed to share winnable nationalist seats between them.

On election day, almost 90 per cent of the electorate came out to vote. The result was a triumph for the Unionist Party, which won forty seats. The Nationalists and Sinn Féin won six seats each, but they refused to recognise the new parliament and did not attend its opening sessions.

ELECTING A SECOND DÁIL

There was also to be an election for the 128 seats in the parliament of 'Southern Ireland'. At first the Sinn Féin leaders wanted to ignore it, but after they put up candidates in the north, they decided to treat it as an election for a second Dáil. But it was not a proper election. With the War of Independence at its height, only Sinn Féin put up candidates. Other parties stood aside, either because of intimidation or to avoid splitting the nationalist vote.

As a result, every one of the 124 Sinn Féin candidates, handpicked by the leaders of Sinn Féin, was elected without a single vote being cast. In an attempt to guarantee a unionist voice in the Southern parliament, four seats were allocated to the graduates of Trinity College. Four unionists

stood for those seats and they too were elected unopposed.

THE NEED TO TALK TO SINN FÉIN

Since 1920 Americans and Europeans had been urging Lloyd George to talk to Sinn Féin. Demands for peace also came from voters in Britain who were disgusted at the behaviour of the Black and Tans. Lloyd George himself wanted to end the violence and now that the unionists were safe in Northern Ireland, his Conservative allies would allow him to negotiate with Sinn Féin.

After the elections the need for talks became urgent.

- The Government of Ireland Act stated that if the government of 'Southern Ireland' did not start to work, the British government would have to take direct control over the twenty-six counties.
- That would cost a great deal of money, which the British government could not afford. It could also involve imposing martial law and perhaps executing thousands of people.
- Lloyd George, a shrewd politician, knew that British people would not stand for that unless he could show that he had made a real attempt to make peace with Sinn Féin.

KING GEORGE APPEALS FOR PEACE

On 22 June 1921, King George V formally opened the Belfast parliament. In his speech he included a heartfelt plea for peace. Lloyd George had encouraged the king to make this plea and it was warmly welcomed in Britain. This gave Lloyd George an excuse to issue a public invitation to de Valera *as the chosen leader of the great majority in Southern Ireland* to *attend a conference here in London in company with Sir James Craig, to explore to the utmost the possibility of a settlement*. (D. MacArdle, *The Irish Republic*, Corgi edition 1968, p. 431)

AGREEING TO A TRUCE

By June 1921, Irish people were desperate for peace. If Sinn Féin did not respond to Lloyd George's offer, they might find the people turning against them. In addition, the IRA was weakening (see page 78). Collins later claimed they only had ammunition for a few more weeks. These factors persuaded de Valera and the IRA to agree to a truce. Prisoners were freed, each side was to keep its arms, and attacks and counter-attacks were to cease so that talks could begin between the British government and the Dáil government.

ASSESSING THE TRUCE

The truce, which began on 11 July 1921, can be seen as a defeat for Lloyd George:

- He had not beaten the IRA as he had hoped. Instead he had to let it stand aside like a real army while he talked to its leaders.

- He had wanted the Sinn Féin TDs to take their seats in Westminster and negotiate from inside the British system, as Parnell and Redmond had done. Instead he had to meet and talk to them as if they were leaders of a separate government.

But by agreeing to a ceasefire, the Sinn Féin leaders also made concessions. If the peace talks were to succeed they would have to accept less than the totally independent republic they said they wanted. This was almost certainly clear to de Valera from the start. Whether it was clear to active IRA men around the country is much more doubtful.

QUESTIONS

1 Why did unionists not want to be ruled by a Dublin government? Did the events between 1916 and 1919 change their attitudes?

2 Were unionists in a stronger or weaker position in 1919 compared with 1914? Explain your answer.

3 What was the attitude of Sinn Féin towards the unionists? Was this attitude realistic? Explain your answer.

4 Describe the violence in the north of Ireland in 1920 and 1921. How did it differ from violence in the south?

5 What was the 'Belfast boycott'? Do you think it was a good idea? Explain your answer.

6 What were the main terms of the Government of Ireland Act? How did this Act affect (a) nationalists in Fermanagh and Tyrone and (b) unionists in Donegal, Cavan and Monaghan?

7 Compare the results of elections for the northern and southern parliaments. How do you account for the differences?

8 Explain the factors which persuaded Lloyd George to propose talks with Sinn Féin in 1921.

9 Explain why de Valera agreed to a truce. Was it a victory or a defeat for Sinn Féin and Lloyd George?

LEAVING CERTIFICATE QUESTIONS

Higher Level
Write an essay on **one** of the following:
1 How did Lloyd George deal with Sinn Féin up to the truce of 1921 and how successful was he in achieving his aims?

2 Why and how was Northern Ireland established?

Ordinary Level
Answer **one** of the following questions:
1 How successful was Dáil Éireann in establishing a government in Ireland?

2 What tactics did the IRA use during the war of independence and how successful were they?

⑤ From Treaty to Civil War

5.1

NEGOTIATING A TREATY: JULY – OCTOBER 1921 (CASE STUDY)

DE VALERA IN LONDON

On 11 July 1921 fighting between the IRA and the British forces in Ireland came to an end so that peace talks between the British government and Sinn Féin could begin.

De Valera went to London on 14 July with several of his ministers. He met Lloyd George alone and told him that Sinn Féin wanted:

- ○ to end partition and
- ○ have a totally independent republic for the whole of Ireland.

Lloyd George refused even to discuss these demands. He offered de Valera a limited amount of independence for twenty-six counties. They would have

- ○ their own parliament and government but
- ○ could not control foreign trade, have an army or navy and they must allow in British forces in time of war.

De Valera turned down these terms. When he took them back to Dublin, the Cabinet and the Dáil supported him.

FINDING A FORMULA FOR TALKS

But neither side wanted to resume fighting. Throughout August and September the two leaders exchanged letters and telegrams, trying to find a formula which would allow talks to start again.

At last Lloyd George came up with a form of words that satisfied de Valera. Irish delegates would go to a conference in London

> 'with a view to ascertaining how the association of Ireland with the community of nations known as the British Empire may be reconciled with Irish national aspirations.' (Longford, Peace by Ordeal, London 1935 p. 88)

This opened the way for more negotiations which began in October. By ongoing talks, each side accepted that they would have to make concessions but each leader had to look over his shoulder at his allies and followers and take their wishes into account.

GOOD ACCOMMODATION.

THE TRAVELLER. "IS THIS 'THE HARP'?"
THE HOST "'CROWN AND HARP,' SIR. BUT I DON'T THINK YOU'LL FIND IT ANY LESS COMFORTABLE FOR THAT."

A Punch cartoon commenting on the Treaty negotiations. Can you explain the symbolism of the name of the inn?

WHAT COULD LLOYD GEORGE OFFER DE VALERA?

Lloyd George knew that he would have to give Ireland more than he offered de Valera in July but he had to keep certain points in mind.

- He was in a coalition government with the Conservative party which was divided about the negotiations. Conservative leaders knew that it was important for Britain to have peace in Ireland but some of their followers did not want any negotiations with Sinn Féin 'murderers'. If Lloyd George tried to force the Ulster unionists into a united Ireland, all Conservatives would unite against him and end the coalition.

- Both Lloyd George and the Conservatives believed that Ireland had been vital to Britain's defence in the recent war against Germany. In any future war, British security might depend on controlling it. Therefore they wanted to keep Ireland in the British Empire and would never agree to an independent republic. The most they would agree to would be **dominion status**, i.e. the same amount of independence as Canada and Australia had.

> **Dominions:** In the British Empire, Canada, Australia, New Zealand and South Africa were **dominions**. The King was their head of state, but they had their own parliaments and their governments had almost total control over their own affairs. The British still claimed the right to interfere in the laws they made but in practice, never did. This kind of independence is known as '**dominion status**'. In 1922 the dominions were in the League of Nations and some people expected they would soon become fully independent states.

WHAT COULD DE VALERA OFFER LLOYD GEORGE?

De Valera too had to keep his followers' wishes in mind. They were divided about what they wanted.

- There were militant republicans who had seen friends and relatives die for a totally independent, thirty-two county republic. They would reject any settlement that gave less. Many TDs in the Dáil and leading IRA men around the country belonged to this group.

- There were pacifist Sinn Féiners like Griffith. They never liked the IRA's violence and would be content with less than complete separation from Britain, provided partition ended and Irish people got real control over their own affairs.

De Valera speaking to the second Dáil in August 1921

● Outside the Dáil and the IRA, many nationalists just wanted an Irish government and peace so that their lives could return to normal. They were not too concerned about the details of how this was achieved.

De Valera had to remember that if the negotiations did not satisfy the needs of these groups, the Sinn Féin movement might split apart.

DIVISIONS IN THE DÁIL CABINET

The divisions in Sinn Féin can also be seen in the Dáil Cabinet which chose the Irish delegation to go to the London talks.

● **Arthur Griffith**, the Vice-President, was a moderate.
● **Cathal Brugha**, the Minister for Defence and **Austin Stack**, the Minister for Home Affairs, were militant republicans.
● **De Valera**, **Collins**, **William Cosgrave**, the Minister for Local Government and **Robert Barton**, the Minister for Agriculture were somewhere between the two extremes.

Robert Barton (1881–1975): A Protestant landowner from Wicklow, Barton joined the British army in 1914. He was stationed in Dublin in 1916 but after the executions he resigned and joined the Republican movement. Elected TD in 1918 de Valera appointed him Minister for Agriculture but he was arrested early in 1920 and remained in prison until the truce.

Courtesy: GAA Museum

Personal quarrels sharpened these divisions. Brugha and Collins disliked and distrusted each other. Stack supported Brugha openly. De Valera claimed to be neutral but since his return from America he usually sided with Brugha.

PICKING THE IRISH DELEGATES

When the Cabinet met to pick the delegates, de Valera astonished them by announcing that he would not be going to London. He gave two reasons:

● If he stayed at home he could control the militant republicans.
● The delegates would have to refer all British proposals back to him in Dublin. That would give them an excuse for not signing anything under pressure from Lloyd George.

Griffith was then appointed to lead the delegation. Brugha and Stack flatly refused to go, so de Valera

Should de Valera have gone to London?
De Valera's decision not to go to London became an important issue during the debate over the treaty.

● Those who opposed him claimed that, after his talks with Lloyd George, he knew that the British would never accept a republic. A compromise was inevitable and he wanted others, especially Collins, to take the blame.
● His supporters argued that his decision was a wise one. They blamed the delegates for failing to follow his instructions and signing the treaty without checking it with him.

It was certainly a strange decision, as Cosgrave said, for the captain of a team not to join in its most important match. But in October 1921 de Valera could not know what was going to happen in December. When he made his decision, it seemed like a good plan. He had seen Lloyd George's enormous power of persuasion and wanted to give the delegates a way out. He underestimated the determination of the British to get their way and the isolation of the delegates in London. He may have got it wrong but it is unfair to blame him for what he could not foresee.

appointed **Robert Barton**, a Protestant landlord with strong republican views, to balance Griffith. De Valera also nominated **Collins** who objected, pointing out that he knew nothing about negotiating. But when de Valera insisted he reluctantly agreed out of a sense of duty. Two lawyers, **Eamonn Duggan** and **George Gavan Duffy**, were included in the delegation to give legal advice.

De Valera appointed **Erskine Childers**, who was Barton's cousin, as the secretary. He was to keep notes during the talks and send reports of progress back to Dublin. Because he had strong republican views, de Valera hoped he would support Barton against the moderates. But Childers' influence was limited because he was not a full member of the delegation. Griffith also disliked and distrusted him and later convinced Collins that he was spying for de Valera.

WERE THEY PLENIPOTENTIARIES?

'Plenipotentiary' is a technical term used in diplomacy. It means *'having full power'* to make agreements.

After the Cabinet picked the delegates, the Dáil appointed them as **plenipotentiaries** to negotiate on its behalf with the British. But confusingly, de Valera also gave them secret instructions that they must not sign anything until they had checked back to Dublin and got the approval of the Cabinet.

'EXTERNAL ASSOCIATION' AND PARTITION

The Irish delegates had two main aims:

- to get a republic (i.e. be fully independent of Britain)
- to restore the unity of Ireland (i.e. undo the Government of Ireland Act by getting the unionists to agree to come under the control of a Dublin government).

But since they could not expect to get everything, they knew they had to make concessions to the British. De Valera had been working on this issue. He knew the British feared an Irish republic in case it would weaken their defences in a war. To remove this worry, he came up with the idea he called "**External Association with the British Empire**". At its simplest it meant that the British would let the Irish leave the Empire and set up their republic. Then the Irish would **voluntarily make a perpetual treaty of alliance** with the Empire and recognise the British king as head of that alliance.

De Valera thought External Association had four advantages.

- It would remove British worries about security.
- It would satisfy British imperialists for whom the king was the symbol of the unity of the Empire.
- It would satisfy the unionists' desire to keep their links with Britain.
- It would satisfy the militant republicans within Sinn Féin by giving them their republic.

De Valera told the delegates to offer External Association to the British in return for ending partition. Unfortunately, it was such a novel idea in 1921 that he and the delegates found it difficult to explain it clearly.

SINN FÉIN'S ATTITUDE TO THE UNIONISTS

Sinn Féin also planned to offer the unionists a local Belfast parliament under the overall control of the Dáil. But they did not make this offer directly to the unionists. Instead, they assumed that once the British made a deal with Dublin, they would force the Ulster unionists to accept Sinn Féin's offer, whether they liked it or not.

This was an unrealistic idea.

- The unionists already had their own parliament under Westminster control. It would be very difficult to remove them.
- The Conservatives would protect the unionists if Lloyd George tried to bully them.

THE BRITISH DELEGATES AND THEIR AIMS

Meanwhile in London, the British Cabinet also selected its delegation. The leaders represented the two parties in the coalition. **Lloyd George** and **Winston Churchill** were Liberals; Austin

Chamberlain and **Lord Birkenhead** were Conservatives.

They had two clear aims:

- to keep Ireland inside in the Empire by making the Irish accept the king as head of the Irish state and swear allegiance to him.
- to protect the unionists in Northern Ireland. But Lloyd George believed this aim mattered less to British people than the first. Therefore he was prepared to make some concessions to the Irish on this point if they could accept the King and Empire.

> **The importance of symbols:** The British obsession with the king seems strange to us today. But in 1921 the 'Crown' (king) symbolised the unity and strength of the Empire for patriotic British people just as the 'republic' symbolised freedom and independence for militant Irish nationalists. Neither symbol had much to do with real life but, unfortunately, men and women were prepared to kill and die for them.

THE UNSEEN PARTICIPANTS: CRAIG AND THE UNIONISTS

Both sides had the Ulster unionists in mind but they were not involved in the talks. Publicly, the Northern Ireland Prime Minister, **Sir James Craig** approved of that. The negotiations, he said, were between the British and the leaders of 'Southern Ireland'. They had nothing to do with him. But privately he feared that the Unionist position might suffer. He relied on his friends in the Conservative Party to keep him in touch with what was going on and to protect him from anything Lloyd George might propose.

QUESTIONS

1 What was the purpose of the Truce of 11 July 1921?

2 What happened during the first phase of the negotiations between de Valera and Lloyd George?

3 What form of words did Lloyd George and de Valera agree on to allow the talks to begin again?

4 How was Lloyd George's dealings with Sinn Féin affected by his coalition with the Conservatives?

5 What divisions within the Sinn Féin movement did de Valera have to keep in mind when negotiating with Lloyd George?

6 Name and comment on the Irish delegation to the London talks. How did de Valera explain his decision not to go?

7 The Irish delegates were called 'plenipotentiaries'. Explain what that means. Was it an accurate description of the delegation?

8 Explain 'dominion status' and 'external association'. (a) What would the Irish dislike about dominion status? (b) What would the British dislike about external association?

9 List four members of the British delegation. Explain their aims.

10 Who was the leader of the Ulster unionists? What was his attitude to the negotiations between the British and Sinn Féin? What did the Sinn Féin delegates plan to offer him? Do you think he would accept it? Explain your answer.

11 Make two columns showing the delegates and their aims facing each other. Can you see any issues which would be likely to cause conflict?

DOCUMENT A

A letter from Tom Jones, Lloyd George's secretary to Andrew Bonar Law, who had recently retired as leader of the Conservative Party. It describes the outcome of the Lloyd George/de Valera meeting.

22 July 1921

De Valera left for Dublin this morning, having had four long interviews with the P.M. [Prime Minister] … His visit has been most helpful to the cause of peace because he and the P.M. have met face to face and alone. The P.M.'s first idea had been to have with him Balfour, Chamberlain and Hamar Greenwood, but luckily de Valera did not want any colleagues with him so the P.M. was able to drop his.

> **Who was Tom Jones?** Tom Jones was Lloyd George's secretary, fellow Welshman and trusted advisor. Lloyd George used him as a go-between with the Irish delegation. He often met them in private, reassuring them about the good will of his boss and good intentions. Jones kept a diary that is a very important source of information about the negotiations.

The P.M.'s account is that de V. is not a big man but he is a sincere man, a white man, and 'an agreeable personality'. He has a limited <u>vocabulary</u>, talks chiefly of ideals, and constantly recurs to the same few dominating notions. He agreed to drop 'the Republic', the P.M. telling him that there was no Irish or Welsh word for it, and therefore it was alien to the spirit of the Celt!

He was willing to be within the Empire, to recognize the King, to go without a Navy. What he chiefly seemed to want was Irish unity – that we should not impose partition … As the negotiations proceeded the P.M. got a draft … of the sort of proposals we should put up to de Valera … It was shown in an early edition to Craig … Grigg and I took it to de Valera … Yesterday there was another interview with the P.M. during which de V., while not accepting our proposals, agreed to make counter-proposals after consulting his colleagues. I think this means that he is not unfavourable to the proposals in substance, but must try and bring his left wing along with him. Michael Collins is all right but some of the gunmen will be irreconcilable. Meanwhile the <u>Hierarchy</u>, the Press, and all moderate opinion in Ireland is yearning for peace, and when de V. reaches Dublin he will come under this influence, it is hoped …

Throughout the P.M. has been superb and the 'Proposals' when they see the light will be accepted by the whole world I think as one of the most generous acts in our history. Briefly it is '<u>Dominion status</u>' with all sorts of important powers, but no Navy, no hostile tariffs, and no coercion of Ulster. There is a Territorial Force for Ulster, and for the South. It is hoped they will contribute to the Debt. Etc. An instrument 'in the form of a Treaty' is proposed. This caused a lot of heart-burning inside and was only got through by the passionate pleading of the P.M.

(T. Jones, *Whitehall Diary*, London 1971)

1 Who wrote this letter and when was it written? Look up the underlined words.

2 How often did de Valera and Lloyd George meet? Why did they meet alone?

3 How did Lloyd George describe de Valera? Do you think Lloyd George was accurate in his estimation of de Valera? Explain your answer. Do these comments tell us anything about Lloyd George?

4 List the things Lloyd George thought de Valera was willing to accept. What, according to Lloyd George, was de Valera most concerned about? How accurate do you consider Lloyd George was on these two points?

5 Jones mentions how different groups in Ireland will respond to the British proposals. List them. Do you think he is accurate? Which group does he hope will influence de Valera?

6 List the content of the 'proposals'? Do you think that Jones is right when he says that the world will see them as 'one of the most generous acts in our history'? Explain why that seems so important to him. Would Irish nationalists agree with him? Explain your answer.

7 Do you think the author of this letter is a reliable witness to the events of July 1921? Set out and explain (a) one reason for trusting and (b) one reason for distrusting his account of these events.

DOCUMENT B

De Valera's reply to Lloyd George

10 August

On the occasion of our last interview I gave it as my judgement that Dáil Éireann could not and that the Irish people would not accept the proposals of your Government as set forth in the draft of July 20th which you had presented to me. Having consulted my colleagues, and with them given these proposals the most earnest consideration, I now confirm that judgement.

… A certain treaty of free association with the British Commonwealth group, as with a partial league of nations, we would have been ready to recommend, and as a Government to negotiate and take responsibility for, had we an assurance that the entry of the nation as a whole into such association would secure for it the allegiance of the present dissenting minority, to meet whose sentiment alone this step could be contemplated …
[*Documents on Irish Foreign Policy*, Vol. 1 pp 254–5, Royal Irish Academy 1998]

1 What, according to de Valera, had he told Lloyd George 'at our last interview'?

2 Explain the term 'the present dissenting minority'?

3 Explain in your own words what de Valera says they 'would have been ready to recommend'?

4 Look back at the British proposals mentioned in Source A. Write alongside them the offer which de Valera makes to Lloyd George in Source B. Comment on the main points of difference.

5 Compare Sources A and B. They give a very different picture of the progress of the negotiations so far. How do you explain that difference?

NEGOTIATING A TREATY: OCTOBER – DECEMBER 1921 (CASE STUDY)

THE NEGOTIATIONS BEGIN

On 11 October 1921, Arthur Griffith led the Irish delegation into No.10 Downing Street to begin the negotiations. The two delegations were unevenly matched.

- **Leadership and experience**
  - Lloyd George was one of the most experienced and ruthless negotiators of his day. A government minister since 1906 and Prime Minister since 1916, he had recently negotiated the peace treaties which ended the first World War.
  - The Irish delegates had no experience. Griffith was a journalist turned politician who had led an underground government for eighteen months. Collins was a post office clerk turned soldier; a brilliant revolutionary leader but with no experience of negotiating.

- **Location of the talks**
  - The British were on their home ground. The visible power of the British Empire lay all around them. Skilled and experienced civil servants and lawyers were at hand to give them help and advice.
  - The Irish were on enemy territory. Their small team of civil servants and advisers lacked experience and resources. In the details of the negotiations they were often out of their depth.

- **The imbalance of power**
  - There was still a large British army in Ireland. If the talks failed, Lloyd George would use it ruthlessly. In recent European war, he had sent millions of men to their death. He would not hesitate to let more die in Ireland, if that would serve Britain's interests.
  - The Irish knew that if they failed it meant war and their people would suffer. That worried Collins in particular. He knew how weak the IRA was and how much of their success depended on secrecy and surprise. Those advantages were now gone.

11–24 OCTOBER: THE TALKS BEGIN

The British began by repeating the offer they made to de Valera in July. Griffith rejected it. Over the next two weeks there were six more meetings. They dealt with issues such as trade, defence and finance. But it became clear that nothing could be agreed until the two key issues – partition and sovereignty (i.e. Ireland's relationship to the British Crown and Empire) – were clarified.

> **Collins on Lloyd George:** *'Lloyd George's attitude I find particularly obnoxious. He is all comradely – all craft and wiliness – all arm around the shoulder – all the old friends' act. Not long ago he would joyfully have had me at the rope's end. He thinks that the past is all washed out now – but that's to my face. What he thinks behind my back makes me sick at the thought of it.'* (T.P. Coogan, *Michael Collins*, London 1990 p. 256)

DISAGREEMENTS AMONG THE IRISH

At the same time, disagreements developed in the Irish delegation. Griffith, who disliked Childers, suspected he was sending hostile reports back to de Valera and won Collins over to his point of view.

The Treaty negotiators in London

Interference from de Valera in Dublin increased the tensions. At one point a furious Collins threatened to go home and make de Valera go to London himself. Only when the other delegates agreed to send a letter of protest, did he cool down.

BREAKING INTO SUB-COMMITTEES

Griffith and Collins suggested to Lloyd George they might achieve more if the two delegations broke up into sub-committees to deal with the various issues. Their aim seems to have been to keep Childers out. Lloyd George, whose secret service told him of divisions in the Irish camp and who also disliked Childers, agreed. From then on, Griffith and Collins met privately with Lloyd George to deal with the key issues of partition and sovereignty.

NEGOTIATING ON PARTITION

On partition, the British offered that, if Ireland agreed to stay in the Empire, they would persuade the Ulster Unionists to join an all-Ireland parliament. While the Irish were considering this, some Conservative MPs in the Commons challenged Lloyd George's Irish policy.

On 2 November he warned that this could bring down his government and asked Griffith to write a letter he could use to reassure them. In it Griffith promised that, if he was satisfied that the 'essential unity' of Ireland was guaranteed, he would recommend

> 'a free partnership of Ireland with the other states associated within the British Commonwealth … [and] that Ireland should consent to a recognition of the Crown as the head of the proposed association of states.' (T.J. Jones, Whitehall Diary, Vol. 3, London 1971, p. 154)

In return for Griffith's letter, Lloyd George promised to make Craig accept an all-Ireland parliament. If he could not do so, he said, he would resign.

PROPOSING A BOUNDARY COMMISSION

But Craig refused even to meet Lloyd George. On 8 November Lloyd George's secretary, Tom Jones, visited Griffith and Collins to tell them this. Clearly, he said, Lloyd George could keep his promise and resign but if he did, the next Prime Minister would be a Conservative who would be even less sympathetic to nationalists.

Jones then suggested a new way to deal with partition. Northern Ireland would remain in existence but a **Boundary Commission** would be set up to redraw the border between it and the South.

Griffith and Collins were unsure about this suggestion.

- Its advantage was that nationalist areas like south Down, south Armagh and Derry city would go to the South as well as Tyrone and Fermanagh.
- Its disadvantage was that accepting it involved admitting that the partition of Ireland was permanent.

They agreed to consider the proposal but only as a way of putting more pressure on the unionists to agree to an all-Ireland parliament.

10 NOVEMBER: LLOYD GEORGE MEETS CRAIG

On 10 November Craig arrived in London. He flatly rejected any deal with Dublin and refused to be intimidated by the threat of a Boundary Commission. Lloyd George and even some Conservative leaders were angry with him but there was nothing they could do. Craig already had Northern Ireland and many Conservative MPs supported him. All he had to do was sit tight and no one could move him.

ACCEPTING THE BOUNDARY COMMISSION

After that, Lloyd George stopped urging the unionists to make a deal with Sinn Féin. He concentrated instead on persuading Griffith and Collins to accept a Boundary Commission. He assured them that it would transfer large parts of Northern Ireland to the South and that the remainder would be too small to survive economically.

The Irish delegates accepted his arguments. They had always known that they could not force one million unionists into a united Ireland against their will. At least it seemed likely that a Boundary Commission would transfer many northern nationalists to the South.

On 13 November Griffith promised not to break off the talks on this issue. When they reported back to Dublin, the other members of the Cabinet also reluctantly accepted a Boundary Commission as the best solution to the issue of partition.

NEGOTIATING ABOUT DOMINION STATUS AND EXTERNAL ASSOCIATION

Talks about the other key issue – sovereignty (independence) – were going on at the same time.
- The British offered Ireland 'dominion status'. They pointed out that the **dominions enjoyed complete freedom from British interference** and were members of the League of Nations.
- The Irish rejected dominion status. They pointed out that the British still had **the legal right to interfere** in the dominions. The Irish did not want that, so they offered External Association instead. That would give **the Irish complete control over everything to do with Ireland** while guaranteeing that they would not side with Britain's enemies in time of war.
- The British rejected External Association. They could not see any difference between it and complete independence. They also brushed aside Irish worries about British interference. The king, they argued, had no power in the dominions. He was just a symbol of unity. And whatever the law said, in practice the British government **never interfered in the dominions' internal affairs**. The Canadians and others would object strongly if they tried.
- But, the Irish replied, Canada is thousands of miles away. It would be almost impossible for Britain to interfere there if the Canadians objected. Ireland is beside Britain. If the king was head of the Irish state, the British government could easily interfere in Irish affairs.

At meeting after meeting Griffith and Collins argued against dominion status and for External Association but the British refused to accept it. Three times the delegates brought this message back to Dublin and each time the Dáil Cabinet told them to go back and try again.

A BREAKTHROUGH ON SOVEREIGNTY

At last, on 28 November, Lloyd George offered to let the Irish use *"any phrase they liked which would ensure that the position of the Crown in Ireland should be* **no more in practice** *than it was in Canada"*.

This was an important breakthrough. The two sides agreed not to spell out how much independence the Irish would have; they would just say it would be the same as Canada's.

1 DECEMBER: A DRAFT TREATY

On 1 December Lloyd George presented the Irish with his final draft of a treaty. The key points were:
- The '**Irish Free State**' was to be a dominion of the Empire with the same independence as Canada.
- The king would be its head of state and all TDs would swear an oath to him.
- Northern Ireland would be allowed to opt out but if it did, a Boundary Commission would redraw the border between North and South.

> **'The Irish Free State':** In July when De Valera met Lloyd George, he was using notepaper headed *Saorstát na hÉireann*. That was Sinn Féin's Irish for '*Irish republic*'. Lloyd George, who spoke Welsh, asked what exactly the words meant and was told 'Free State of Ireland'. He then used those words in the Treaty, hoping it would appeal to the Irish, while disguising from the British how near to a republic dominion status really was.

3 DECEMBER: THE DÁIL CABINET DISCUSSES IT

The delegates took the draft treaty back to Dublin and the Cabinet met to discuss it. All accepted the

Boundary Commission as a solution to partition but they disagreed about dominion status and the oath to the king.

The meeting lasted for seven exhausting hours. During it, the bitterness among Cabinet members came into the open, with Griffith and Brugha almost coming to blows. Griffith made it clear he thought the offer was a good one. If it was rejected, he wanted de Valera to go to London himself to tell Lloyd George. Only reluctantly did he finally agree to return.

The meeting ended abruptly because the delegates had to rush away to catch their boat. De Valera hurriedly drew up a different form of oath and told the delegates not to sign anything until they had brought it back for approval.

4 DECEMBER: THE NEGOTIATIONS BREAK DOWN

The weary delegates arrived back in London on Sunday morning. Collins refused to go to Downing Street with their rejection but Griffith and the others went to tell Lloyd George. He was angry and the talks broke off in disagreement. It seemed as if two months of negotiations had achieved nothing.

5 DECEMBER: LLOYD GEORGE SEES COLLINS

But Lloyd George was not ready to give up. The next morning he sent Tom Jones to persuade Collins to see him. Collins explained that he feared the Boundary Commission would not end partition. Lloyd George assured him that it would remove so much of Northern Ireland that the remainder could not survive economically. This satisfied Collins. After Lloyd George promised to re-examine the trade clauses and the oath, Collins agreed to another session of talks in the afternoon.

5 DECEMBER: THE FINAL TALKS

At this final session, Lloyd George showed his brilliance as a negotiator, skilfully mixing threats and concessions to get what he wanted.

First he set a deadline. The Northern Ireland parliament was due to meet next day and he had promised to let Craig know its fate before then. What was he to say? Did they accept the Boundary Commission?

Griffith replied that they must first know Craig's attitude. Lloyd George rejected this. Producing Griffith's undertaking of 13 November, he demanded to know if Griffith was about to break his promise not to repudiate the Boundary Commission. Always touchy about his honour, Griffith angrily denied the suggestion. After that, it was no longer possible to break off the talks on partition.

LLOYD GEORGE'S FINAL CONCESSIONS

Then Lloyd George softened his line. He offered the Irish something dear to Griffith's heart — the right to protect Irish industry with tariffs on British imports.

He also agreed to re-write the oath. In the new version it read.

> 'I ... ... do solemnly swear **true faith and allegiance to the Constitution of the Irish Free State** as by law established, and that **I will be faithful to His Majesty King George V** in virtue of the common citizenship of Ireland with Great Britain and her adherence to and membership of the group of nations forming the British Commonwealth of Nations.'

These words were very similar to the version of the oath de Valera had drawn up at Saturday's Cabinet meeting. It was also an important symbolic climb down by the British.

- In other dominions, MPs swore 'true faith and allegiance' to the king.
- In the Irish Free State, they would swear **allegiance** to their own constitution and only to be **faithful** to the king.

Allegiance: The Irish objected to swearing 'allegiance' (i.e. loyalty) to the king because it would have made them subjects of the king and not citizens of Ireland.

This was very close indeed to de Valera's External Association, though Lloyd George could not say so out loud in case it annoyed the Conservatives.

THE THREAT OF WAR

That, Lloyd George insisted, was as far as he could go. Would the Irish accept it? Griffith replied that they must check with Dublin before they signed anything. Lloyd George objected. He pointed out that their papers described them as 'plenipotentiaries' so they had power to sign. If they did not, war *'immediate and terrible'* would follow within three days.

Griffith then said that he would accept the terms. The rest insisted on withdrawing to discuss their position. Outside, Collins said he too would sign and Duggan agreed with him. Barton and Gavan Duffy held out for several hours but at last they reluctantly agreed to sign.

WHY DID COLLINS ACCEPT THE TERMS?

Up until this time, many believed Collins was a committed republican, so why did he accept these terms? Perhaps it was because he was a realist. He may have believed that the terms on offer were the best they could get and he knew that if war began again the IRA was unlikely to win against the much stronger British forces. But if the British left, it would be very difficult for them to come back, whatever the Irish did.

Collins had also studied the development of the dominions while he was in London. He knew that their independence was expanding rapidly. As a Dominion, the Irish Free State's independence would expand too.

6 DECEMBER: SIGNING THE TREATY

At 2.10am on the morning of 6 December the delegates went back to Downing Street and signed the *'**Articles of Agreement for a Treaty between Great Britain and Ireland**'*. It contained eighteen articles. The most important were:

- Articles 1 and 2 recognised the Irish Free State as a Dominion of the British Commonwealth. Its position *'in relation to the Imperial (British) Parliament and Government… shall be that of the Dominion of Canada'…* This wording was important. If Canada got more independence, so did the Irish Free State; if the British interfered in the Irish Free State, the Canadians would protest because that would affect them too.

- Articles 3 and 4 provided that the king would be represented in Ireland by a **governor-general** and that all members of the Irish parliament would take an oath to him (see above).

- Article 5 said the Free State would pay a share in the UK war debt.

- Articles 6 to 9 covered coastal defence: the British navy would have permanent use of the ports of Queenstown (Cobh), Berehaven and Lough Swilly, with additional facilities in time of war.

- Articles 11 to 15 covered the position of Northern Ireland. If the parliament of Northern Ireland opted out of the treaty settlement, Article 12 laid down that:

    'a Commission consisting of three persons, one to be appointed by the Government of the Irish Free State, one to be appointed by the Government of Northern Ireland, and one, who shall be the chairman, to be appointed by the British Government, shall determine, in accordance with the wishes of the inhabitants so far as may be compatible with the economic and geographical conditions, the boundaries between Northern Ireland and the rest of Ireland.'
    (For a full text of the Treaty, see Longford *Peace by Ordeal*, Appendix 1)

1 Name the members of the two delegations which met in Downing Street on 11 October 1921. Write a brief comparison between them.

2 What caused conflict (a) within the Irish delegation and (b) between the delegates and the Cabinet in Dublin.

3 Outline the way the discussions over partition developed. Explain what a 'Boundary Commission' meant. What advantages and disadvantages did Griffith and Collins see in this proposal?

4 (a) Explain the British objections to external association. (b) Explain the Irish objections to dominion status. (c) What did Lloyd George offer on 28 November which got around the Irish objections to dominion status?

5 Describe the meeting of the Dáil Cabinet on 3 December.

6 How did Lloyd George keep the talks going after the Irish rejection?

7 Describe what happened in Downing Street during the final session. What deadline did Lloyd George set? What two last-minute concessions did he make? What threat did he offer?

8 Which Irishman agreed to sign first? Explain why he did so. Who was the second to agree? Why did he do so? Who held out longest against signing? Why did they do so?

9 Outline the main terms of the Treaty.

DOCUMENT A

ARTHUR GRIFFITH TO ÉAMON DE VALERA

London, 24 October 1921

A Chara,

Míceal and I were asked to see Lloyd George and Chamberlain this evening at the conclusion of the Conference. They talked freely – Chamberlain frankly. The burden of their story was that on the Crown they must fight. It was the only link of the Empire they possessed.

They pressed me to say that I would accept the Crown provided we came to other agreements. It was evident they wanted something to reassure the Die-Hards. I told them I had no authority. If we came to an agreement on all other points I could recommend some form of association with the Crown …

Told them the only possibility of Ireland considering association of any kind with the Crown was in exchange for essential unity.

Míceal got Chamberlain to admit that the general feeling in England was for a settlement. He countered their arguments on defence, etc. all the time. But they always fell back on the impossibility of peace except with the acceptance of the Crown. We agreed to proceed on the basis of settling all other points, leaving the Crown to last.

Meet again at 4 tomorrow,

Art Ó Griobhtha

(*Documents of Irish Foreign Policy*, Royal Irish Academy 1998, Vol. 1, 1919–22, pp 290–1)

1 Who wrote this document and why did he write it?

2 The letter describes a meeting between four men. Name them and in each case say who he was.

3 What did the two British men mean when they spoke of 'the Crown'. What did they say about it? Explain why it was so important to them.

4 Explain what Griffith meant by saying 'they wanted something to reassure the Die-Hards'.

5 What did Griffith reply to their request? Explain what he meant when he referred to 'agreement on all other points'?

6 What did 'Míceal' get Chamberlain to admit? Why did Griffith consider that important?

7 What does this document tell us about the main British concerns during the negotiations? Do you think Griffith is reflecting these accurately?

DOCUMENT B

When the Dáil met to debate the Treaty, Robert Barton gave this account of how the Treaty was signed.

… On Sunday, 4 December, the Conference had precipitately and definitely broken down. An <u>intermediary</u> effected contact next day, and on Monday at 3pm, Arthur Griffith, Michael Collins, and myself met the English representatives. In the struggle that ensued Arthur Griffith sought, repeatedly to have the decision between war and peace on the terms of the Treaty referred back to <u>this assembly</u>.

This proposal Mr. Lloyd George directly negatived. He claimed that we were <u>plenipotentiaries</u> and that we must either accept or reject. Speaking for himself and his colleagues, the English Prime Minister with all the solemnity and the power of conviction that he alone, of all men I met, can impart by word and gesture … declared that the signature and recommendation of every member of our delegation was necessary or war would follow immediately. He gave us until 10 o'clock to make up our minds, and it was then about 8.30.

We returned to our house to decide upon our answer. The issue before us was whether we should stand behind our proposals for external association, face war and maintain the Republic, or whether we should accept inclusion in the British Empire and take peace.

Arthur Griffith, Michael Collins, and Eamonn Duggan were for acceptance and peace; Gavan Duffy and myself were for refusal – war or no war. An answer that was not unanimous committed you to immediate war, and the responsibility for that was to rest directly upon those two delegates who refused to sign.

For myself, I preferred war. I told my colleagues so, but for the nation, without consultation, I dared not accept that responsibility. The alternative which I sought to avoid seemed to me a lesser outrage than the violation of what is my faith. So that I myself, and of my own choice, must commit my nation to immediate war, without you, <u>Mr. President</u>, or the Members of the Dáil, or the nation having an opportunity to examine the terms upon which war could be avoided. I signed, and now I have fulfilled my undertaking I recommend to you the Treaty I signed in London.
(*Dáil Debates*, 19 December 1921)

QUESTIONS ON THE DOCUMENT

1. Explain the three underlined words and name the 'Mr President'.

2. What was 'the struggle' on Monday, 3 December and what did Griffith try to get the 'English representatives' to agree to?

3. What did Lloyd George tell the Irish representatives? What does Barton say about his manner? Does this throw any light on the signing of the Treaty?

4. What options did the Irish delegates have to consider after they left Downing Street? How did the delegates line up on these issues?

5. Which option did Barton say he preferred? What reason does he give for signing despite that?

6. Barton, a republican, is explaining to the Dáil why, despite his beliefs, he signed the Treaty. Do you think this might have influenced the way he told the story of these events? Explain your answer.

DIVIDING OVER THE TREATY: DECEMBER 1921 – JANUARY 1922

JULY TO DECEMBER 1921: THE IRA DURING THE TRUCE

When the truce was signed in July, no one expected the peace talks to last until December. This long delay did not help the cause of peace.

The IRA grew rapidly during the truce. Men who were afraid to fight the Black and Tans now rushed to share in the reflected glory of the few who had. Known as 'truceleers', they were despised by the fighting men and IRA leaders found it hard to control them.

Law and order began to break down. There was no police force. The RIC was destroyed but there was not yet an Irish police force to replace them. Local IRA commanders filled the gap but some used the opportunity to seek personal gain or pursue personal grudges. They robbed banks, forced people from their homes or murdered them as 'spies' or 'traitors'. In Cork and some border areas, Protestants were killed or expelled merely because of their religion.

REACTIONS TO NEWS OF A TREATY

As a result most people greeted news of an agreement in London with relief. Peace would mean that life could return to normal.

But when dedicated republicans heard the terms, they were dismayed and angry. They had fought for an independent republic. A Treaty that gave less was not acceptable. It was reported that some IRA men talked about arresting the returning delegates for treason.

De Valera was furious when he heard the delegates had signed a Treaty without his permission. He proposed that the Cabinet sack Griffith, Collins and Barton and throw out the Treaty. But when a vote was taken, Cosgrave supported the delegates' demand that the Treaty be sent to the Dáil for a final decision.

TAKING SIDES ON THE TREATY

Before the Dáil met each side tried to rally support.

- Collins was president of the IRB. On 10 December he got its Supreme Council to back the Treaty, though it left TDs who were in the IRB free to vote according to their consciences.
- De Valera came out publicly against the Treaty.

On 9 December he issued a statement, saying: *'The terms of this agreement are in violent conflict with the wishes of the majority of this nation as expressed freely in successive elections during the past three years.'* (Longford and O'Neill, *Eamon de Valera*, Dublin 1971 p. 169)

With this statement de Valera broke a tradition that disagreements within the Cabinet were confidential.

THE SECOND DÁIL: A VERY PECULIAR PARLIAMENT

On 14 December 1921 the Second Dáil met to debate the Treaty. This Dáil was unique in Irish history. Its members had been chosen in May while the fighting was still going on. Only Sinn Féin put up candidates so it contained only Sinn Féin TDs who got their seats without a single vote being cast.

This made the Second Dáil an unelected, one-party assembly such as any dictator might have admired. Its members were hand picked by the Sinn Féin leaders and naturally they chose men and women who were dedicated republicans. As a result, this Dáil had far more committed republicans than the country as a whole.

But there was no dictator to tell these TDs what to do. They were free to make up their own minds. While some had taken sides before the debate began, there were quite a few who listened carefully to the arguments, thought hard about the issues, changed their minds back and forth and in the end voted according to their consciences.

14 DECEMBER: A SECRET SESSION ON DE VALERA'S DOCUMENT NO. 2

The debate began in secret. De Valera called on TDs to reject the Treaty and offer the British an alternative treaty which he called 'Document No. 2'. It repeated his External Association proposals. This pleased no one. Supporters of the Treaty pointed out that the British had already rejected these demands; republicans thought it was no better than the Treaty. As a result de Valera withdrew it.

19 DECEMBER TO 7 JANUARY: THE PUBLIC DEBATE

On 19 December the Dáil began to debate the Treaty in public.

- Griffith, supported by Collins, proposed that TDs accept it.
- De Valera, seconded by Stack, wanted them to reject it.

The debate that followed lasted until 7 January, with a week's break for Christmas. Every deputy insisted on speaking. Very few mentioned partition, apparently accepting the argument that the Boundary Commission would reduce Northern Ireland to an unviable area. Instead most of the debate focussed on the oath to the king and Ireland's status as a Dominion of the British Empire.

THE CASE AGAINST THE TREATY

Opponents of the Treaty can be divided into two camps, the hard-line republicans and the moderates.

- **The arguments of the hard-line republicans**
For hard-line republicans, belief in the republic was more like a religious faith than a political argument. They claimed that:
  — The republic had been declared in 1916. It was confirmed by the election of 1918 and the Dáil's declaration in 1919. It was sanctified by the blood of martyrs who had died for it. No one had the right to overthrow it.
  — All TDs had taken an oath to uphold the republic. To take an oath to the king was to betray that oath.
  — The Treaty must be rejected. If war was the only alternative, then war it must be.

These views were passionately expressed by, among others, **Stack, Brugha** and the six women TDs, including **Mary MacSwiney** and **Constance Markievicz**. Ominously for the future, they made it clear that if they lost, they would not accept the decision of the Dáil. As Liam Mellows said: *'We who stand by the republic still will, I presume, rebel against the new government that would be set up if this Treaty is passed'*. (Dáil Debates, p. 243)

The arguments of the moderate republicans

Moderate republicans were more reasoned in their opposition to the Treaty, though they too felt that the oath to the king violated their oath to the republic.

— Their main objection was that the Treaty made the British king head of the Irish Free State and this, **de Valera** said, *makes British authorities our masters in Ireland.* (Longford and O'Neill, *De Valera*, London 1971, p. 175)

— When supporters of the Treaty pointed out that the British did not interfere in Canada **Erskine Childers** replied that Canada and the other Dominions were thousands of miles from Britain, while Ireland was on its doorstep.

— Letting the British navy use three Irish ports would make it impossible for an Irish government to have a foreign policy independent of Britain's.

The moderate republicans did not want to return to war and accepted that they had to compromise with Britain. They just felt that the Treaty terms were not good enough. They urged the Dáil to reject them and send delegates back to London to try again.

THE CASE FOR THE TREATY

Not many TDs who supported the Treaty actually liked it. They supported it mainly because they could see no alternative.

The military argument.

Their main argument was military. If, as Lloyd George said, the alternative to the Treaty was war, could the Irish win? **Collins** and several IRA leaders, like **Richard Mulcahy** and **Seán MacEoin** argued that they could not.

— Lloyd George did not agree to talk because of the IRA's military victories. As Mulcahy pointed out *'we have not yet been able to drive the enemy from anything but a fairly good-sized police barracks'.* (D. MacArdle, *The Irish Republic*, p. 568). He talked because decent British people were embarrassed by the behaviour of the Black and Tans. If the Dáil turned down the Treaty they would lose British and world sympathy.

— If war began again, the British military could be more ruthless than before and their people would support them. That would bring more suffering to Irish people. Would nationalists, whose backing had been vital to the IRA's earlier success, still support them if the Dáil threw away the chance of peace?

— And if they did start fighting again, as **Collins** and others pointed out, the IRA would be weaker than before. Its leaders were now well known and its spy network was exposed.

The 'step by step' argument

Some republicans accepted the Treaty because they saw it as the first step towards full

DUBLIN OPINION.   APRIL, 1922 APRIL, 1922.   DUBLIN OPINION.

What IS a Poor   Journalist to do?

St. Michael Driving Bad Angel out of Paradise.
CARTOON CREATED AFTER ATTENDING FREE STATE MEETING.

The Butchery of Ireland.
CARTOON EXECUTED AFTER ATTENDING REPUBLICAN GATHERING.

Courtesy: Trinity College Library

1 Explain the conclusion a 'poor journalist' came to 'after attending a Free State meeting'.

2 Explain his conclusion 'after a republican meeting'.

3 What point was the cartoonist making about the two sides?

independence. Collins made this point most clearly. The Treaty, he said, *'gives us freedom, not the ultimate freedom that all nations desire and develop to, but the freedom to achieve it'*.

The advantage of dominion status

Collins also argued that a small, militarily weak country, like Ireland would be more secure as a dominion. Alone and isolated, it would be easy for the British to bully us but as a dominion, the other dominions would protect us. *'They are, in effect, introduced as guarantors of our freedom, which makes us stronger than if we stood alone'*. (Dáil Debates, p. 35)

The Treaty compared to Home Rule

Finally a few TDs compared dominion status, not with the idealised republic but with the Home Rule that nationalists had welcomed only ten years before. **Griffith** listed gains which would have seemed impossible then.

> *'We have brought back the flag; we have brought back the evacuation of Ireland after 700 years by British troops and the formation of an Irish army. We have brought back to Ireland her full rights and powers of fiscal control. We have brought back to Ireland equality with England, equality with all nations which form that Commonwealth and an equal voice in the direction of foreign affairs in peace and war.'* (Dáil Debates, p. 21)

THE DIVISION OUTSIDE THE DÁIL

Around the country people followed the debate closely. Like TDs they were divided about the Treaty. Many who had been active in the IRA opposed it but most people wanted peace so that they could resume their normal lives. The economy was shattered and rebuilding it seemed more important than abstract ideas like an oath to the king or the difference between a dominion and a republic.

All national newspapers and most local ones urged TDs to accept the Treaty. Twenty county councils, all democratically elected unlike the Second Dáil, passed resolutions in favour of it.

Some republican TDs proudly insisted they would make up their own minds, whatever their constituents thought. But others listened when they went home at Christmas. If the vote had been taken before that, the Treaty might have been rejected. But a small number of TDs changed their minds when they realised how strong the popular support for it was.

7 January 1922: the Dáil accepts the Treaty

The vote finally came on 7 January 1922. It was very close with sixty-four TDs voting for the Treaty and fifty-seven against. De Valera resigned as President and Griffith was elected in his place. De Valera and his followers withdrew from the Dáil in protest, though they returned later.

QUESTIONS

1 After the Treaty was signed, how did the two sides try to rally support?

2 Why was the Second Dáil 'unique in Irish history'?

3 Name two hard-line republicans who opposed the Treaty and explain the reasons they gave for opposing it. Do you agree with the view that their opposition was 'more like a religious faith than a political argument'? Explain your answer.

4 Name two of the moderate opponents of the Treaty and explain the reasons they gave for opposing it. Do these arguments seem reasonable to you? Explain your answer.

5 Name three of the people who supported the Treaty. Set out the main arguments they put forward in favour of it. Which do you think is the most convincing? Explain your answer.

6 List the things Griffith claimed the Treaty brought. Is this a fair assessment of its merits?

7 What happened on 7 January 1922?

CIVIL WAR: JUNE 1922 – MAY 1923

TAKING OVER FROM THE BRITISH

The Treaty allowed for a twelve-month transition period – to 6 December 1922 – during which the British would hand over, step by step, to a Provisional Irish government, headed by Griffith and Collins.

Michael Collins arriving at Dublin Castle by taxi to take over the government of Ireland from the British

On 16 January, Collins went to Dublin Castle, which for seven hundred years, had been the seat of British rule in Ireland. He formally took possession of it from men who, only months before, would have executed him as a traitor to the king. Over the weeks that followed, similar scenes took place at government offices and army barracks around the country. Slowly, like a receding tide, the British withdrew, until the last troops finally left in December.

SETTING UP THE INSTITUTIONS OF THE IRISH FREE STATE

The Provisional government also had to set up the institutions the new state would need.

- A police force was essential. They decided to call it the **Garda Síochána** and that it should be unarmed. Most of the men who joined it had been in the IRA.

- Once it became clear that the majority of the IRA opposed the Treaty, they also set up a **Free State army**. Organised by Richard Mulcahy, who was now Minister for Defence, it was made up of pro-Treaty IRA men plus Irish men who had served in the British army.
- They began to set up a civil service.
- They began to draw up a constitution for the Irish Free State.

THE ANTI-TREATY IRA

While working on these things, Collins was also desperately trying to stop the split over the Treaty degenerating into violence. His most urgent problem was the IRA.

- Most of the Headquarters staff in Dublin followed Collins and Mulcahy, but a minority, including **Rory O'Connor** and **Liam Mellows**, were anti-Treaty.
- Among the IRA commandants around the country, only **Seán MacEoin** in Longford supported it.
- Opposition was strongest in Munster where most of the fighting in the War of Independence had taken place. **Seamus Robinson** in Tipperary and **Tom Barry** and **Liam Lynch** in Cork were all hard-line republicans. Rank and file IRA men probably followed their local leaders.

MAY FLOWERS

What point about the Treaty debates is this cartoon making?

Courtesy: Trinity College Library

Their reasons for opposing the Treaty varied. Some had risked their lives for a republic and would settle for nothing less. For others, peace was not attractive. Since 1918 their guns and their role as heroes of the revolution gave them status in their neighbourhoods. Peacetime civilian life had little to offer them.

At first the anti-Treaty IRA was better armed than government supporters. When the British started to withdraw, they had handed over arms to local IRA leaders without asking their politics. This changed later but by then it was too late.

26 MARCH: THE ARMY CONVENTION REPUDIATES THE DÁIL

In January, after the Dáil accepted the Treaty, Mulcahy agreed to let the IRA hold an Army Convention to discuss it, despite protests from Griffith that it was undemocratic. When he realised it would be strongly anti-Treaty he cancelled it but it went ahead anyway.

Two hundred IRA men attended the Convention on 26 March. Led by Liam Mellows and Rory O'Connor they rejected the authority of the Dáil and set up their own sixteen-man Executive. Afterwards a reporter asked Rory O'Connor if they acknowledged any other government in Ireland apart from the IRA Executive. He replied,

> 'No'. 'Do we take it that we are going to have a military dictatorship, then?' he was asked and replied, 'You can take it that way if you like'. (Robert Kee, *The Green Flag*, London 1972, p. 733)

14 APRIL: THE FOUR COURTS SEIZED

On 14 April O'Connor and his followers seized the Four Courts and other buildings around Dublin. This was a challenge to the Provisional Government but Collins chose to ignore it. He still hoped to avoid a war and he needed time to build up the Free State army. Recruitment and training went ahead rapidly and by June it contained 8,000 men.

COLLINS AND CRAIG MEET ABOUT VIOLENCE IN NORTHERN IRELAND

Another problem for Collins was the situation in Northern Ireland (see section 11.1). Violence had continued there during the truce as the IRA resisted partition and the Unionist government tried to tighten its hold. Catholics in Belfast were driven from their jobs and often their homes. There was evidence that the police were either directly involved in the attacks or were making no attempt to stop them.

To protect nationalists, Collins met Craig three times between January and March. In return for Collins's promise to end the boycott of Belfast goods, Craig promised to ensure greater protection for Catholics. But Craig was unable to control his own extremists and the violence continued.

In April the Northern parliament passed the **Special Powers Act**, which imposed the death penalty for possessing arms. The number of British troops was increased and Sir Henry Wilson, who had just retired as Commander of the British army, was engaged as a military adviser. These forces were used exclusively against the nationalist community.

This made Collins extremely angry. Unknown to Griffith, he arranged with the anti-Treaty IRA to send arms to the IRA in the north. As well as helping northern Catholics, he seems to have hoped that co-operation on the north between pro- and anti-Treaty IRA factions would prevent the split in the South.

DE VALERA'S TACTICS

Meanwhile de Valera's attitude was unclear. He formed an anti-Treaty party, **Cumann na Poblachta**, and in a number of speeches said that those who wished to finish the work of the last four years would have to wade through Irish blood to do so. When a delegation from the Labour Party met him to beg for peace, he repeatedly stated that *'the majority have no right to do wrong'*.

His opponents accused him of being anti-democratic and of inciting violence. He replied that he was trying to control the extreme republicans. Yet at the same time he angered them by leading his followers back into the Dáil. That seemed to recognise the Provisional government, which they refused to do.

COLLINS AND DE VALERA

It was important to have elections to allow the people to vote on the Treaty. But would the anti-Treaty IRA, which suspected it would lose, try to stop them? To ensure they went ahead, Collins needed de Valera's support. To win him over he left out all reference to the oath and the king from the Free State Constitution which he was drawing up.

20 MAY: THE COLLINS–DE VALERA 'PACT'

Elections were set for June and as they approached, the two leaders announced a 'Pact'. The pro- and anti-Treaty factions would fight the election jointly and form a coalition government afterwards. This was an undemocratic arrangement which would have prevented the voters from giving their opinion on the Treaty. Griffith was angry at it but Collins was desperate to avert civil war.

For De Valera, the Pact was better than a free election that he was sure to lose. Fortunately for Irish democracy the Pact left other parties free to fight the election. The Labour Party and other parties, which had stood aside in 1921, put up candidates this time.

THE BRITISH AND THE NEW CONSTITUTION

Under the Treaty the British government had to approve the Free State Constitution. On the eve of the elections, Griffith and Collins took it to London. Lloyd George was horrified at the absence of the oath and the king. He threatened to scrap the Treaty and impose an economic blockade unless the necessary changes were made.

Collins and Griffith had no choice but to submit. The king and the oath were put back. Two days before the election was due, Collins returned to

Ireland and announced that the pact with de Valera was off. The Constitution was only published on the morning of the election. That allowed de Valera to claim that the voters did not have time to read it before they cast their votes.

18 JUNE 1922: THE TREATY ELECTION

It is unlikely if that would have made any difference. The result was clear. Pro-Treaty candidates won fifty-five seats compared with thirty-five for the anti-Treaty side. Other parties, all of which supported the Treaty, also won thirty-five seats. The same picture emerges when we look at number of votes cast.

Table A

Seats won and votes cast in 'Treaty election' June 1922			
Parties	Pro-Treaty	Anti-Treaty	Labour, and other parties (almost all pro-Treaty)
Seats won	58	35	35
First preference votes cast	239,193	133,864	247,226

28 JUNE: ATTACK ON THE FOUR COURTS STARTS THE CIVIL WAR

The election showed clearly that a large majority of Irish voters accepted the Treaty. It also gave Collins a mandate to move against the IRA in the Four Courts. Whether he would have done so voluntarily is not clear, for two events forced his hand.

The first was the assassination of Sir Henry Wilson in London on 22 June. The two IRA men involved were captured but they refused to say who sent them. Everyone assumed that it was the extreme IRA in the Four Courts. Outraged, the British demanded that Collins act against them.

This made it difficult for Collins who did not want to be seen to act on the orders of a British minister but on 27 June he got the excuse he needed. The Four Court garrison seized J.J. O'Connell, Deputy Chief of Staff of the Free State Army. Collins issued an ultimatum to Rory O'Connor and early on 28 June, using field guns borrowed from the British army, opened fire on the Four Courts.

These were not the first shots in the Civil War. There had been clashes between pro- and anti-Treaty IRA in several places already. But after this, what had been a quarrel had become a war. People now had to take sides. De Valera and other moderate republicans joined the anti-Treaty 'Irregulars' while the supporters of the Treaty rallied to the Free State army.

CIVIL WAR IN DUBLIN

The fighting in Dublin lasted less than a week. The republicans failed to learn the military lessons of the past three years. Like the 1916 rebels, they took up fixed positions and were as easily defeated. The Four Courts fell on 30 June, but only after the IRA blew up the building that held many of the irreplaceable records of Ireland's history. Other buildings they held were soon taken. Cathal Brugha was among those who died in the fighting. Hundreds of republicans, including O'Connor and Mellows, were imprisoned.

The images of Collins

What did Collins look like? This (in army uniform) is the image most people have of him. But it was only during the last two months of his life that he regularly wore a uniform. That is the only time he was a soldier. Up to the truce, he worked secretly as an intelligence expert  and a finance minister. He carefully avoided having his photograph taken but we know he wore business suits. He did the same while negotiating in London. But after he became Commander-in-Chief of the army in 1922 he always appeared in uniform and had his portrait painted like that. As a result he left behind an image that does not reflect the reality of his life.

CIVIL WAR IN MUNSTER

Collins resigned from the government to take command of the Free State army. His next task was to gain control of Munster, where the republicans controlled most of the area from Waterford to Limerick. He divided his troops in two. Some were sent by sea to attack the republicans from behind; others moved south across the midlands. By the end of July he had driven the republicans from every town in Munster. They then fell back on guerrilla tactics.

12 AUGUST: THE DEATH OF GRIFFITH

On 12 August, Arthur Griffith died suddenly. Collins took over from him as President. Other members of the Cabinet, especially Kevin O'Higgins, were worried at one man having both military and civilian power and they feared Collins's tendency to take decisions without consulting them.

22 AUGUST: COLLINS DIES AT BÉAL NA MBLÁTH

After Griffith's funeral, Collins returned to Munster. He may have been trying to start peace talks when he was killed in an ambush at Beal na mBláth in Co. Cork. His death at the age of thirty-two shattered the country.

De Valera and Collins's death: The film, Michael Collins, has many serious inaccuracies and distortions. Among them is the suggestion that de Valera played some part in Collins's death. While he was in the area at the time, there is no historical evidence to support this claim.

PRESIDENT W.T. COSGRAVE

A frightened Cabinet met to pick a new President. Mulcahy, who took over as Commander-in-Chief of the army, seemed the obvious choice but members of the Cabinet were reluctant to let one man have so much power again. Instead they chose **W.T. Cosgrave**. At forty-two, he was the oldest man in the Cabinet.

W.T. Cosgrave (1880–1965): A Dubliner and member of Sinn Féin from its foundation, he had served on Dublin Corporation for many years. A prominent member of the Irish Volunteers, he had been sentenced to death in 1916 and elected an MP after his release. In 1919 de Valera had appointed him Minister for Local Government and his was one of the Dáil's more successful ministries.

This photograph illustrates how the civil war affected friends. It shows Kevin O'Higgins at his wedding, with de Valera and Rory O'Connor standing on either side of him. Not long afterwards O'Higgins signed the warrant sentencing O'Connor to death

COSGRAVE'S GOVERNMENT FIGHTS THE CIVIL WAR

Cosgrave accepted the leadership from a sense of duty. He took over a demoralised government that had lost its two most respected leaders. In September the Third Dáil gave Cosgrave's government special powers to combat the IRA. These included the right to set up army courts and to execute people caught carrying guns.

By this stage the Civil War had degenerated into a brutal guerrilla campaign with atrocities on both sides. As part of its campaign the IRA murdered Free State supporters and burned many houses. Among its victims was the elderly father of Kevin O'Higgins. In December they killed a Free State TD, Seán Hales, and badly injured another.

The Free State government retaliated with executions, some of them of doubtful legality. After Hales was killed, Rory O'Connor, Liam Mellows

and two other republicans arrested in the Four Courts were shot, even though none of them could have been involved in his murder. It was an act of revenge, not justice. In all, the Free State government executed over seventy republicans, among them Erskine Childers executed for possessing a small handgun.

DE VALERA'S ANTI-TREATY 'GOVERNMENT'

De Valera and the anti-Treaty TDs refused to recognise Cosgrave's government. They claimed the June election was not valid because Collins had broken the 'Pact' and had not informed the people about the new Constitution.

They also pointed out that the Second Dáil never formally dissolved itself so that it was still the lawful government. In October Anti-Treaty TDs from it set up a 'republican government' with de Valera as President. In theory de Valera's 'government' was in charge of the republicans during the Civil War but in practise the anti-Treaty IRA paid little attention to them.

MAY 1923: THE END OF THE CIVIL WAR

By the end of 1922 it was clear that the republicans had no hope of winning. De Valera urged the IRA to call a halt but Liam Lynch, the IRA leader, paid no attention to him. In April 1923 Lynch was killed. The new leader, **Frank Aiken**, a more moderate man, accepted de Valera's advice. In May he called on the IRA to put away its arms. For republicans it was not a surrender but a pause; they planned to fight again another day. For the Free State it was victory and a chance at last to begin to build for the future.

QUESTIONS

1 How long did the Treaty allow for the British to hand over to the Irish Free State? Who did they hand power to?

2 List and write a short account of the main tasks the Provisional government had to see to in order to set up the new state.

3 Describe how the IRA split over the Treaty. What was the IRA Convention and why did Griffith say it was 'anti-democratic'? What was the result of the IRA Convention?

4 Why was Collins so tolerant of the IRA men who took over the Four Courts?

5 What was the 'Collins-de Valera Pact'? Why did it not work?

6 Describe the events leading to the Free State attack on the Four Courts. Do you think it was justified?

7 Outline the main course of the civil war up to Collins's death.

8 Describe how Cosgrave and his ministers handled the remaining months of the civil war.

LEAVING CERTIFICATE QUESTIONS

Higher Level

1 'The delegations that negotiated the Anglo-Irish Treaty of 1921 were unevenly matched.' Do you think the progress and outcome of the negotiations justifies this opinion?

2 Outline the main stages in the negotiation for the Anglo-Irish Treaty and say how far each side achieved its aims.

3 Did the terms of the Anglo-Irish Treaty make a civil war inevitable?

Ordinary Level

A Look at the cartoon on page 86.
   1 Who is the man on the right?
   2 What was his attitude to the Anglo-Irish Treaty?
   3 Who is the man on the left and what was his attitude to it?
   4 Which of them won the support of 'Éire' in the June 1922 election? Give figures to support your answer.

B Write a paragraph on **one** of the following:
   1 The Irish delegation to the London talks.
   2 The republican arguments against the Treaty.

C Answer **one** of the following questions:
   1 What were the two main aims of the Irish delegates in the London talks and how successful were they in achieving them?
   2 What part did Michael Collins play in the civil war?

6 Building a State and Consolidating Democracy 1922-1937

6.1

THE INSTITUTIONS OF THE IRISH FREE STATE

INTRODUCTION: A BAD TIME FOR DEMOCRACY

On 6 December 1922, exactly one year after the Anglo-Irish Treaty was signed, the Irish Free State came into existence. Like the other new states set up after the first World War, it was a liberal democracy, one of twenty-eight democratic states in Europe at that time. But it was born in the middle of a vicious civil war and many people, both in Ireland and abroad, doubted that it could survive either as an independent state or as a democracy.

The 1920s and 1930s were not good years for European democracy. Many democratic states became fascist dictatorships. By 1939 only seventeen still had democratic governments. Ireland was one of them. In this chapter we will try to explain how it was able to survive its traumatic birth and establish a stable democracy in such difficult times.

BUILDING ON THE BRITISH MODEL

The men and women who set up the Irish Free State based its institutions – form of government, civil service, legal system, local government, etc. – on the British model. This may seem strange. After all, they had fought to free themselves from British rule. But in the 1920s there were good reasons for copying Britain:

- It was still the greatest power in the world and people everywhere respected and admired its institutions.
- Most Irish politicians, lawyers and civil servants grew up and received their training in the British system. They knew it and had no experience of any other.
- Some British people believed that the Irish were unfit to govern themselves. What better way for the leaders of the Free State to prove them wrong than to develop a government along British lines and make it work?

THE FREE STATE CONSTITUTION

In October 1922, the third Dáil adopted a constitution for the Irish Free State. It included the Treaty, whose terms also dictated many features of the Constitution. Its main points were:

- The Irish Free State was a **dominion of the British Commonwealth**. The head of state was the British king. All TDs and Senators had to take an oath to him and he had to sign all bills passed by the **Oireachtas**. The king was represented in Ireland by the **Governor-General**.
- An elected parliament, **the Oireachtas** made all laws for the Irish Free State. It consisted of two houses, the **Seanad** (Senate) and the **Dáil**:
  — The **Senate** had sixty members, elected by men and women over thirty. It could delay bills for 270 days but not stop them. The first Senate was not elected; the Dáil chose thirty Senators and the President chose the other thirty. Griffith used this power to appoint fifteen leading unionists to the Senate as a gesture of reconciliation. They included Sir Horace Plunkett, the founder of the co-operative movement. Others Senators were the poet W.B. Yeats and Jenny Wyse-Power, a prominent Sinn Féiner and campaigner for women's rights.
  — The **Dáil** had much more power than the Senate. It consisted of **Teachta Dála** (TDs), one to represent every 20,000–30,000 people. All men and women over twenty-one could vote for TDs and voting was by **proportional representation** (**PR**). Graduates of the two universities, Trinity and National, also elected two TDs each. The Trinity College TDs were usually unionists.

The Free State government was too poor to afford a special parliament building, so it took over Leinster House which had belonged to the Royal Dublin Society, for the Dáil and Senate

Courtesy: Corbis

- The Dáil elected the **President** of the Executive Council (Prime Minister). He appointed ministers who together formed the **Executive Council** (Cabinet). Each minister headed a government department (e.g. Finance, Local Government, Education, etc.)
- The Constitution guaranteed that citizens (which it defined as *'every person without distinction of sex'*…) should have freedom of speech and assembly. It also guaranteed freedom of religion and forbade the government to favour one religion over another.
- For the first eight years (later extended to sixteen) the Constitution could be changed by the Oireachtas without a **referendum**. If 75,000 voters signed a petition demanding a referendum, one had to be held. This rule was removed from the Constitution in 1928 after Fianna Fáil tried to organise a referendum on the Oath and it was not included in de Valera's 1937 Constitution.

THE CIVIL SERVICE

The Irish Free State needed a civil service and the British lent **C.J. Gregg**, a Kilkenny man who had worked as a British civil servant in London, to advise them. As one historian has noted, *'he, more than any other single man, was responsible for the organisation of … the new civil service'.* (R. Fanning, *The Irish Department of Finance*, p. 43)

His work was completed when the 1924 **Ministers and Secretaries Act** was passed. It created eleven departments, each responsible for one area of government. Each department had its own minister, who was answerable to the Dáil for its activities.

THE CIVIL SERVICE COMMISSION

An important reform was the **Civil Service Commission**. It set examinations for entry to the civil service. A boy or girl could only become a civil servant if they passed. This guaranteed that civil servants had a good level of ability and education and it reduced the opportunities for bribery or political favouritism.

CONTINUITY AND CONSERVATISM

Only 200 new people, mostly Sinn Féin supporters, joined the civil service in 1922. The remaining 20,000 civil servants were people who had worked for the British as clerks, administrators, cleaners, postmen and so on. They were offered a choice. They could retire on a pension, move to Britain or Northern Ireland or stay and work for the Free State. 98 per cent opted to stay.

These people, trained in the British system, naturally continued to do things more or less as they had before. As a result, less changed in the Irish Free State after independence than might have been expected. The political leaders were new but the civil servants who advised them and carried out their policies were not.

This remained true after Fianna Fáil won the election in 1932. De Valera replaced Cosgrave as President of the Executive Council but the same civil servants worked for him as had worked for Cosgrave.

- This had advantages. It provided stability. It gave inexperienced leaders people with experience to advise them and made it less likely that they would try dangerous experiments.
- It also had disadvantages. It made it difficult for new ideas to get a hearing or new policies to be tried. From 1922 to the late 1940s all Irish governments followed policies based on what Britain was doing, rather than seeking policies that might have been more suited to the very different conditions in Ireland.

THE LEGAL SYSTEM

The legal system also changed very little. The Free State took over all the British laws which were in force in 1922 and only gradually did the Oireachtas bring in new ones to replace them.

The law courts also remained largely unchanged. The Free State government did not keep the informal Sinn Féin courts (see page 69) which had been one of the successes of the Dáil government. The **Courts of Justice Act** of 1924 abolished them and established a new system of courts:

- **District Justices** replaced British Magistrates and Justices of the Peace. They dealt with minor crimes.
- **Circuit Courts**, each covering an area with a population of 400,000, replaced the British Assize courts and dealt with major crimes.
- People could appeal from the decisions of these courts to the **Court of Criminal Appeal, the High Court** and **the Supreme Court**. The Supreme Court could also decide if laws passed by the Oireachtas were in line with the Constitution. This point was borrowed from the Americans and was the main difference between the Irish legal system after 1922 and the British system.

The changes to the legal system were all on the surface. Irish District Justices enforced the same laws as British magistrates had up to 1920. Irish barristers still wore British-style wigs and Irish judges still liked to be called 'my lord'.

Excited Suburbanite : " Are you one of the Civic Guard ? "
Civic Guard : " Yes."
Excited Suburbanite : " My house has been broken into. Can you tell me where I'll find a policeman ? "

This cartoon appeared in 1922:

1. *What has happened to the little man and what does he want?*
2. *Why did he not ask the Civil Guard to help him with his problem?*
3. *This cartoon is meant to be funny, but it makes a serious point about the changes in Ireland in 1922. Explain what it was.*

THE JUDICIAL COMMITTEE OF THE PRIVY COUNCIL

The British Commonwealth had its own supreme court in London. It was called **the Judicial Committee of the Privy Council**. Any Commonwealth citizen had the right to appeal to it from his or her local courts. This was a part of the Treaty that no one liked because it was a restriction on Irish independence. The Cosgrave government took care to prevent Irish citizens making appeals to it and the right to do so was abolished by the de Valera government in the 1930s.

LOCAL GOVERNMENT

Local government had been reorganised in 1898 and the Free State government did little to change it. Elected county and urban councils dealt with sewerage, water supplies, housing and roads and raised a local tax on property (the **rates**) to pay for them. Until 1934 only ratepayers and their wives were entitled to vote for these councils. Voting for them was by Proportional Representation.

Income from the rates was never enough to pay for everything the councils had to do, so grants from the central government made up the difference. In 1923–24 these grants amounted to 22.5 per cent of local revenue, but by 1931–2 they amounted to 42 per cent.

This reduced the independence of local councils and increased the control central government had over them. Before 1920 many local councils were corrupt (i.e. councillors accepted bribes or gave jobs to their friends). Cosgrave's government tried to stamp out corruption and to improve the councils' efficiency. During the 1920s it dissolved several local authorities and replaced them with Commissioners. To improve efficiency, some councils appointed '**managers**' to work with the elected councillors. This was made compulsory in the **County Managers Act** of 1940.

HELPING THE POOR

Under British rule, care of the old, sick or orphaned was left to specially elected bodies called **Poor Law Unions**. The Dáil abolished them in 1923 and gave the task to local councils.

To keep rates low, the councils spent as little as possible helping the poor. Workhouses, bleak old buildings where the Poor Law Unions had housed their charges, were renamed County Homes but were still used to house orphans and old people. Unemployed adults got 'home assistance'. It had to be approved by council officials who enquired into people's circumstances and often took the view that being poor was a sign of laziness. Those who passed this humiliating 'means test' received only the most limited help.

QUESTIONS

1. Write a paragraph on the 1922 Constitution. You should cover the following points: Head of State, Oireachtas and how it was elected, Executive Council, freedoms guaranteed, changing the Constitution.

2. Explain (a) the Ministers and Secretaries Act, (b) The Civil Service Commission.

3. What was the background of the civil servants who worked for the Irish Free State in its early years? Explain one advantage and one disadvantage of this.

4. Outline the main features of the legal system of the Irish Free State. In what ways was it (a) different from and (b) the same as the British system?

5. Give two significant changes in local government introduced by the Irish Free State.

6. How were the old and the poor treated in the Irish Free State?

THE DEVELOPMENT OF DEMOCRATIC PARTIES: 1922–1926

COULD IRELAND BE A DEMOCRACY?

One reason people worried about democracy in Ireland was that up to 1922 there was only one nationalist party. Until 1918 that was the Home Rule Party; after 1918 it was the Sinn Féin Party. This deprived voters of the choice that exists in normal democracies, where different parties draw up different programmes and the voters choose the one they like.

Unexpectedly that problem was solved when Sinn Féin split over the Treaty. The split produced the two parties which have dominated Irish politics ever since. Cumann na nGaedheal and later Fine Gael grew from those who accepted the Treaty, while Sinn Féin and later Fianna Fáil grew from those who opposed it.

CIVIL WAR THREATENS DEMOCRACY

But while the Treaty split removed one threat to democracy, the civil war that followed raised new, more serious, ones:

- In 1922 the elected parliament, the Dáil, voted to accept the Treaty. Later, in a free election, the voters supported that decision. Yet a large section of the Sinn Féin party and of the IRA refused to accept these democratic votes and went to war against the legally elected government. That violated a basic principle of democracy: **political leaders must accept defeat when the majority votes against them and must not use violence to try to change the situation.**
- The Free State government itself was not without fault. During the civil war it executed some republican leaders without trial. It also turned a blind eye when some of its police and army tortured and murdered republicans. These actions violated another basic principle of democracy: **that the government itself must obey the law, just like everyone else.** (This is called 'the rule of law'.)

This disrespect for democracy and for the rule of law grew out of the revolutionary period. The IRA, fighting British forces for Irish freedom, felt entitled to ignore British law. IRA men, armed and unelected, lorded it over their areas and despised the elected politicians of Sinn Féin. They also felt entitled to murder and rob in the name of Ireland. During the civil war, individuals on both sides went on behaving in the same way.

After peace was restored the Free State government faced the problem of changing these attitudes:

- It had to restore respect for the law.
- It had to bring its own army, which was used to running its own affairs, back under civilian control. Otherwise there was the danger of a military dictatorship.
- It had to find a way to persuade the large minority that opposed the Treaty to give up violence and return to peaceful, constitutional and democratic politics.

THE FIRST ELECTION IN THE IRISH FREE STATE

The Civil War ended in May 1923 when de Valera called on republicans to lay aside their arms. At once Cosgrave called an election. The pro-Treaty part of the old Sinn Féin party had recently formed itself into a new party called **Cumann na nGaedheal**. Led by Cosgrave and Kevin O'Higgins it promised voters a return to peace, order and stability.

A number of small parties also put forward candidates. Of these, the **Labour Party** was the most important. Led by **Thomas Johnson**, it promised improved social welfare and greater social justice. There was also a **Farmers' Party** and a large number of Independent candidates, some of whom were former unionists.

But the biggest party opposing Cumann na nGaedheal was the anti-Treaty **Sinn Féin**, led by de Valera. Cosgrave could have stopped it putting up candidates but he preferred the democratic option. So long as Sinn Féiners had given up violence, he left them free to seek the support of the voters. But many Sinn Féin candidates were still in prison because of their role in the civil war and during the election campaign de Valera, who had remained free until then, was also arrested.

A FAIR RESULT SURPRISES SINN FÉIN

Voting in the election was by Proportional Representation (PR). Sinn Féin did better than expected, winning forty-four seats (see Table A). People's unease at the behaviour of some of the Free State forces may partly explain their success. But the use of PR, which was much fairer than the British 'first past the post' voting system, also helped.

The leaders of Sinn Féin were surprised. They expected that the voting would be rigged against them. When it was not, the more moderate among them began to see advantages in democracy.

A GOVERNMENT WITH LITTLE OPPOSITION

To enter the Dáil, all TDs had to take the oath to the king. The Sinn Féin TDs refused to take the oath and remained outside the Dáil. Their abstention gave Cosgrave and his Cumann na nGaedheal party an easy time. The other parties criticised Cumann na nGaedheal but never had enough votes to defeat them (see Table A). As a result between 1923 and 1927 the Free State lacked what every democracy needs – an opposition big enough to offer the voters an alternative set of policies and an alternative government to vote for.

W.T. COSGRAVE

W.T. Cosgrave was the leader of Cumann na nGaedheal and President of the Executive Council from 1922 to 1932 (see page 93). A small, quiet man, he had not sought the leadership but had it thrust upon him by Collins' death. He took over in the chaos and bitterness of civil war and that made him cautious and conservative.

Cosgrave's aims were modest: to re-establish order, maintain democracy and prove to the sceptics that the Irish could rule themselves. He had no ambition to change society or to introduce major reforms. But perhaps that was just what the Irish Free State needed after the turbulent years of its birth. As J.J. Lee says of him:

> 'His vision was limited ... He had neither a capacious intellect not a commanding personality. What he did have was a basic decency, a sense of public service and a sound judgement on matters of state.' (J.J. Lee, Ireland 1912–1985, London 1989, p. 174)

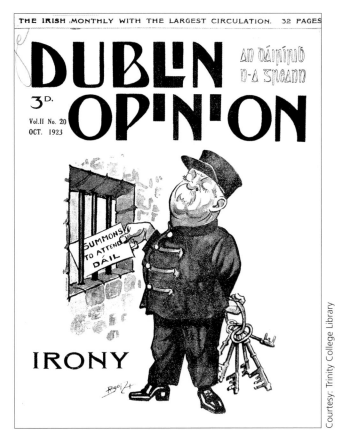

Courtesy: Trinity College Library

Explain what this 1923 cartoon means by 'Irony'.

Table A

Results of the 1923 election					
In the Dáil				Abstaining	
Cumann na nGaedheal	Labour	Farmers	Independents	Sinn Féin	Total number of seats
63	14	15	17	44	153

Kevin O'Higgins (1892–1927): Born in Laois, he studied law in UCD before joining Sinn Féin. Elected a TD in 1918, he worked with Cosgrave in the Dáil Department of Local Government and was a strong supporter of the Treaty.

KEVIN O'HIGGINS

Cosgrave's Vice-President was Kevin O'Higgins. He was also Minister for Home Affairs (later called Justice) and was therefore responsible for restoring and maintaining law and order. During the civil war it was his job to sign death warrants and this made him a hate-figure among republicans. Even after the Civil War ended, O'Higgins feared that the order, stability and obedience to the law which are the hallmarks of democracy were missing in Ireland. He wanted to restore them.

OTHER CUMANN NA NGAEDHEAL MINISTERS

Other members of the Cumann na nGaedheal government included:

- **Richard Mulcahy**, Collins' friend and successor as Commander-in-Chief of the army. He was Minister for Defence responsible for the Free State army.
- **Ernest Blythe**, an Ulster Presbyterian, was Minister for Finance (see page 173).

- **Eoin MacNeill**, a Catholic from Antrim and one of the founders of the Gaelic League, was Minister for Education.
- **Desmond FitzGerald** was Minister for External Affairs.
- **Patrick Hogan**, was Minister for Agriculture and Lands (see page 131).

WEAKNESS OF CUMANN NA NGAEDHEAL AS A POLITICAL PARTY

Cumann na nGaedheal ruled the Free State for ten years, but it was never developed a successful political machine in the way that Fianna Fáil later did. There were several reasons for this:

- Cosgrave, though good as the leader of the country, was not a skilful politician. He also lacked the charismatic personality of his rival, de Valera.
- The leaders of the party spent their first ten years running the country. That left them little time to organise a party that could get out the voters at election time.
- The party was not united. In 1923 its members agreed to back the Treaty but on little else. Some saw the Treaty as the first step to a republic; others were content to remain a dominion of the British Commonwealth. Some wanted to reform social welfare and introduce new economic policies; others wanted to change as little as possible. Some wanted to protect Irish industries; others wanted to keep free trade with Britain.

As a result of these weaknesses, Cumann na nGaedheal never won an overall majority in Dáil elections. But this did not matter so much up to 1927 because de Valera's party stayed out of the Dáil.

THE LABOUR PARTY

That left the Labour Party as the main opposition to Cumann na nGaedheal. It was set up by Connolly and Larkin in 1912 to fight for seats in the Home Rule parliament which never came. Larkin left Ireland for America in 1914 and Connolly was executed in 1916. After that the leadership of the labour movement passed to

Thomas Johnson who became leader of the Labour Party and to **William O'Brien** who took over the Irish Transport and General Workers' Union (ITGWU) which Larkin had set up. These men were moderate socialists working for a gradual improvement in the wages and working conditions of their followers.

LABOUR AND THE STRUGGLE FOR INDEPENDENCE

In the 1918 election, Johnson gave way to pressure from Sinn Féin and the Labour Party did not put up any candidates (see page 61). During the War of Independence, trade unionists supported Sinn Féin and the IRA with strikes and other forms of direct action. They too suffered at the hands of the Black and Tans. When the Treaty came, it divided the labour movement:

- More extreme socialists sided with the republicans and wanted to continue what they saw as a fight against British imperialism.
- Johnson, O'Brien and most party and trade union leaders accepted the Treaty. The Labour Party put up candidates in the Treaty election of June 1922 and won seventeen seats. Johnson insisted that they must take the oath and enter the Dáil, and all but one did so.

LABOUR OPPOSES CUMANN NA nGAEDHEAL

In the Dáil, the Labour Party attacked Cumann na nGaedheal's conservative social and economic policies, especially its decision to cut old age pensions (see page 178). They also objected to the cost of reviving Irish or sending Irish diplomats abroad when so little was spent to develop industry, clear out the slums or improve health or education. A comment from Seán O'Casey highlights the difference between the myths that children were being taught in school and the daily reality of their lives:

> 'Children who are rickety in their legs are to be told of Cúchulainn's hero's leap over walls as high as Nelson's Pillar. Children who are fed on tea and margarine are to be told of the wine and venison feasts of the Fianna.' (*The Irish Statesman*, 29 November 1924, p. 362)

WHY THE LABOUR PARTY DID NOT DO WELL IN THE IRISH FREE STATE

But the Labour party had difficulty winning support. There were many reasons for this:

- Labour mainly spoke for industrial workers but there were few of them in the Free State where 60 per cent of the people worked on the land. Farmers shared none of the aims of the labour movement and distrusted many of its policies.
- The economic slump of the 1920s and internal quarrels in the ITGWU reduced support for trade unions. Membership fell from 175,000 in 1924 to 92,000 in 1929.
- The Catholic Church and the owners of property viewed 'godless communism' with horror. In fact most Irish Labour politicians were anti-communist but it was easy for their opponents to link them to it. This 'red smear' discouraged conservative Catholics from voting for Labour candidates.
- Sinn Féin and later Fianna Fáil included promises of social reform in their election programmes. That took voters away from the Labour movement.

THE LARKIN AND O'BRIEN SPLIT WEAKENS THE LABOUR MOVEMENT

A bitter internal quarrel also weakened the Labour movement. In 1923 James Larkin returned to Ireland after spending ten years abroad, partly in the US and partly in the Soviet Union. A convinced communist, he opposed the conservatism of

Jim Larkin speaking in Dublin's O'Connell Street in 1923

Courtesy: RTÉ Stills Library

O'Brien and Johnson. The quarrel between O'Brien and Larkin split the labour movement until Larkin's death in 1947.

OTHER PARTIES AND INDEPENDENTS

Other political parties appeared on the scene from time to time. In the 1920s a **Farmers' Party** represented the views of the bigger farmers. In the Dáil it usually supported Cosgrave. Independents were also numerous in the early days of the state. Some of them were former unionists or former Home Rulers who were able to win seats through the PR system. In the Dáil they usually supported the conservative Cumann na nGaedheal against the left-wing Labour Party or the nationalist Fianna Fáil.

6.3

MOVING TOWARDS DEMOCRACY: 1922–1927

TWO CRISES

In its early years, Cumann na nGaedheal faced two major crises, the so-called 'army mutiny' and the report of the Boundary Commission.

THE 'ARMY MUTINY'

The event known as the 'army mutiny' was an important step in consolidating democracy in the Free State. It grew from the need to cut the size of the army, which had grown very big during the Civil War. It was also complicated by differences between two of Cosgrave's most powerful ministers, **Richard Mulcahy** and **Kevin O'Higgins**.

THE ARMY AT THE END OF THE CIVIL WAR

When the civil war ended, the Irish army had 55,000 men with 3,300 officers. Some of them had been in the IRA; many others were Irishmen who had previously served in the British army.

As Minister for Justice, O'Higgins was in charge of the Garda Síochána. His aim was to restore respect for the law in the chaos of the Civil War

Richard Mulcahy (1886-1971): Born in Waterford, he joined the IRB and later the Volunteers. In 1916 he was second in command to Thomas Ashe whose effective actions in Co. Meath pointed the way to guerrilla war. In 1917 he was elected commander-in-chief of the Volunteers (IRA) and tried to impose a central control on their campaign. A close associate of Collins he supported the Treaty on the grounds that the IRA could not continue fighting.

and he blamed the Free State army for some of that chaos. He also feared that a powerful army might attempt to seize power, as had happened in other newly independent countries.

RESENTMENT AT THE ARMY CUTS

The Free State could not afford a big army so when fighting ended the government decided to cut it back. Mulcahy and the Army Council loyally carried out this policy. By the start of 1924 only 13,000 men and 2,000 officers were left. Those who were let go got only a small compensation payment or pension and other jobs were hard to find.

The cuts caused resentment. Former IRA men felt that the ex-British soldiers were being kept on while they were let go. There was some truth in this. Mulcahy and the Army Council were trying to build a professional, peacetime army. They needed well-disciplined officers but some of the men who had worked for Collins as assassins and guerrilla fighters were not ideal for that role.

To defend their interests, **Liam Tobin**, who had been close to Collins, formed the '**Old IRA**'. To counter them, Mulcahy encouraged the re-emergence of the old secret society, the IRB, amongst the officers. O'Higgins disapproved because he did not think army officers should belong to secret societies.

THE ARMY MUTINY, MARCH 1924

On 6 March 1924 the Old IRA, led by Tobin, sent an ultimatum to Cosgrave. They wanted him to end demobilisation and dismiss Mulcahy and the Army Council. To give credibility to their complaints, they also protested that nothing had been done to deliver Collins' promise that the Treaty was the first step towards a republic.

Mulcahy wanted to take action against them but Cosgrave preferred negotiation. O'Higgins saw a chance to outmanoeuvre Mulcahy. He got the Cabinet to appoint Eoin O'Duffy, the Garda Commissioner, as Supreme Commander of the army. Some days later some of the Old IRA men met in a Dublin pub, apparently to plot another

move. A senior army officer, after consulting Mulcahy but not O'Duffy, ordered their arrest.

Cosgrave was ill with flu (some have speculated that it was a 'diplomatic illness') and O'Higgins was in charge. He forced the Army Council to resign and in protest, Mulcahy also resigned as Minister for Defence.

O'Higgins claimed that he was acting in the national interest by establishing civilian control over the army. From now on, he insisted, the military must obey the orders of their elected masters.

THE BOUNDARY COMMISSION

A much bigger crisis blew up in 1925. It was about the vital issue of partition. Under Article 12 of the Treaty, a Boundary Commission would decide the border between the Irish Free State and Northern Ireland. The Commission would contain three men:

- ◉ One unionist appointed by the Northern Ireland government.
- ◉ One nationalist appointed by the Free State government.
- ◉ A neutral chairman appointed by Britain.

They were to decide the border *'in accordance with the wishes of the inhabitants, so far as may be compatible with economic and geographic conditions'*.

Courtesy: National Library of Ireland

The Boundary Commission's first sitting in Ireland

In the Treaty debates, Collins and Griffith had argued that the Commission would transfer large areas of Northern Ireland to the south. The anti-Treaty side accepted this interpretation without serious question. But it reflected wishful thinking rather than hard reality. The terms were very vague and many vital questions were not even discussed. For example:

- Who were the 'inhabitants'?
- How were their wishes to be discovered?
- Which economic and geographical considerations had their wishes to be compatible with?

DELAYING THE COMMISSION

Civil War in the South and unionist resistance in the North delayed the Commission until 1924. By then a great deal had changed:

- Northern Ireland had been in existence for four years. It would be much harder to take territory away from it then than it would have been in 1922, when partition had barely begun.
- In Britain, Lloyd George fell from power towards the end of 1922. The Conservative government which took over was unlikely to support the Free State government's interpretation of Article 12 against its unionist friends.

SETTING UP THE COMMISSION

The Dublin government appointed its Minister for Education, **Eoin MacNeill**, a Catholic from Co. Antrim, as its representative. Craig refused to appoint anyone, so the British took power to appoint the unionist representative. He was **J.R. Fisher**, a Belfast lawyer and a staunch unionist. They also appointed **Justice Richard Feetham** of the South African Supreme Court to be the neutral chairman.

A LEAK OF THE COMMISSION REPORT

The Commissioners began work in November 1924 (see pages 164–66 for their work in Northern Ireland). They promised not to let any government know of their decisions. MacNeill rigidly kept his promise, so Cosgrave got a nasty surprise on 7 November when a London newspaper published a leaked version of the Commission's report. This claimed that:

- The Free State was to get small parts of south Armagh and some minor areas in Fermanagh, moving about 25,000 Catholics from North to South.
- Part of east Donegal, where about 2,000 Protestants lived, was to go from the Free State to Northern Ireland. This was totally unexpected. No one imagined that the Free State would actually lose territory.
- Apart from these minor changes, the border established in 1920 would remain unaltered (see map page 165).

Nationalists were outraged. Most voters had not expected this result though some politicians may have feared it. A storm of angry criticism arose. On 20 November MacNeill resigned from the Cabinet. Officers in the army threatened to fight if any part of Donegal were transferred to Northern Ireland, while in the North, unionists made it clear they would resist any change by force.

DECEMBER 1925: THE ANGLO-IRISH AGREEMENT

Before the Commission began its work, all sides had agreed to accept its decision as final. Now Cosgrave needed to stop it publishing its report. With some of his ministers he hurried to London to urge the British to bury it. If not, he warned, a sectarian civil war might break out in border areas and de Valera might win the next election.

The British accepted these arguments. On 3 December the two sides signed an Anglo-Irish Agreement, which modified the Treaty. Under it:

- The Commission report would be suppressed and the border between the six and the twenty-six counties would remain as it had been in the 1920 Government of Ireland Act.
- The Council of Ireland, which that Act set up to maintain a link between the two Irish states, would be abandoned. By giving it up, Cosgrave acknowledged that partition was permanent.
- The British agreed to cancel the Free State's commitment to pay part of the British war debt. This was worth between £6 and £8 million a year to the Irish Free State.

- The British also agreed that the Northern government no longer had to repay land annuities to the British Treasury. Cosgrave's failure to demand a similar concession for the Free State was to cost him dearly.

REACTIONS TO THE AGREEMENT

The Agreement was unpopular because it accepted partition. In protest some members of Cumann na nGaedheal resigned from the party. De Valera's Sinn Féin Party also attacked it. They claimed it showed that they were right to reject the Treaty. If they had been in the Dáil, they might have been able to exploit the divisions in Cumann na nGaedheal. But they were abstaining, so they could do nothing.

The myth of the Treaty and partition

Today, many people believe that the Treaty was responsible for partition. That is not true. Partition began in 1920 with the Government of Ireland Act. In 1921, the delegates in London were trying to undo what was already done.

In the Treaty debates, de Valera accepted that Ulster unionists could not be forced under a Dublin government against their will. Most anti-Treaty people also believed that the Boundary Commission would give large areas of Northern Ireland to the South and that what was left would be unworkable. Their main objection to the Treaty was dominion status and the oath to the king, not partition.

After the Boundary Commission dashed these hopes in 1925, the anti-Treaty side encouraged the myth that the Treaty was to blame for partition. They found it easier to justify fighting a civil war to defend Irish unity than to oppose the oath, especially after de Valera decided it was just 'an empty formula'.

MARCH 1926: DE VALERA'S BREAK WITH SINN FÉIN

The result of the Boundary Commission strengthened the Sinn Féiners who wanted to end abstention. A special Ard Fheis was called for 10 March 1926 to discuss the issue. At it, de Valera proposed that, if the oath were removed, Sinn Féin's entry into Dáil Éireann would be *'a question not of principle but of policy'*. But the extremists, mobilised by MacSwiney and Stack, defeated him.

The party resolved:

> *'that it is incompatible with the fundamental principles of Sinn Féin, as it is injurious to the honour of Ireland, to send representatives into any usurping legislature set up by English law in Ireland.'* (P. Pyne, 'The Third Sinn Féin Party' in *Economic and Social Review*, Vol. 1, p. 45)

This was immediately followed by a unanimous vote declaring de Valera *'the greatest Irishman of the century'*. Despite that, he resigned as leader of Sinn Féin.

MAY 1926: THE FOUNDATION OF FIANNA FÁIL

Two months later, de Valera set up a new party, which he called **Fianna Fáil** (Soldiers of Destiny). The advantage of this name was its lack of meaning, leaving him free to follow any policy he liked. Asked if the new party would take the oath to the king, he replied: *'That oath, no republican will take, for it implies acceptance of England's right to overlordship in our country.'* (Quoted in T.P. Coogan, *De Valera: Long Fellow, Long Shadow*, London 1993, p. 386)

Fianna Fáil grew rapidly over the next year as young enthusiasts like Seán Lemass and Gerard Boland toured the country and persuaded many Sinn Féin branches and most Sinn Féin TDs to join them. As Lemass recalled later:

> *'Within a year of the first Fianna Fáil executive being set up, we had a nation-wide organisation, the strongest in the country, fully geared for action. The speed with which the Fianna Fáil organisation came into being, from a group sitting in Dublin to a nation-wide organisation extending to every parish in the country, was quite phenomenal.'* (Brian Farrell, *Seán Lemass*, Dublin 1983, p. 18)

Fianna Fáil promised that if the oath were removed, they would enter the Dáil. They also developed an economic policy designed to appeal to people suffering from unemployment and poverty. Late in 1926 de Valera went on a fundraising tour of

America. Irish-Americans were more republican than Irish people at home and they contributed generously to Fianna Fáil, ensuring that it would not be short of funds at the next election.

1926–27: UNPOPULAR DECISIONS BY CUMANN NA NGAEDHEAL

A general election was due in 1927. The poor state of the economy and the result of the Boundary Commission made Cosgrave and his ministers unpopular. Yet in the year before the election they made several decisions which made them more unpopular still:

- Their economic policy (see chapter 8.1) involved keeping taxes and spending low. To achieve that they cut the old age pension by 10 per cent. They also reduced the number of people entitled to social welfare.
- In March 1926 they made the 'Ultimate Financial Agreement' with Britain. In it they committed themselves to paying **land annuities**. This was money collected from farmers to repay loans from the British government which allowed them to buy their farms. Cosgrave's government saw the annuities as a debt of honour, but the Labour Party and Fianna Fáil disagreed. The £5 million a year sent to Britain should, they claimed, be spent on developing the Irish economy.
- As IRA violence increased in 1926, they brought back detention without trial. To many people this seemed an unnecessary infringement of civil liberties.
- In February 1927 O'Higgins brought in the **Intoxicating Liquor Bill**. It proposed reducing the number of public houses by half and limiting opening hours. Some Cumann na nGaedheal TDs resigned in protest and formed the **National League**, led by William Redmond, son of the Home Rule leader.

JUNE 1927: THE GENERAL ELECTION

The election was held in June:

- Cumann na nGaedheal asked for support because it had given the country stability and good government. Voting for Fianna Fáil would, it warned, endanger that stability. But neither achievements nor threats could overcome their unpopularity. The party did badly, falling to forty-seven seats.
- Fianna Fáil, well organised and well funded, won forty-four seats, exactly what Sinn Féin won in 1923. But it might have done better had it not still been following an abstentionist policy.
- Constance Markievicz followed de Valera when he left Sinn Féin. Elected a Fianna Fáil TD in June 1927, she died shortly afterwards.
- The hardline republicans who remained in Sinn Féin did badly. Mary MacSwiney and Austin Stack lost their seats.
- The Labour Party, which had opposed Cumann na nGaedheal within the Dáil, was rewarded by increasing the number of its seats to twenty-two.

Overall, the result was inconclusive. If Fianna Fáil and Sinn Féin continued to abstain, Cosgrave's government remained in power. But if Fianna Fáil entered the Dáil, it was in danger. Would de Valera take the oath?

De Valera and other Fianna Fáil TDs entering Leinster House in 1927

Table B

Results of the June 1927 election (1923 results in brackets)							
In the Dáil					Abstaining		
Cumann na nGaedheal	Labour	National League	Farmers	Independents	Fianna Fáil	Sinn Féin	Total number of seats
47 (63)	22 (14)	8 (–)	11 (15)	16 (17)	44 (–)	5 (44)	153 (153)

DE VALERA'S CAMPAIGN AGAINST THE OATH

On 23 June the new Dáil met. De Valera led his TDs to Leinster House and demanded to be let in. He was asked to sign the book containing the oath to the King and he refused.

De Valera then began a campaign to have the oath removed. He took advantage of a clause in the 1922 Constitution which said that the government must hold a referendum if 75,000 people signed a petition requesting one. Fianna Fáil began to collect the necessary signatures.

10 JULY 1927: THE ASSASSINATION OF KEVIN O'HIGGINS

Some days later, an event occurred which totally changed the situation. On Sunday, 10 July three IRA men saw Kevin O'Higgins walking home from Mass and shot him. They acted alone. The IRA disapproved of the killing but everyone assumed they were responsible. Fianna Fáil too might have been blamed because they still had close ties to the IRA, even though de Valera at once condemned the murder.

Cosgrave could have used the murder to outlaw Fianna Fáil but he chose a more far-sighted and democratic option. He put before the Dáil the **Electoral Amendment Bill**. Under it, any candidate for election to the Dáil or Senate had to swear that, if elected, he or she would take the oath. And an elected member who refused to take the oath would lose his or her seat.

Cosgrave's aim was to force de Valera and the anti-Treatyites to play their part in the institutions of the Free State or to leave politics. If they accepted his challenge, he might well lose power but Irish democracy would be healthier. With Fianna Fáil in the Dáil, voters would have two strong parties to choose between, either of them capable of forming a government.

FIANNA FÁIL TAKES THE OATH

This put de Valera in a difficult position:
- On the one hand many Fianna Fáil members knew abstention was futile. Two Fianna Fáil TDs had already taken the oath. Even before O'Higgins's death, the Labour Party had approached de Valera to suggest an alliance in the Dáil to get Cosgrave out.
- On the other hand he had always insisted that he could never take the oath. If he did, the extreme republicans, with whom he still had close links, would think he had betrayed the republic.

On 11 August, the Fianna Fáil Executive met and issued a statement that:

> 'the required declaration is not an oath … that it is merely an empty political formula which Deputies could conscientiously sign without … involving their nation in obligations of loyalty to the English crown.' (quoted in T.P. Coogan, *De Valera: Long Fellow, Long Shadow*, London 1993, p. 404)

Then they went back into Leinster House. Once again, de Valera was presented with a book to sign. Before he did so, he said:

> 'I want you to understand that I am not taking any oath nor giving any promise of faithfulness to the King of England or to any power outside the people of Ireland. I am putting my name here merely as a formality to get the permission necessary to enter among the other Teachtaí that were elected by the people of Ireland, and I want you to know that no other meaning is to be attached to what I am doing.' (Longford and O'Neill, *Eamon de Valera*, Dublin 1971, p. 256)

He then carried the Bible to the far side of the room in case anyone might think he was swearing on it. Leaving it there, he returned and signed the oath. The rest of his party followed suit. *'Thus,'* a modern historian has written, *'seeing no oath, hearing no oath, speaking no oath and signing no oath, the Soldiers of Destiny shuffled into Dáil Éireann.'* (J.J. Lee, *Ireland 1912–85*, London 1989, p. 155)

SEPTEMBER 1927: ANOTHER ELECTION

With Fianna Fáil in the Dáil, Cosgrave's government was in danger. De Valera put down a motion of no confidence in the government. Labour, the National League and some Independents voted with Fianna Fáil and the result was a dead heat. Cosgrave then called another election in September.

Results of the September 1927 election (June 1927 results in brackets)								Table C
Cumann na nGaedheal	Fianna Fáil	Labour	Sinn Féin	National League	Farmers	Independents	Total seats	
62 (47)	57 (44)	13 (22)	0 (5)	3 (8)	6 (11)	14 (16)	153	

The result showed that voters had abandoned small parties (Table C) to rally behind the two big 'Treaty' parties:

- Cumann na nGaedheal went up from forty-seven to sixty-two seats. Sympathy for O'Higgins, worry about stability and fear of Fianna Fáil probably explain the change.
- Fianna Fáil rose from forty-four to fifty-seven seats. Now that it was in the Dáil the party could give voters what they wanted, a strong opposition and an alternative to Cumann na nGaedheal.
- Smaller parties lost seats. Voters preferred strong parties that were capable of forming a government.
- Sinn Féin did not even put up candidates. From now on it played little part in politics, though the IRA remained strong.

THE SIGNIFICANCE OF 1927

The dramatic events of 1927 were very important in establishing Irish democracy:

- However reluctantly, the opponents of the Treaty had accepted the existence of the Free State. For the first time all elected TDs were in Dáil Éireann. From now on, political debate could take place where it should in a democracy – in the elected parliament.
- With Fianna Fáil in the Dáil, there was a better balance between government and opposition. The large minority that had voted for the anti-Treaty side could now make its voice heard within the institutions of the Free State.
- Many within that minority were poor and disadvantaged. With a bigger party to represent them some of the social and economic reforms they needed might be undertaken.

But another big hurdle remained to be crossed. Would it be possible for the Free State to change its government after a democratic election?

QUESTIONS

1 Write a paragraph about the army mutiny, explaining what caused it and how it was handled. Do you think it was an important episode? Give reasons for your answer.

2 What was the Boundary Commission and what did Irish leaders think it would do? Give three reasons why these hopes were unlikely to be fulfilled.

3 Describe how the Commission did its work (for this see also page 164). How did Cosgrave get to hear about their conclusions and why did they come as a 'nasty shock' to him?

4 Describe how the 1925 Anglo-Irish Agreement came about and what it contained. How did it affect Cumann na nGaedheal?

5 What was meant by 'abstention'?

Who followed this policy and why did they do so? Why, by 1925, did de Valera want to change this policy?

6 Describe how de Valera broke with Sinn Féin and set up Fianna Fáil.

7 Give the results of the June 1927 election for each of the three main parties and explain how each party did compared with the 1923 election.

8 How did Fianna Fáil finally enter the Dáil and how did that affect Cosgrave's government?

9 Compare the results of the June and September 1927 elections and explain the changes you see. Do you agree that the events of these months are 'very important in establishing Irish democracy'? Give reasons for your answer.

CONSOLIDATING DEMOCRACY: 1927–1936

1927–32: FIANNA FÁIL, THE 'SLIGHTLY CONSTITUTIONAL' OPPOSITION

Between 1927 and 1932 Fianna Fáil was the official opposition party within Dáil Éireann. Its TDs opposed Cumann na nGaedheal's social and economic policies and ridiculed their involvement in the Commonwealth. They hoped to win the support of the voters and form the government after the next election.

But although they took part in the institutions of the Free State, Fianna Fáil TDs remained ambivalent towards it. They refused to attend state functions, especially those involving the king's representative, the Governor-General. They also made it clear that they had entered the Dáil only as a first step on the road to a republic.

In 1928 Seán Lemass said in the Dáil:

> 'Fianna Fáil is a slightly constitutional party ... but before anything we are a republican party. We have adopted the method of political agitation to achieve our end, because we believe, in the present circumstances, that method is best in the interests of the nation and of the Republican movement, and for no other reason ... Our object is to establish a republican government in Ireland. If that can be done by the present methods, we will be pleased, but if not we will not confine ourselves to them.' (R. Fanning, *Independent Ireland*, Dublin 1978, p. 99)

FIANNA FÁIL AND THE IRA

Lemass' words appear to threaten to use force again. This reflects the close links Fianna Fáil still had with the IRA. They had a lot in common:

- Close ties of friendship and understanding bound members of the two organisations. They had fought side by side against the Free State and suffered imprisonment and death. As de Valera put it: *'Those who continued in that organisation can claim exactly the same continuity as we claimed up to 1925.'* (B. Bell, *The Secret Army*, Dublin 1981, p. 97)

- Both wanted a republic. The IRA still used violence. Fianna Fáil had abandoned violence for politics but, as Lemass implied, might use it again if politics failed.

THE IRA AFTER DE VALERA LEFT

After de Valera left Sinn Féin in 1925 the IRA's Army Council prepared for a 'second round' against the Free State. IRA men engaged in occasional acts of violence, such as arms raids, bank robberies and attacks on the Gardaí. But some republicans thought this random violence was futile. It achieved little except public disapproval and government retaliation.

By 1930 the great depression which followed the Wall Street crash in the USA began to affect Ireland. As jobs disappeared and poverty increased, some IRA leaders like Peadar O'Donnell and Seán MacBride suggested that they adopt a socialist policy based on the writings of James Connolly.

The Army Council rejected these suggestions but not all IRA men obeyed them. In 1931 O'Donnell helped set up **Saor Éire**, a socialist republican movement. It aimed to overthrow *'the British empire and its ally capitalism'*. Meanwhile in his native Donegal he supported small farmers in a campaign against paying land annuities.

THE IMPACT OF THE DEPRESSION

In 1931, the depression grew worse. Like most democratic governments at the time, Cosgrave and his ministers had no idea what to do about it. They followed the example of other governments and cut the wages of public servants like guards and teachers. This did not improve the economy. It just made them more unpopular.

The depression also encouraged the growth of extremist groups across Europe – fascists on the right, communists on the left. In Ireland, apart from Saor Éire a number of left-wing groups emerged, among them a tiny Communist Party. Although they had few followers, they frightened property owners. IRA violence also increased. In 1931 it was responsible for a number of violent incidents, culminating in the murder of a Garda superintendent in Tipperary.

ARTICLE 2A

These developments worried Cosgrave. To deal with them, he introduced the **Constitution (Amendment) Bill**. This inserted **Article 2A** into the Constitution. Under it, a five-man Military Tribunal (court) was set up to try political offences and the government had power to declare certain organisations illegal. In the Dáil, Fianna Fáil and the Labour Party attacked this as an overreaction to a minor problem and a threat to civil liberties.

Once the Bill passed, Cosgrave outlawed twelve groups, including the IRA, Saor Éire and the Communist Party. Members of these organisations, among them O'Donnell, were arrested and imprisoned.

FEBRUARY 1932: AN ELECTION CALLED

In February 1932 Cosgrave called an election. This was to be one of the most important elections in the history of the state. Would Fianna Fáil win and if they did, would Cumann na nGaedheal or their supporters in the army and the Gardaí let them take power?

FIANNA FÁIL IN THE 1932 ELECTION

Fianna Fáil went into the election with a number of advantages. De Valera was a charismatic leader and it had a big campaign fund that he had raised in the United States. The party was well organised with over 1,400 branches whose members were full of enthusiasm and hungry for power. Above all it had drawn up a programme which was designed to appeal to a large section of the community.

THE FIANNA FÁIL PROGRAMME

Knowing many people feared another civil war, Fianna Fáil played down its republicanism and it concentrated on its economic programme, which promised to protect Irish industry and jobs. It did not use the word 'republic', merely it promised to free IRA prisoners and abolish the oath, the Governor-General and the Senate. There were also some cautious words on partition.

DE VALERA'S *IRISH PRESS*

In the 1920s Fianna Fáil had difficulty in getting its message over to voters because the main daily newspapers – the *Irish Independent*, the *Irish Times* and the *Cork Examiner* – were all hostile to it. To counter this, de Valera set up the *Irish Press* in 1931. He funded it with money he collected in the United States. A lively paper with lots of pictures and extended sports coverage, it was an immediate success. Through it the Fianna Fáil programme reached people who up to then seldom read a daily paper.

CUMANN NA NGAEDHEAL AND THE 1932 ELECTION CAMPAIGN

Cumann na nGaedheal did little to counter the Fianna Fáil promises. After ten hard years, its leaders were tired and the party was poorly organised. The members lacked the unity and intensity of Fianna Fáil.

Cosgrave asked voters to look at his record. Since 1923 he and his ministers had brought stability out of the chaos of the Civil War and given the country honest government. But by 1932 this was no longer enough. They had no answer to the economic crisis, and the policy of cutting wages cost them votes.

A RED SMEAR

To make up for their lack of policies, Cumann na nGaedheal tried to frighten the voters. Electing Fianna Fáil, they warned, would undermine the country's stability, provoke a new war with Britain, even bring in 'godless communism'.

Some Cumann na nGaedheal leaders genuinely believed that Fianna Fáil had communist leanings. They also hoped to frighten Catholic businessmen and farmers who knew that in the Soviet Union, Stalin was persecuting Christians, collectivising farms and killing *kulaks* (medium-sized farmers).

The election campaign was reasonably peaceful but during it Cumann na nGaedheal made a major blunder. They used Article 2A to bring the editor of the *Irish Press* before the Military Tribunal. This looked like a serious interference with the freedom of speech and was unpopular, even among their own supporters.

DON'T LET THIS HAPPEN
VOTE FOR
CUMANN NA
nGAEDHEAL

A Cumann na nGaedheal poster for the 1932 election. Explain its message in your own words

THE RESULT

When the votes were counted (see Table D), Fianna Fáil had won fifteen more seats than in 1927. Cumann na nGaedheal lost five seats and all other parties lost ground too. Although Fianna Fáil did not have an overall majority, it had enough seats to form a minority government with the backing of the Labour Party, which supported many of its social policies.

WOULD THERE BE A PEACEFUL HANDOVER OF POWER?

This result provided the greatest test of democracy yet faced by the Free State. Would the losers in the election hand power peacefully to the winners? There were some in Ireland and abroad who doubted it. They recalled that only ten years earlier the two sides had fought a vicious civil war.

The Garda Commissioner, **Eoin O'Duffy**, did suggest to some army officers that they might stage a coup to stop de Valera. He got no support. The army had suffered redundancies and wage cuts under Cumann na nGaedheal; the officers may have reckoned they would do no worse under Fianna Fáil.

9 MARCH 1932: A PEACEFUL TRANSITION

The new Dáil met for the first time on 9 March. People waited tensely to see what would happen. A grim-faced de Valera entered the Dáil, accompanied by his son, who carried a gun. Other Fianna Fáil TDs also had guns in their pockets.

Cosgrave, however, was determined to uphold the democratic principles he and his party had preached since the Treaty vote. Already he had warned the British that they must respect the people's decision. He also instructed the heads of the army, the Garda Síochána and civil service to accept their new masters. In the Dáil chamber, he stepped aside and de Valera was elected President of the Executive Council.

Once in power, de Valera behaved with the moderation appropriate in a democracy. Many of his followers wanted revenge but he did not satisfy them. The officers in the army and the Gardaí, who had fought him in the Civil War, were not sacked. A few civil servants in sensitive positions

Table D

Results of the 1932 election (September 1927 in brackets)					
Cumann na nGaedheal	Fianna Fáil	Labour	Farmers	Independents	Total
57 (62)	72 (57)	7 (13)	3 (6)	16 (14)	153

were moved to other jobs, but the rest remained where they were. The British-trained civil service which had worked for Cumann na nGaedheal continued to work for Fianna Fáil.

A CONTINUING DISTRUST

But it would take time for de Valera's moderation to become clear. Meanwhile, Fianna Fáil and Cumann na nGaedheal still deeply distrusted each other:

- In spite of the peaceful handover of power, many in Fianna Fáil still feared the pro-Treaty side would stage a coup. They could not believe they would give up power so easily.
- Many in Cumann na nGaedheal still distrusted de Valera. They had acted democratically by handing over power but they did not trust him to behave in a similar manner. Some feared that he planned a communist revolution or a fascist dictatorship, such as Hitler was setting up in Germany.

A good deal of what happened in the next two years was the result of this mutual distrust.

A VICTORY FOR REPUBLICANISM?

At first Cumann na nGaedheal's worst fears seemed justified. Republicans greeted Fianna Fáil's election as a belated victory in the Civil War. The day after they took over, the new Ministers for Defence and Justice went personally to see IRA prisoners in jail and freed over 100, among them Peadar O'Donnell. On 18 March the Military Tribunal was suspended and the ban on the IRA and other organisations was lifted. The IRA became popular and its numbers grew to over 30,000.

IRA ATTACKS ON CUMANN NA NGAEDHEAL

IRA men then attacked Cosgrave and Cumann na nGaedheal as traitors to Ireland:

- At a rally in Dublin Peadar O'Donnell said he was *'glad the murder-government was put out of power, but these men must be put finally out of public life'*. (M. Manning: *The Blueshirts*, Dublin 1971, pp. 32–3).
- Another said Cumann na nGaedheal leaders were *'a menace to society and the independence*

of Ireland and it behoved all Republicans to unite and wipe out this menace at all costs …' (T.P. Coogan, *De Valera, Long Fellow, Long Shadow*, London 1993, p. 463).

- IRA-led mobs broke up Cumann na nGaedheal meetings and stopped its leaders from speaking. Their behaviour was very similar to that of Hitler's Brownshirts in Germany.
- Gardaí, uncertain what their new masters wanted, did little to protect the speakers or arrest republicans involved in violence.
- All this strengthened Cumann na nGaedheal's distrust of Fianna Fáil. In December 1932 their newspaper, *United Ireland*, wrote: *'It has become all too apparent that Mr de Valera is leading the country straight into Bolshevik servitude.'* (M. Manning, *The Blueshirts*, Dublin 1971, p. 44).

THE ARMY COMRADES' ASSOCIATION

Since the Gardaí did not protect them, Cumann na nGaedheal turned for help to the **Army Comrades' Association** (**ACA**). It was an organisation of former soldiers in the Free State army, founded to campaign about army pensions.

In August 1932 T.F. O'Higgins, a Cumann na nGaedheal TD and a brother of Kevin O'Higgins, became its leader. He declared that the ACA would defend free speech and oppose communism. It provided stewards at Cumann na nGaedheal meetings. Fights between it and the IRA became common and tension rose sharply.

THE NATIONAL CENTRE PARTY

Meanwhile some independent TDs tried to get away from civil war politics by founding a new party. Called the **National Centre Party**, it was led by **Frank MacDermot** and **James Dillon**, and drew support from bigger farmers and people who wanted to be on good terms with Britain.

JANUARY 1933: ANOTHER GENERAL ELECTION

The party grew quickly, especially as the economic war began to affect farm prices. But before it became established, de Valera called a sudden

Results of the 1933 election (1932 results in brackets)					
Fianna Fáil	Cumann na nGaedheal	Labour	Centre Party	Independents	Total seats
77 (72)	48 (57)	8 (7)	11 (–)	9 (16)	153

election in January 1933. He hoped to secure a majority of Dáil seats so that he would have a clear mandate for his economic war with the British (see page 123).

Taken by surprise, his opponents had little to offer the voters. Fianna Fáil gained seventy-seven seats, which gave it an overall majority. Cumann na nGaedheal fell to forty-eight, while Labour won eight seats and the Centre Party achieved eleven (Table E).

EOIN O'DUFFY RESIGNS

Rioting between the IRA and the ACA increased during the election. After it, de Valera called in the Garda Commissioner, Eoin O'Duffy. Unhappy with the way the Gardaí had handled the violence, he asked O'Duffy to move to another job. O'Duffy refused and resigned in a blaze of publicity. Cumann na nGaedheal regarded him as a martyr to de Valera's desire for power.

THE BLUESHIRTS

In July O'Duffy became leader of the ACA. He began to make it more like the fascist movements developing elsewhere in Europe:

- He changed the name to the **National Guard**, made a uniform of blue shirts, already worn by some members, which were compulsory, and adopted the fascist-style straight-arm salute. He encouraged sporting activities and set up a women's section which quickly became known as the 'blue blouses'.
- Membership was limited to: *citizens of Irish birth or of Irish parentage who profess the Christian faith*. This was clearly a coded way of excluding Irish people who happened to be Jews. It reflects the anti-semitism which was common in Ireland as in most other countries

at the time. It may also have been a hidden attack on de Valera, as there were persistent rumours (which he was at pains to deny) that his father had been Jewish. However, unlike the German and British fascist movements, open anti-semitism played little part in the Blueshirt agenda.

- O'Duffy also denounced political parties as a relic of English rule. He wanted the Dáil remodelled, so that TDs would be elected to represent **vocational groups** – e.g. farmers, workers, etc. – rather than territorial constituencies. This had echoes of Mussolini's corporate state in Italy.

Eoin O'Duffy (1892–1944): An engineer from Monaghan, O'Duffy fought in the War of Independence. A close associate of Collins, he supported the Treaty and was made Garda Commissioner in 1922. A tough disciplinarian, he built the unarmed Gardaí into respected police force. During the 1924 army mutiny, O'Higgins put him in charge of the army for a time but he later returned to the Gardaí.

Blueshirts salute

DE VALERA AGAINST THE BLUESHIRTS

O'Duffy announced that in August 1933 the National Guard would parade outside Leinster House to commemorate the deaths of Griffith, Collins and O'Higgins. To de Valera this posed a problem. The IRA would almost certainly try to stop the march and there would be riots. Could he count on the loyalty of the Gardaí and the army? He took decisive action.

He ordered politicians, including former Cumann na nGaedheal ministers, who held guns for their own protection, to surrender them.

He ordered the formation of a special police unit, mainly recruited from IRA men. Nicknamed the 'Broy Harriers' after O'Duffy's replacement, Éamon Broy, they were armed and guarded government buildings against what Fianna Fáil implied was a Mussolini-style 'march on Rome'.

Finally he banned the march to Leinster House and, reviving Article 2A, declared the National Guard an illegal organisation.

THE FORMATION OF FINE GAEL:
3 SEPTEMBER 1933

O'Duffy never intended to seize power. True to the law-abiding traditions of Cumann na nGaedheal, he called off the march. But he and his friends thought de Valera's actions were the first step

towards the dictatorship they feared. They were deprived of their guns and their protectors while the IRA was allowed to go armed and unmolested. Hitler used similar tactics to destroy German democracy earlier that year.

The leaders of Cumann na nGaedheal, the National Centre Party and the National Guard felt they had to stand together against the threat. On 3 September 1934 they combined to form a new party, the **United Ireland Party – Fine Gael**. O'Duffy was elected leader with Cosgrave, Dillon and MacDermott as vice-presidents. The National Guard was renamed the Young Ireland Association and became the youth wing of the new party.

Fine Gael's programme made no reference to vocationalism or to O'Duffy's attack on political parties. Instead it called for an end to PR voting, the reunification of Ireland within the Commonwealth and a series of social reforms.

1933–34: GROWING VIOLENCE

During the new party's first year the country remained tense. De Valera continued to put pressure on his opponents. When O'Duffy changed the name of the National Guard to the Young Ireland Association, it too was banned. Gardaí searched his house and those of other Fine Gael leaders. Some Blueshirts were arrested and put on trial on very flimsy charges. A bill to prevent the wearing of uniforms passed the Dáil but was blocked by the Senate in May 1934.

The economic war (see page 136) added to the tension. The price of cattle fell as exports to Britain declined. Big farmers of Munster and Leinster who supported Cumann na nGaedheal were the worst hit. In retaliation, they refused to pay their rates (local taxes) to the county councils.

By the spring of 1934, 36 per cent of rates were unpaid. The government used the 'Broy Harriers' to seize animals and machines from farmers and sell them at public auctions. Blue-shirted farmers tried to stop the auctions, leading to fights with the police.

21 SEPTEMBER 1934: O'DUFFY REPLACED

O'Duffy supported the farmers but the violence embarrassed other Fine Gael leaders. They were also uncomfortable with his erratic behaviour and his clear admiration for fascism. They had always prided themselves on upholding democracy and the rule of law and this was not what they wanted for their new party.

When he talked wildly about invading Northern Ireland, they had to act. At Fine Gael's first annual conference in September 1934, O'Duffy was forced to resign the leadership and Cosgrave was elected in his place. O'Duffy tried to keep the Blueshirts going as a separate movement but it quickly faded into insignificance. In 1936 he made his last political gesture when he led a brigade of 700 men to fight with General Franco in the Spanish Civil War.

DE VALERA AND THE IRA

De Valera had defeated the Blueshirts but the IRA was also a threat to democracy. No democratic government can tolerate private armies, so once he was in charge of the Free State, he had to deal with them.

In 1932 the IRA had about 30,000 members. Since the civil war they had not recognised the Free State, but de Valera set out to win them over:

- He gave pensions to men who had served on the anti-Treaty side in the Civil War and compensated republicans who had lost property.
- Several hundred republicans were recruited into the 'Broy Harriers'. Many more became part of a Volunteer force, set up as a branch of the Free State army in 1934. With the Free State paying their wages, these people found it harder to deny its right to exist.
- Republican objections to the Free State were reduced by his removal of the oath and other traces of British rule (see page 122).

But hardline republicans refused to be won over. They had expected that de Valera would declare a republic overnight and probably invade Northern Ireland, so they were not impressed by his slow dismantling of the Treaty.

After the 1933 election, de Valera instructed the Gardaí to prosecute IRA men for violence. But he was still tied to them by shared memories, experiences and friendships, and he did not want an open breach. In 1934 he met some leading republicans and tried to persuade them to lay aside their arms. They refused and increased their pointless violence.

- In 1935 the IRA was responsible for a number of murders and de Valera used the Military Tribunal, revived to deal with the Blueshirts, against them.
- In 1936, the IRA in Cork shot the seventy year old Admiral Somerville for giving references to young men going to join the British navy.
- Soon after in Waterford, they shot a young man whom they accused of spying.

This was more than de Valera would tolerate. On 18 June 1936 he banned the IRA. Its chief-of-staff, Maurice Twomey, was brought before the Military Tribunal and given three years' hard labour. The IRA drifted, leaderless and impotent, for the next few years, seeking a new policy.

AN ESTABLISHED DEMOCRACY

With the IRA outlawed, the last serious threat to democratic government within the Irish Free State was laid to rest. By then almost everyone accepted that democracy was as safe in de Valera's hands as in Cosgrave's. The proof of this can be seen in the Constitution which de Valera produced in 1937. Whatever its strengths and weaknesses, it was clearly the Constitution of a democratic state.

1. In 1928 Seán Lemass said Fianna Fáil was a 'slightly constitutional party'. Do you think this is a good description of Fianna Fáil's attitude to the Irish Free State between 1927 and 1932? Give reasons for your answer.

2. What economic and political changes did the Great Depression produce? How did Cosgrave and his ministers respond to these changes?

3. Set out four reasons to explain why Fianna Fáil won the 1932 election. Why is the result such an important landmark in Irish history?

4. In 1932–33 Cumann na nGaedheal continued to distrust Fianna Fáil. Explain the reasons for this. What did the leaders of Cumann na nGaedheal do to protect themselves?

5. Who was Eoin O'Duffy? Describe his role in the Blueshirt episode.

6. Were the Blueshirts Irish fascists or was the whole episode just a hang-over from the Civil War? Give reasons for your answer.

7. How did de Valera deal with the IRA?

8. By 1936 'almost everyone accepted that democracy was as safe in de Valera's hands as in Cosgrave's'. Do you agree with this opinion? Give reasons for your answer.

6.5

CONFIRMING DEMOCRACY: BUNREACHT NA hÉIREANN: 1936–1937

THE NEED FOR A NEW CONSTITUTION

After Fianna Fáil won power in 1932, de Valera dismantled the Treaty step by step (see chapter 7.2). That involved making big changes in the 1922 Free State Constitution. The oath to the king was removed and the Senate abolished. In 1936 the External Relations Act had removed the king and the country no longer had a head of state. De Valera decided to write a new Constitution that owed nothing to the Treaty. He hoped a fully Irish-made Constitution would at last persuade republicans to accept the Irish state.

BUNREACHT NA hÉIREANN

De Valera worked on the Constitution through 1936 and the early months of 1937. Although he consulted a wide range of people, the final version was very much his own. The following are some of its main points.

The Irish state

The Constitution declares the right of the Irish people to decide their own form of government. The Irish state is called '*Éire or in the English language, Ireland*'. The territory of the state was defined as '*the whole island of Ireland*' (Article 2) but '*pending the reintegration of the national territory*' its laws would apply only to the twenty-six counties (Article 3). These articles reflected de Valera's opposition to partition.

The status of Irish

Irish is the '*first official language*' of the state. This reflected his commitment to reviving Irish.

The President

The head of state is a President, elected by all voters for a seven-year term. The position is mainly ceremonial, but the President has some special powers.

— Before signing a bill, he/she can refer it to the Supreme Court to see if it is in accordance with the Constitution.

— He/She can refuse to allow a Taoiseach, who had lost his/her majority in the Dáil, to call a general election.

Having an elected head of state makes Ireland a republic, though the word is not used in the Constitution.

● The Oireachtas

There are two houses of **the Oireachtas** that make the laws, agree to taxes and elect the government.

— The **Dáil** is elected by all citizens over twenty-one, voting by proportional representation (PR). There must be elections at least every five years. This was the same as in the 1922 Constitution.

— The **Seanad** of sixty members is elected by a complex and undemocratic process. Forty-three are elected by county councillors, TDs and Senators to represent vocational groups. De Valera borrowed this idea from Mussolini's corporate state. Six are elected by graduates of Trinity College and the National University. Eleven more are nominated by the Taoiseach of the day. This means that the Senate would always reflect the Dáil and was unlikely to challenge the power of the government in the way the Free State Senate did.

● The Taoiseach and the Cabinet

The head of the government is called the **Taoiseach** (another echo of fashionable 1930s ideas). She/he appoints other members of the Cabinet, who have to be approved by the Dáil.

● Civil rights

The Constitution guarantees freedom of speech, assembly and association to citizens. It also protects the right to own private property and to education. But the value of these rights is undermined because they are '*subject to public order and morality*'.

● Relations between Church and State

The 1922 Constitution simply stated that the state would not favour one religion above another. But de Valera, a devout Catholic, wanted his Constitution to reflect the dominant position of the Catholic Church within the twenty-six counties.

He consulted a number of Catholic clergymen. The most important was his friend, John C. McQuaid. But he resisted pressure from them to make the Catholic Church the country's official religion or to ignore the rights of religious minorities. He also consulted the leaders of the Protestant Churches and the Jewish Community about their wishes.

In the end the Constitution recognised the '*special position of the Roman Catholic Church*' as the '*religion of the great majority of citizens*' (Article 44). It then went on to guarantee '*freedom of conscience and the free profession and practice of religion*' to all other religious groups in Ireland in 1937, listing them by name.

This satisfied other religious leaders but drew criticism from some Catholics. They had hoped that de Valera would create a Catholic state for a Catholic people. It is believed that among those who expressed dissatisfaction was Pope Pius XI.

● The ban on divorce

Article 41 outlawed divorce. This reflected the Catholic Church's views, though de Valera insisted that he included it because divorce injured the family, not because it was Catholic teaching. It could be seen as denying the civil rights of those who accepted divorce, but in 1937 such people were rare. Protestant Churches too disliked it as can be seen from the abdication of King Edward VIII in Britain, though they were less absolute on the issue that the Catholic Church. At the time the ban caused little debate.

● Women and de Valera's Constitution

In 1937, the most controversial part of de Valera's constitution was its references to women. To many women it seemed that he was trying to take away the constitutional guarantee of equality that they got in the 1922 Constitution.

WOMEN IN THE STRUGGLE FOR INDEPENDENCE

This guaranteee had grown out of the prominent part women took in the struggle for independence:

● Griffith's Sinn Féin was the first political party to admit women as full members. From the start women such as Jenny Wyse Power were among its leaders.

● Women set up **Cumann na mBan** in 1914 as an auxiliary to the Irish Volunteers. During the 1916 rising they acted as nurses and couriers. In the Irish Citizen Army women were enrolled directly as soldiers and several, like Constance Markievicz, were involved in the fighting.

- In 1916 Connolly, a supporter of women's rights, insisted that the Proclamation speak to 'Irish men and Irish women'; it was the first public document to do so.
- In 1918, Sinn Féin was the only party to take advantage of a new law that allowed women to stand for parliament. It nominated two women and one, Markievicz, was elected. De Valera made her Minister for Labour in the first Dáil Cabinet.
- During the War of Independence women in Cumann na mBan were active in resisting the Black and Tans.
- Sinn Féin nominated six women to the Second Dáil. In the debates surrounding the Treaty they all took an extreme republican position, but they were not representative. Other women like Jenny Wyse Power, supported the Treaty and it seems likely that women were divided over it in much the same proportions as men.

THE STATUS OF WOMEN IN THE 1922 CONSTITUTION

The 1922 Constitution gave women equal citizenship in the new state. Article 3 stated simply that: *'every person without distinction of sex shall … enjoy the privileges and be subject to the obligations of citizenship.'* That article, which made women full and equal citizens of the Irish Free State, was in advance of its time. British women under thirty did not get the vote until 1928 and French women did not get the vote until 1945.

FEAR OF WOMEN'S EQUALITY

However, no sooner was the Free State set up than attempts began to pull back from this commitment to equal citizenship. This was because many men and some women viewed the idea of equality for women with alarm. They still shared the Victorian ideal of women as wives and mothers. They believed it was contrary to nature and the divine order, for a woman to play a public part in the political or economic life of the nation. The woman's place was at home looking after her husband and children, while the man's role was as the breadwinner who supported them.

In Ireland, Catholic clergy were especially vigorous in expressing these views but they were not alone. Political leaders and many trade unionists also put them forward. Similar views were also expressed in Europe and America, where the advances women had made earlier were also being undermined.

REDUCING WOMEN'S PUBLIC ROLES: THE CUMANN NA nGAEDHEAL YEARS

In Ireland views like these led to various attempts to stop women playing a full part in society. They began under Cumann na nGaedheal, with Kevin O'Higgins taking a lead.

- In the **1924** and **1927 Juries Acts** he made it much more difficult for women to serve on juries. O'Higgins justified this by claiming that women were reluctant to serve. So were men, but no one took that 'obligation of citizenship' away from them. This decision also did a grave injustice to women defendants who, as a result, were tried by all-male juries.
- In 1925, an attempt was made to prevent women sitting examinations for senior posts in the civil service. It was dropped after protests from Jenny Wyse Power in the Senate and a campaign by some women's groups who argued that promotion should be on merit, not gender.
- In 1929, the Censorship of Publications Act banned the publication of information about contraception. While this affected men and women equally, it imposed an especially heavy

GENTLEWOMEN PREFER BLANDS.

Courtesy: Trinity College Library

One reason given for removing women from juries was that they were likely to favour good looking men. This cartoon is a comment on that argument. Do you think this is a good reason for taking women off juries?

burden on women who at that time often had very large families.

REDUCING WOMEN'S PUBLIC ROLES: THE FIANNA FÁIL YEARS

Fianna Fáil took power in the great Depression. Jobs were scarce and this was used as an excuse to limit women's opportunities to work. Lemass in particular claimed that if there was only one job it should go to a man with a family to support. This overlooked the fact that many women also had families to support and that almost a quarter of women were single.

- In 1932, a 'marriage bar' was introduced in the civil service. It was later extended to primary teachers. This forced women to retire on marriage, whether they wanted to or not. In practice few women at that time wanted to work outside the home, but compulsion was unjust to those who wanted to continue working.
- As new industries were set up in the 1930s trade unionists were concerned that jobs in them were going to women instead of men. To reassure them, Seán Lemass created powers, in the **Conditions of Employment Act**, to limit the number of women working in any industry.

WHAT DE VALERA'S CONSTITUTION SAID ABOUT WOMEN

When the first draft of de Valera's Constitution appeared in 1937, women were dismayed.

- The words '*without distinction of sex*' was dropped from the articles dealing with voting rights.
- The article that said that all citizens were equal added that this did not mean that the state would not give '*due regard to differences of capacity, physical and moral and of social function*'.
- Further on it stated that '*by her life in the home, woman gives to the state a support without which the common good cannot be achieved*'.
- Finally it added that '*mothers shall not be obliged by economic necessity to engage in labour to the neglect of their duties in the home*', that the state must ensure that '*the inadequate strength of women and the tender age of children*' must not be exploited, and that

citizens should not have to do work '*unsuited to their sex, age and strength*'.

Taken together, these phrases seemed to relegate women to the status of second-class citizens. The **Irish Women Workers' Union**, the **Women Graduates' Association** and various other women's organisations tried to have changes made. They succeeded in getting the phrase '*without distinction of sex*' restored and the words '*the inadequate strength of women*' dropped. But the rest remained.

1 JULY 1937: THE FIRST REFERENDUM

A referendum was needed for the new Constitution to come into effect. This would be the first referendum in Irish history. To get the voters out, de Valera held a general election and referendum on the same day. Women's groups campaigned for a 'No' vote. They argued that '*women … demand to be treated as human beings with full rights. Do not vote away those rights*'.

In spite of this the Constitution was accepted by a small margin (see table F) and Fianna Fáil won the election. Afterwards all political parties agreed to nominate Douglas Hyde, the founder of the Gaelic League, as the first President of Ireland.

Table F

Referendum results, July 1937	
For the new Constitution	Against the new Constitution
685,105	526,176

All parties agreed that Douglas Hyde should be the first President, and he was inaugurated in 1938

ASSESSING DE VALERA'S CONSTITUTION

In his Constitution, de Valera tried to reconcile a number of opposing views:

- It gave Ireland the form of a republic, with an elected President. But de Valera did not use the word 'republic' so as not to annoy the unionists or the British.

- By claiming that it applied to the whole island, he hoped to satisfy nationalists but at the same time he accepted the reality of partition by limiting its operation to the twenty-six counties.

- Although many aspects are liberal and democratic, its attitude to the Catholic Church, divorce and women is very conservative. In this it reflected the political fashions of the 1930s.

- A major weakness was that, instead of dealing with general principles, it contained too much detail. The women's issue illustrates this. He replaced the simple statement of the 1922 Constitution with a lot of opinions that really do not belong in a Constitution. The Constitution neither stopped women being exploited in the workplace, as de Valera claimed was his aim, nor did it deprive women of full citizenship rights, as his opponents feared. In fact since 1937 these clauses have made no practical difference to women's lives.

QUESTIONS

1 Why did de Valera want a new Constitution in 1937?

2 How does Bunreacht na hÉireann deal with the following points: (1) the state, (2) the President, (3) the Oireachtas, (4) civil liberties?

3 How did de Valera treat the issue of religion in his Constitution?

4 Outline the part played by women in the independence movement. How was that acknowledged in the 1922 Constitution?

5 To what extent had women's claim to equal citizenship been undermined by the 1937 Constitution?

6 Write a brief assessment of de Valera's Constitution.

LEAVING CERTIFICATE QUESTIONS

Higher Level

1 'The Constitution and institutions of the Free State were based on a British model.' Do you agree or disagree with this statement?

2 What were the major threats to democracy in the Irish Free State up to 1932 and how successful was Cumann na nGaedheal in overcoming them?

3 What happened to those who opposed the Treaty from 1922 to 1932?

4 Explain why the events of 1927 and 1932 are central to the development of Irish democracy.

5 'With his Constitution, de Valera showed that Irish democracy was safe.' Do you agree with this statement? Explain your answer.

Ordinary Level

A Write a paragraph on **one** of the following:
1 The Boundary Commission.

2 The Blueshirts.

B Answer **one** of these questions.
1 What happened in the 1932 election and why is that important in Irish history?

2 Who was responsible for the 1937 Constitution (Bunreacht na hÉireann) and what are its main features?

7 Foreign and Anglo-Irish Policy 1922–1939

7.1

MAKING THE TREATY WORK: 1922–1932

WHY IRELAND NEEDED A FOREIGN POLICY

In 1923 a Cumann na nGaedheal TD said in the Dáil:

> 'I do not see why we want a Minister for External Affairs … We are concerned with no foreign affairs. We have no colonies and have no interests to clash with any other nation. I think it is ridiculous to be playing with theatricals like this … This Ministry of Foreign Affairs ought to be scrapped.' (Quoted in Dermot Keogh, *Ireland and Europe 1919–48*, Dublin 1988, p. 18)

This was a shortsighted view. Ireland may be small, but it exists in a large and complicated world. Its government needs to 'speak' to other countries. It needs to know what their governments think and to make them aware of Irish views. The best way to do this is to send Irish diplomats abroad and to receive foreign diplomats in Ireland.

THE START OF THE IRISH DIPLOMATIC SERVICE

The first Irish diplomats were the delegation Dáil Éireann sent to the Paris Peace Conference in 1919. Led by Seán T. O'Kelly, their mission failed but they stayed in Paris to try to influence French politicians and people in Ireland's favour. The Dáil government appointed other people to do the same in Rome and Berlin. De Valera's trip to the United States in 1919 had the same aim.

THE IMPORTANCE OF ANGLO-IRISH RELATIONS

Once the Irish Free State was set up, Cosgrave and his ministers had to decide what their **foreign policy** should be. The most important part of it would have to be **Anglo-Irish relations** (i.e. Ireland's relationship with Britain). There were four reasons for this:

- Britain is Ireland's nearest and most powerful neighbour.
- A very large proportion of Ireland's trade was with Britain, and many Irish people had emigrated there.
- It controlled Northern Ireland.
- The Treaty made Ireland a 'dominion of the Commonwealth' of which Britain was the head.

WAS THE FREE STATE SOVEREIGN?

An important aim of Cumann na nGaedheal's foreign policy was to find out how much independence the Treaty gave the Irish Free State. It was a '**dominion of the British Commonwealth**', but were the dominions sovereign (i.e. fully independent) states like France or Belgium or were they still under British control? That had been a key issue during the Treaty debates but the answer could not be found in Ireland alone. It would have to be tested through Ireland's relations with Britain and with other countries.

WHAT IS A SOVEREIGN STATE?

Sovereignty is a matter of international law. Under it, every sovereign state has certain characteristics:

1 It has clearly defined borders.
2 It has one government which makes and enforces the laws and collects the taxes within those borders.
3 No outside government is allowed to interfere in affairs within a sovereign state.
4 Other countries recognise the state's boundaries and government. They send diplomats to it and accept diplomatic representatives from it. They allow it to join international organisations.
5 When citizens travel abroad, they carry a passport from their government, which other countries accept.

THE RESTLESS DOMINION

As a Dominion, the Irish Free State had the first two characteristics of sovereignty, but what about the others? Collins had argued that the Treaty gave Ireland the freedom to achieve them and Cumann na nGaedheal used foreign and Anglo-Irish policy to prove him right. That meant that, unlike the other dominions, which were reasonably content as they were, the Free State was constantly trying to expand the amount of sovereignty that dominion status had conferred on it.

CHOOSING THE GOVERNOR-GENERAL

Opponents of the Treaty had argued that, because King George V was still head of state, the British government would be able to interfere in internal Irish affairs. To guard against this, Cosgrave insisted on controlling the appointment of the king's representative. Other dominions might accept a British-named aristocrat as their Governor-General, but for the Free State government, only an Irish man and a commoner would do.

The first Governor-General was **Timothy Healy**, a long-serving Home Rule MP. He held the office from 1922 to 1928 when he was replaced by **James MacNeill**, brother of Eoin MacNeill. In theory, the Governor-General had power to influence government decisions, but in practice neither of them tried to do so.

SENDING DIPLOMATS TO OTHER CAPITAL CITIES

The Cosgrave government also wanted other countries to recognise the separate existence of the Free State. Up to then, the British ambassador spoke for the dominions in Washington, Paris, Berlin, etc. but the Free Sate wanted its own diplomats in these capitals.

This was a bit embarrassing for other countries. They did not want to annoy the British by treating the Free State as a sovereign state while its status was still unclear. In the end they agreed to accept the Irish representatives as 'ministers', not ambassadors. Only after the second World War were Irish diplomats accepted as ambassadors. Foreign diplomats sent to Dublin were also called 'ministers'.

JOINING THE LEAGUE OF NATIONS AND REGISTERING THE TREATY

Cosgrave's government also joined the League of Nations in September 1923. Members of the League were supposed to register agreements between them at the League and in 1924 the Free State registered the Anglo-Irish Treaty. The British objected strongly. A 'treaty', they argued, is an agreement between two sovereign states and Ireland was not a sovereign state. Cosgrave's government rejected this interpretation and in the end the British had to back down.

Exterior of League of Nations in Geneva, Switzerland

IMPERIAL CONFERENCES

Even though Cosgrave and his ministers had supported the Treaty, they at first distrusted the British: perhaps they might go on interfering in Irish affairs. By joining the League and having direct contacts with foreign governments, the Irish leaders hoped to counter British power. But within two years they realised that their suspicions were unfounded. The British were relieved to be out of Ireland and had no wish to involve themselves again in Irish problems.

This became clear at the **1923 Imperial Conference**. These Conferences were held every few years to allow British and dominion leaders to discuss problems. Kevin O'Higgins led the Irish delegation to it. Because of the Civil War they did not have time to prepare properly, so they took little part in the discussions. But they were impressed that Britain treated the dominions as equals.

Britain, however, was not legally obliged to do so. O'Higgins wanted that changed. Before the next Conference in 1926 the Irish made contact with the South Africans and Canadians who wanted the same thing. In 1926 they got Britain to accept the **Balfour Declaration**, which stated that the Dominions were:

'autonomous [i.e. self-governing] communities within the British Empire, equal in status, in no way subordinate one to another in any aspect of their domestic or external affairs, though united by a common allegiance to the Crown and freely associated as members of the British Commonwealth of Nations.' (D.W. Harkness, *The Restless Dominion*, London 1969, p. 96)

THE STATUTE OF WESTMINSTER, 1931

The Irish pushed for the Declaration to be made legally binding. After the 1930 Conference the British agreed to have the parliament pass the **Statute of Westminster** in 1931:

- It gave up the British claim to make laws that bound the dominions without their consent.
- It declared that a dominion parliament could repeal laws previously passed for them by the British parliament.

THE ADVANTAGES OF COMMONWEALTH MEMBERSHIP

For the Free State, this was a very important expansion of sovereignty. The British no longer claimed the right to interfere in internal Irish affairs and the Free State could legally dismantle the Treaty if it wished. Winston Churchill pointed this out when the Statute of Westminster was being debated in parliament. The Prime Minister, Ramsay MacDonald, reassured him that he had every faith in Cosgrave and his government.

His faith was justified. By 1932, the Cosgrave government had no wish to leave the Commonwealth. In fact they saw advantages in being members. In a dangerous world, a small, country like Ireland needed friends, and Britain and the other dominions provided them.

AN UNDERVALUED ACHIEVEMENT

By 1932 it was clear that Collins had been right. The Treaty was indeed the first step to full sovereignty. Historians consider that proving this was one of the main achievements of Cosgrave's government. But it was a very abstract achievement. It did not provide jobs for voters or make up for Blythe's cut in old age pensions. And the outward signs of British power remained. In the 1932 election de Valera could claim that the fact that the oath to the king and the Governor-General were still there proved that the Free State was not fully sovereign.

But the reality was different, as de Valera admitted in private. Years later his son, Vivion, told how, soon after Fianna Fáil won the 1932 election, he:

> 'had been waxing eloquent on the iniquities of the "Free Staters" in the approved Fianna Fáil fashion … His father stopped him frowningly. "Yes, yes, yes," de Valera said testily, waving his forefinger, "we all said that, I know, I know. But when we got in and saw the files … They did a magnificent job, Viv. They did a magnificent job".' (T.P. Coogan, De Valera, *Long Fellow, Long Shadow*, London 1993, p. 426)

QUESTIONS

1 What is meant by 'foreign policy' and 'Anglo-Irish policy'? Explain why they are important for Ireland.

2 Explain what is meant by a 'sovereign state'. Which characteristics of sovereignty did 'dominion status' confer on the Irish Free State? Which did it not have?

3 List and explain three ways in which the Free State government tried to assert Irish sovereignty. Which do you think was the most important? Explain your choice.

4 Describe the role of Irish representatives in the Imperial Conferences of the 1920s. What was the most important result of these Conferences?

5 What did the Statute of Westminster say? Explain its importance for the Irish Free State.

6 Write a paragraph explaining how the attitude of the Cosgrave government changed towards Britain and the Commonwealth between 1922 and 1932.

7 De Valera's son reported him as saying: 'They did a magnificent job.' Do you agree or disagree with this statement? Explain your answer.

DISMANTLING THE TREATY: 1932–1939

DE VALERA AS FOREIGN MINISTER

During the 1932 election, Fianna Fáil promised that if it won it would dismantle the Treaty and introduce protection. That meant relations with Britain were going to be tense. Probably for that reason, de Valera kept the job of Minister for External Affairs for himself. He may have remembered the mistake of 1921 when he left the task of negotiating with Britain to others.

De Valera took foreign policy more seriously than Cosgrave. He did not discuss it with other Fianna Fáil ministers. It seems the only person he consulted was **Joseph Walshe**, the Secretary of the Department of External Affairs. Although Walshe had worked closely with Cumann na nGaedheal, de Valera kept him on and valued his advice.

DE VALERA AND THE LEAGUE OF NATIONS

In 1932, it was Ireland's turn to chair the General Assembly of the League of Nations. De Valera went to Geneva for the meeting and in a speech bluntly criticised the failings of the League and the limited role it gave to small states. Relayed by radio to Ireland, the speech impressed many naïve voters who thought his influence was much greater than it really was.

After that, de Valera often travelled to Geneva. He believed in the League as the protector of small nations and he backed it in the various crises of the 1930s:

- After Mussolini invaded Ethiopia, he supported sanctions on Italy even though that was unpopular at home.

- He also favoured non-intervention in the Spanish Civil War, even though the Catholic bishops pressed him to recognise Franco's regime.

- During the Munich Crisis in 1938, he supported the British policy of appeasing Hitler but after that he, like most others, lost hope that the League could prevent another war.

De Valera was active in the League because:

- It emphasised Irish sovereignty.
- He gained prestige at home by playing the role of world statesman in Geneva.
- Membership ensured that Ireland would not be friendless if Britain reacted badly when he dismantled the Treaty.

DE VALERA'S AIMS IN ANGLO-IRISH RELATIONS IN THE 1930s

But although de Valera valued the League, Anglo-Irish relations had to be at the centre of his foreign policy. His aim was to reshape the Free State's relationship with Britain so as to get the External Association he had wanted in 1921. Until he achieved that with the 1937 Constitution, a kind of cold war existed between the two countries, with neither talking much to the other.

REMOVING THE OATH

In 1932, some of de Valera's followers expected him to declare a republic at once but he disappointed them. Fearing that Britain might retaliate if he acted too swiftly, he took the Treaty apart bit by bit.

First to go was the hated oath to the king. On 22 March 1932 de Valera told the British government that the Irish people wanted to get rid of this 'relic of medievalism'. The bill to abolish it quickly passed through the Dáil but the Senate, which Cumann na nGaedheal still controlled, rejected it. As a result, the final abolition of the oath was delayed until May 1933.

DOWNGRADING THE GOVERNOR-GENERAL

As soon as they came to power, Fianna Fáil ministers launched a campaign of insults against the Governor-General, James MacNeill. After a few months, he resigned in protest. De Valera did not want to appoint anyone in his place but his legal advisers warned that he needed someone to sign bills passed by the Dáil.

He then gave the job to **Dónal Ó Buachalla**. A faithful Fianna Fáil man, Ó Buachalla cycled to work, did not occupy the Governor-General's official residence in the Phoenix Park and never performed any public duties.

ECONOMIC WAR

Meanwhile as part of its economic policy, Fianna Fáil refused to pay the land annuities (see page 104) and imposed duties on imports, almost all of which came from Britain. Although de Valera claimed these actions were not part of an attack on Britain, the British thought they were.

The British government had no representative in Dublin and knew little about Irish politics. The Dominions Secretary, **J.H. Thomas**, believed de Valera was a dangerous revolutionary who planned to take Ireland out of the Commonwealth, declare an independent republic and default on his debts. Because of the Statute of Westminster he could not do anything about the Treaty, but the land annuities were a debt and the British could insist on being paid.

To collect the money they imposed duties on Irish cattle and other agricultural exports. Secretly their aim was to make Fianna Fáil so unpopular that they would lose the next election. In fact, it had the opposite effect. De Valera was able to blame Britain for the country's economic woes and he won another election in 1933.

REMOVING MORE OF THE TREATY

With this proof of popular support, de Valera then:

- Stripped the Governor-General of the power to withhold consent from bills.
- Ended the right of an Irish citizen to appeal from Irish courts to the Privy Council, the highest court in the Commonwealth.

The British protested strongly. Reversing what they had claimed in 1924, they now insisted that the Treaty was an international agreement that could only be changed with the consent of both sides. But when they brought a case against de Valera to the Privy Council in 1935, it decided that he was within his rights under the Statute of Westminster.

ABOLISHING THE SENATE

In Ireland resistance to de Valera's policies was strongest in the Senate, where Cumann na nGaedheal still had a majority. Time and time again it voted against the changes introduced by Fianna Fáil. It could only delay them, but that was exasperating to a party in a hurry. In March 1934 de Valera retaliated with a bill to abolish the Senate itself. The Senate delayed that too, but it finally passed and in May 1936 the Free State Senate ceased to exist.

EXTERNAL ASSOCIATION AT LAST

By 1936 the objectionable parts of the Treaty were almost gone. De Valera was starting to write a new constitution when a dramatic development in London allowed him to achieve External Association at last.

Edward VIII, who became king some months earlier, wanted to marry an American divorcée. His ministers disapproved and he was forced to abdicate on 11 December 1936. His brother replaced him, as King George VI. Edward was also King of Ireland so the Dáil too had to approve of his abdication and accept his successor. That gave de Valera his opening.

On the day of the abdication he got the Dáil to pass two Acts:

- The first was the **Constitution (Amendment) Act**. It removed all reference to the king and the Governor-General from the Free State Constitution.
- The second was the **External Relations Act**. It stated that as long as Ireland was associated with the nations of the Commonwealth and

  'so long as the King, recognised by those nations as the symbol of their co-operation, continues to act on behalf of each of these nations ... for the purpose of the appointment of diplomatic and consular representatives and the conclusion of international agreements, the King ... is hereby authorised to act on behalf of Saorstát Éireann for the like purposes, as and when advised by the Executive Council to do so.' (Longford and O'Neill: *Eamon de Valera*, London 1971, pp. 293–4)

King Edward VIII with Wallis Simpson, the American divorcée. He gave up his throne to marry her, thereby giving de Valera the chance to remove the King from the Irish Constitution

Courtesy: Corbis picture library

With these two acts de Valera achieved the external relationship with the Commonwealth he wanted in 1921. From then until the External Relations Act was repealed in 1949, the only power the King still had was to sign the letters which Irish diplomats presented to foreign governments.

BUNREACHT NA HÉIREANN CREATES 'A REPUBLIC IN ALL BUT NAME'

These actions had changed the Free State Constitution considerably and de Valera decided in 1936 that the country needed a new one. In 1937 he produced **Bunreacht na hÉireann** (see page 114). With an elected President as head of state, this made the country a republic, though that word was not used anywhere in the document.

De Valera did not consult the British about the External Relations Act or the new Constitution. They were unsure what these moves meant. Was Ireland still in the Commonwealth or not? After some debate they decided to ignore them, simply stating that the new Constitution did not produce *'a fundamental alteration in the position of the Irish Free State as a member of the British Commonwealth of Nations'*. (N Mansergh 'Ireland: External Relations 1926–1939' in F. MacManus (ed) *The Year of the Great Test*, Dublin 1968, p. 135)

NEVILLE CHAMBERLAIN

This mild response was mainly due to **Malcolm MacDonald**, who became Dominions Secretary in 1935. He wanted to reach an understanding with de Valera, and met him secretly a number of times.

De Valera with Malcolm MacDonald

In 1937 MacDonald won the backing of the new Prime Minister, Neville Chamberlain. He was preoccupied with developments in Europe, where Hitler was looking more and more dangerous. He appeased Hitler in the hope of avoiding a war in Europe and he hoped that appeasing de Valera would keep him on Britain's side if war did come.

TOWARDS RECONCILIATION WITH BRITAIN

The economic war with Britain had eased in 1935 when the two countries signed the Coal-Cattle Pact. Secret talks also took place on other issues but only in 1938, with his new Constitution safely in place, was de Valera ready to negotiate publicly. By then war threatened in Europe and he wanted a settlement with Britain before it began.

Talks opened in London on 17 January 1938. Because there were also economic problems to sort out, de Valera was accompanied by his economic ministers Seán Lemass, Seán MacEntee and James Ryan:

- De Valera had four aims: an agreement on land annuities, to restore trade between the two countries, to end the British occupation of the Treaty ports and to end partition.
- The British wanted to settle the land annuities, restore trade and reach an agreement with the Irish about defence in case there was war with Germany.

THE 1938 ANGLO-IRISH AGREEMENTS

The talks lasted until 25 April when three Anglo-Irish Agreements were signed:

- The land annuities issue was easily dealt with. The British had claimed £100 million but settled for a single payment of £10 million from the Irish.
- The economic war was ended with a three-year trade agreement (see page 138).
- The British handed the Treaty ports to the Irish government without conditions. This was a

Neville Chamberlain (1869–1940): Son of Joseph Chamberlain, who had opposed Home Rule after 1886. A leading Conservative, his time as Chancellor of the Exchequer convinced him that Britain was unprepared for war, and he tried to avoid it by appeasing Hitler.

surprise, but Chamberlain was acting on the advice of his armed forces. Since 1921 the British had done nothing to maintain the ports. To make them usable again would have been costly and Britain would then have to guard them against a possible IRA attack. The British military chiefs thought it better to let the Irish government carry the burden. In return de Valera promised that no foreign power would be allowed to use Ireland for an attack on Britain.

Chamberlain hoped that his generous gesture would encourage de Valera to make a defence treaty, allowing Britain to use the ports if war broke out. But de Valera responded to this proposal by asking for a declaration against partition. The British refused to give that. They pointed out that the unionists ruled Northern Ireland and that he should talk to them about ending partition. Thus the talks ended without dealing with partition and de Valera considered them a failure.

ASSESSING DE VALERA'S ANGLO-IRISH POLICIES

By 1939 de Valera had succeeded in his aim of dismantling the Treaty, though he still kept a link with the Commonwealth through the External Relations Act. Apart from that Ireland was a completely sovereign state.

The Anglo-Irish Agreements showed that the British government had at last accepted the reality of Irish independence, something they could not face up to in 1921. In international law, the relationship between Britain and Ireland was the same as between any two independent states. This was confirmed when they accepted Irish neutrality after the second World War began.

But in reality, the ties of geography, history, trade and people meant that no Irish government could regard Britain as just another country. Britain is too powerful and too close to be ignored and therefore Anglo-Irish relations must always be at the centre of Irish foreign policies. This reality became uncomfortably clear once war broke out in 1939.

QUESTIONS

1 Who controlled Irish foreign policy while Fianna Fáil was in power? Why did he choose to do so?

2 Outline the part played by de Valera in the League of Nations. What did he gain from this?

3 List and explain the first steps which de Valera took to dismantle the Treaty.

4 Write a short paragraph on the External Relations Act. Why was it important?

5 Describe how the British responded to de Valera's policies between 1932 and 1938. Can you suggest any reasons why they did not do more?

6 Outline the main terms of the 1938 Anglo-Irish Agreements. De Valera was unhappy with the outcome. Why? Do you think his view was justified?

7 Compare de Valera's Anglo-Irish policies with those of Cumann na nGaedheal. Which do you consider the more successful? Explain your answer.

Higher Level

1 Explain the limitations which the Treaty placed on full Irish sovereignty and discuss how far Cumann na nGaedheal had succeeded in removing those limitations by 1932.

2 Within the Commonwealth, Ireland has been described as the 'restless Dominion'.
How fair is that description of Irish attitudes to the Commonwealth between 1922 and 1938?

3 Compare the Anglo-Irish policies of Cumann na nGaedheal and Fianna Fáil from 1922 to 1938.

4 How successful was de Valera's handling of Anglo–Irish relations between 1932 and 1939?

Ordinary Level

A Read this passage and answer the questions that follow.
'The effect of that Agreement is to hand over to the Irish state complete control of its defences… The ports are handed over unconditionally… These Agreements … remove from the field of dispute between Great Britain and ourselves all major items except one…' (De Valera speaking in the Dáil in 1938)

1 Name the Agreements de Valera was talking about.

2 How many ports were handed over?

3 Why did the British and Irish governments make these Agreements at that time?

4 What, in de Valera's view, was the one major item of dispute remaining between Ireland and Britain?

B Write a paragraph on one of the following:
1 The Statute of Westminster.

2 De Valera and the League of Nations.

C Answer **one** of the following questions:
1 What steps did Cumann na nGaedheal take up to 1932 to extend Irish independence?

2 How did de Valera handle Anglo-Irish relations between 1932 and 1938?

8 Economic and Social Policy 1922–1939

8.1

THE ECONOMIC AND SOCIAL POLICIES OF CUMANN NA nGAEDHEAL: 1922–1932

HOPING FOR PROSPERITY

Since the Union with Britain in 1800 only the north-east of Ireland had prospered. The rest of the country had suffered economic decline. Jobs in industry disappeared, millions emigrated and the population fell. Even people who stayed in Ireland had a relatively low standard of living. In 1914 Irish workers earned only about 75 per cent of what British workers earned.

Nationalists blamed the Union with Britain for Ireland's poor economic performance. They believed that an Irish government, which had only Irish interests at heart, was bound to do a better job developing the economy. But when independence finally came in 1922, partition and the depressed state of the world economy in the 1920s and 1930s made it almost impossible that these expectations could be fulfilled.

THE MEN WHO MADE ECONOMIC POLICY

Cosgrave appointed **Ernest Blythe** as Minister for Finance in 1923. It was his task to manage the economy. But neither he nor any of his Cumann na nGaedheal colleagues had any experience. As a result they relied heavily on the advice of two civil servants, **Joseph Brennan** and **J.J. McElligott**.

Joseph Brennan (1887–1963) was a Cork man who had worked for the British Treasury (Department of Finance) in Dublin Castle. During the Treaty negotiations, he secretly advised Collins about financial issues. In 1922 Collins made him Secretary (head) of the new Department of Finance. Brennan remained as Secretary until 1927, when he resigned, possibly because of quarrels with Blythe. He then became Chairman of the Currency Commission up to 1943 and then Governor of the Central Bank until he retired in 1953. In all these positions he was able to influence government economic policy.

J.J. McElligott (1893–1974) was a Kerry man who had also worked for the British civil service until sacked for taking part in the 1916 rising. After that he worked as a financial journalist. Collins had sought his advice on economic issues and he was the obvious man to become Assistant Secretary in the Department of Finance in 1923. When Brennan left in 1927, he became Secretary and held the post through various changes of government until he retired in 1953.

Ernest Blythe (1889–1975): A Presbyterian from Co. Antrim, Blythe joined the Gaelic League and later the IRB. In the Dáil government he was minister for Trade and Commerce. Cosgrave appointed him Minister for Finance, a post he held up to 1932.

THE POWER OF THE DEPARTMENT OF FINANCE

In Britain, the Treasury controlled how all other departments spent the taxpayers' money. With Blythe's support, Brennan and McElligott applied this policy in the Irish Free State. That made the Department of Finance and the men who ran it, the most powerful figures in the Irish government.

THE ECONOMIC REALITIES BEHIND AN ECONOMIC POLICY

Before they could decide on an economic policy these men had to take certain harsh economic realities into account:

- Partition meant that Ireland's only industrial area was now in Northern Ireland. As a result, the Free State depended heavily on agriculture at a time when the prices for agricultural produce were low.
- This left the Free State government poor. In a population of 3 million, only 6,000 people were rich enough to pay income tax. Most of its money came fom indirect taxes, such as those on alcohol and cigarettes but with a small

population, these did not bring in large amounts either. In the 1920s it only had about £20 million to spend each year.

- The government also had high costs. Years of emigration and unemployment had left a large group of dependants – children, old age pensioners and the unemployed – whom the government had to look after. It also had to spend a lot on repairing the damage caused during the War of Independence and the Civil War.

POLITICAL INDEPENDENCE, NOT ECONOMIC INDEPENDENCE

Another problem the Free State government faced was that political independence did not bring economic independence. For 120 years the economies of Ireland and Britain had been united. Goods moved freely between the two islands and they shared taxes, a currency and a banking system.

Independence did not change that. In the 1920s:

- Over 90 per cent of the Free State's trade was with Britain or Northern Ireland.
- The Free State used the British currency – the pound sterling – and its international value (the exchange rate) was set in London, not Dublin.
- Irish banks had their headquarters in London and kept their foreign currency reserves there.

All this meant that economic decisions made in London, where Ireland now had no voice, could still seriously affect the Irish economy and there was little a Dublin government could do about it.

THE IMPORTANCE OF EXPORTS AND IMPORTS

Overseas trade had to be at the centre of any economic policy. A country is like a person: it must earn the money it spends. Its income comes from the goods it sells abroad (**exports**). It spends that income to buy things it needs but does not produce at home (**imports**). It is important for a country to keep a balance between imports and exports. If it spends more on imports than it earns in exports it is in trouble.

A BRIDGE PROBLEM.

Jarvey : " Stiffish work driving up hills, Sir, but the down hills has their compensations."

Courtesy: Trinity College Library

This cartoon comments on one of the results of civil war. How did this sort of thing affect the Free State's economic policy?

- In the 1920s, 86 per cent of the Free State's exports were agricultural produce – beef, butter, pork, poultry, barley – and a small number of processed items – beer (especially Guinness), whiskey and Jacob's biscuits. They were based on agricultural produce. The most important non-agricultural exports came from a factory that Henry Ford set up in Cork in 1917. Over 90 per cent of all exports went to Britain.

- With the income earned from these items the country paid for fuel (coal, oil), food (wheat, tea, sugar, fruit, etc), raw materials (cotton, steel, etc) and anything else it did not make at home. Over 90 per cent of imports also came from Britain or were carried on British ships.

ADVISING ON AN ECONOMIC POLICY

As the figures above show, the British market was vital to the Irish economy. Brennan and McElligott advised the Cosgrave government to concentrate on that:

- The Free State exported a great deal of food to Britain, but in 1924 Irish farmers were selling less than in 1914. Brennan and McElligott urged the government to concentrate on improving agriculture so as to win back the British markets and increase earnings from exports.

- They felt that the large successful export industries like Ford, Guinness and Jacob's could look after themselves and advised the government to leave them alone.

- They wanted the free trade between Britain and Ireland, which existed up to independence,

to continue because they did not think any other country would buy what Ireland produced.

- They wanted taxes kept as low as possible, so as not to put up the costs for farmers or industrialists who were selling to Britain.

- They wanted to keep the Irish pound linked to the pound sterling. In 1927 separate Irish notes and coins were produced, but they had the same value and names as those of the British currency. Sterling was a world currency, so this seemed like a good idea. But at that time sterling was overvalued and that made life difficult for exporters.

THE PROBLEMS WITH FARMING

Agriculture was central to the economic policy. In a total labour force of 1.3 million, 670,000 people worked in agriculture, and agricultural produce made up 86 per cent of the country's exports. Cosgrave appointed **Patrick Hogan** as Minister for Agriculture with the task of developing the farming industry and improving exports.

In 1922 Irish farming had many weaknesses:

- The majority of farms were small (see Table A on page 131). This meant that many farmers were poor because it was hard to make a decent living on less than thirty acres. Small farms were also not very productive because a farmer with less than fifty acres did not have the money to invest in new technology (tractors, etc) or more expensive methods of farming.

Patrick Hogan (1891–1936): Was Minister for Agriculture from 1922–1932. He opposed protection and tried to raise farming standards so as to improve exports.

- In the 1920s, over a quarter of farmers were over sixty years old. Fathers were often reluctant to hand over to their sons, many of whom were in their forties before they got the farm. Elderly men were less likely to make the changes needed to improve the quality and productivity of farming.

PROBLEMS WITH THE BRITISH MARKET

Farmers also had problems with the British market. During the first World War, when the British were desperate for food, Irish farmers had sold them substandard produce. After it, exports fell as British consumers turned with relief to other sources of supply.

They had plenty of choice. To keep the food prices down, the British government encouraged farmers from around the world to sell their produce to Britain. Thus, food from Ireland had to compete with food from many other countries. Some governments even gave subsidies to their farmers to encourage them to export to Britain, a practice known as 'dumping'. As a result, prices for agricultural produce in Britain fell after the war and stayed low.

AGRICULTURAL POLICIES

Hogan was determined to improve the quality and quantity of Irish agricultural produce and to win back the British market:

- His Department set standards for production and presentation in eggs, meat and butter.
- Advisers were appointed to visit farmers and show them how to improve quality and productivity. There were also attempts to improve animals through selective breeding.
- Farmers distrusted banks and were reluctant to borrow money to make improvements. In 1927 Hogan set up the **Agricultural Credit Corporation** to offer them cheap loans. Few farmers took advantage of it and loans were small, averaging £100.
- To make all farms big enough to allow a family to make a decent living and to improve productivity, the **Land Commission** bought land and divided it among small farmers.
- Before 1914 most Irish farmers had bought their farms but in 1922 about 20,000 were still renting their land from landlords. In 1923 Hogan got the Dáil to pass a **Land Act** which forced the remaining landlords to sell their land to the tenants.

TAXATION AND THE FARMERS

To keep farmers' costs down so that they would be competitive in Britain, Ernest Blythe cut income tax by 40 per cent. This was good for the few big farmers who earned enough to pay income tax, but it did nothing for the vast majority of poor farmers (see Table A). Blythe's other cost-cutting decision, to reduce old age pensions, affected far more farmers but not in a way which made them vote for Cumann na nGaedheal.

Table A

Size of farms in the Irish Free state in 1931						
Total number of farms	1 to 14 acres	15 to 29 acres	30 to 49 acres	50 to 99 acres	100 to 199 acres	Over 200 acres
335,000	104,000	90,000	62,000	50,000	21,000	8,000

CUMANN NA nGAEDHEAL'S INDUSTRIAL POLICY

Industry was also important in the Irish Free State because it provided over 60 per cent of export earnings. There were two kinds of industries:

- Big, efficient and successful companies like Guinness or Jacob's in Dublin or Ford's in Cork, who exported most of their produce to Britain and its empire.
- Small factories making footwear, furniture, textiles, clothing, etc, which they sold on the home market. Many of them were inefficient. They were unable to compete with cheap imports coming into Ireland from bigger, more efficient British factories and they feared for their survival.

PROTECTION OR FREE TRADE?

In 1923, the smaller companies asked the Free State government to protect them from foreign competition by putting tariffs (taxes) on imports. Griffith had always said an Irish government should do this but the big companies opposed it. They feared that Britain might retaliate by putting tariffs on goods from Ireland and that that would damage them. They urged Cosgrave's government to keep free trade with Britain.

Brennan and McElligott supported the bigger companies. So did the government but they had to be careful. The small firms had more workers and so more votes than the big ones. To avoid giving an immediate decision, Blythe set up the **Fiscal Inquiry Committee** to look into the question. It recommended that the government keep free trade.

In spite of that Blythe did put tariffs on boots, shoes, confectionery, soap, bottles, clothing and furniture in 1924 and 1925. The small companies wanted more and in 1926 the government set up the **Tariff Commission** to investigate each request for protection on its merits. By 1930 it had only reported on a small range of industries.

THE SHANNON SCHEME AND THE ESB

A big problem for Irish industry was the lack of cheap power. Coal was used to run factories and make gas and electricity but it had to be imported.

The Shannon scheme

By 1922 there were small electricity schemes in many towns, but they were inadequate for industrial purposes.

Water power seemed the obvious answer. In 1923 the German firm, Siemens, offered to develop and distribute electric power from the Shannon. It involved an investment of £5 million. The government agreed, despite the opposition of Brennan and McElligott. The project, the Shannon Scheme, a great feat of engineering, was completed by 1929.

To distribute electricity the government set up the Electricity Supply Board (**ESB**). It took over the small electricity plants and established one of the first national grids in Europe to carry electricity around the country. By 1939 every town in Ireland had an electricity supply. The ESB was owned by the state (i.e. the taxpayers) and became the model for later 'semi-state companies'.

SOCIAL POLICY

Before 1914 the British government had introduced unemployment pay and old age pensions. Because of Ireland's high unemployment and emigration, more people claimed these benefits here than in Britain. To make up for this Britain, as the richer partner in the United Kingdom, subsidised the payments in Ireland. With independence, these subsidies ended. Now the Irish government had to pay for them out of its own limited resources. In 1922-23 old age pensions alone cost £3.3 million a year out of a total expenditure of £20 million.

Blythe's and McElligott's desire to keep taxes low meant they also had to reduce the amount spent on social welfare:

- In his first budget Blythe cut the old age pension from 10 shillings to 9 shillings a week.
- The means test that decided which poor people were entitled to a pension or to unemployment pay was also made much tougher.
- Throughout the 1920s the Cosgrave government spent little to improve health services or to replace the dreadful slums which existed in many towns.
- In 1930–31, when the great Depression hit the Free State, Blythe also cut wages to civil servants, teachers and Gardaí.

This low-tax, low-spending policy was popular with businessmen and bigger farmers but it did little for the poorest people in society. It made Cumann na nGaedheal unpopular and helps to explain their loss of power in 1932.

CUMANN NA nGAEDHEAL'S SUCCESS TO 1929

By 1929 Cumann na nGaedheal could point to some success with their economic policies:

- Exports to Britain, especially agricultural produce, had recovered to the levels they had been at before the war.
- Between 1926 and 1930 industrial employment rose by 5,000.
- Government spending had been cut and the budget was balanced (i.e. spending was equal to the government's income from taxes).

These successes showed to a sceptical world that the Irish could manage their economy prudently, but they were also due to improvements in the world economy in the late 1920s.

In October 1929 the Wall Street stock exchange crashed. That started a world economic crisis. All democratic governments were in difficulties as they

This is a Fianna Fáil election poster.

1 Who is the two-headed man?
2 Explain what he is saying to the people on the left and to the people on the right.
3 Is this a fair view of Cumann na nGaedheal's economic policy? Explain your answer by referring to decisions they made.

struggled to cope with this unprecedented economic collapse. One common response was to move from free trade to protection. Even the British government, which had supported free trade for almost a century, began to impose tariffs on imports.

The Free State did not escape the depression:

- In 1930–31 its exports to Britain declined by 10 per cent and prices paid for agricultural produce fell even faster.
- Unemployment rose but emigration ceased because there were no jobs in Britain or America.
- The demand for protection grew stronger. By 1930 even the farmers wanted tariffs to protect them from cheap imports dumped by countries in eastern Europe. In response in 1931, Blythe imposed tariffs on bacon, butter and oats as well as on a range of industrial products.

FIANNA FÁIL'S ECONOMIC CHALLENGE

The Depression also allowed Fianna Fáil to attack Cumann na nGaedheal's economic performance and to offer voters an alternative economic policy. Seán Lemass, who was mainly responsible for it, drew on Griffith's protectionist ideas:

- If elected, Fianna Fáil promised to protect jobs by imposing tariffs on imports.
- They promised they would keep the land annuities (annual payments) owed to Britain to pay for land bought from the landlords before 1914. The money would be used to develop new, Irish-owned industries and create jobs.
- Fianna Fáil TDs also attacked the cuts in old age pensions and wages for civil servants. It promised to spend more than Cumann na nGaedheal on social welfare and housing.

This economic programme was attractive to voters worried about their income and their jobs. Fianna Fáil won the election and set about implementing its economic policies.

QUESTIONS

1 Name and write briefly about the two civil servants who influenced Irish economic policy in the 1920s.

2 List and explain four economic problems that the Free State government faced in 1922.

3 Why did Cumann na nGaedheal concentrate on developing agriculture? Who was the agriculture minister? Write about five of his main policies.

4 Explain the difference between free trade and protection. In 1923 (a) which groups wanted protection and (b) which wanted free trade? What reasons did they have? What did the government decide?

5 Describe the Shannon Scheme and explain why Cumann na nGaedheal accepted it.

6 What did Ernest Blythe do about income tax? What effect did that have on Cumann na nGaedheal social policy?

7 Assess Cumann na nGaedheal's economic policies and explain how they were affected by the great depression.

THE ECONOMIC AND SOCIAL POLICIES OF FIANNA FÁIL: 1932–1939

THE MEN IN CHARGE

The change of government in 1932 brought in new economic policies. De Valera was the dominant personality in Fianna Fáil, but his main interest was foreign policy and Anglo-Irish relations. While keeping a general eye on things, he left the details of economic policy to his economic ministers.

Seán MacEntee was **Minister for Finance** from 1932 to 1939. In his budgets he imposed tariffs on imports and increased taxes. J.J. McElligott remained in his civil service post as Secretary of the Department of Finance. He disapproved of the Fianna Fáil policy. At first MacEntee ignored his views but as time passed, McElligott won him over. By 1938 MacEntee was prepared to follow the more conservative policies that McElligott favoured.

Seán Lemass had drawn up the Fianna Fáil economic policy. De Valera made him **Minister for**

Seán Lemass (1899–1971): A Dublin man who at sixteen was in the GPO during Easter Week. He fought with the IRA and rejected the Treaty. When imprisoned by the Free State he studied economics and after Fianna Fáil was founded, helped draw up its economic policies.

Industry and Commerce, a post he held until 1948. He was in charge of developing Irish industry behind the protective tariffs. An extremely dynamic administrator, he took on the job with great energy.

James Ryan was Minister for Agriculture from 1932 to 1947. Agriculture was less important for Fianna Fáil than it had been for Cumann na nGaedheal. Farm exports and farmers' incomes were badly hit by the economic war with Britain.

Ryan tried to encourage **self-sufficiency** by getting farmers to grow wheat and sugar beet to replace imported flour and sugar. These policies were not a success and by the end of the 1930s Fianna Fáil leaders had realised that Ireland had to export agricultural produce to Britain if it was to earn the money needed to pay for imports.

WHAT INFLUENCED FIANNA FÁIL'S ECONOMIC POLICY?

Three things influenced Fianna Fáil's economic policy:

- The world depression: it made most countries adopt protection. Even Cumann na nGaedheal had begun to protect Irish industries and jobs before 1932. Fianna Fáil planned to increase protection substantially.
- Nationalism: Fianna Fáil's leaders were nationalists who wanted to make the Irish economy less dependent on Britain. During the election campaign they spoke of making the country 'self-sufficient', that is producing most of what it needed at home and importing as little as possible from Britain.
- The quarrel with Britain: Fianna Fáil also planned to dismantle the Treaty and refuse to pay the land annuities. That provoked a quarrel with Britain and led to the so-called 'economic war'.

THE 'ECONOMIC WAR'

As soon as they took over Fianna Fáil began to carry out their political and economic promises:

- De Valera announced that he was removing the oath to the King and would not pay the land annuities.

- In his first budget, Seán MacEntee imposed tariffs on many imports, almost all of which came from Britain.

These actions enraged the British. They were especially upset by the removal of the oath, but they could do nothing about it because of the Statute of Westminster. However, they could attack the Irish economy and they hoped this might make Fianna Fáil so unpopular that it would lose power. They put a tax, equal to the land annuities on Irish cattle going into Britain. Fianna Fáil responded by putting more tariffs on imports from Britain. This is known as the 'economic war'.

THE IMPACT OF THE DEPRESSION AND THE ECONOMIC WAR

The depression was bad in Britain. Unemployment rose sharply and cut the demand for agricultural produce, even before Fianna Fáil took over. The value of agricultural exports fell from £47 million in 1929 to £36 million in 1931. The economic war made things worse. By 1934 agricultural exports were down to £18 million. This had a devastating impact on farmers, especially the more prosperous cattle farmers who had supported Cumann na nGaedheal.

FIANNA FÁIL AGRICULTURAL POLICY

To deal with the crisis:
- Ryan gave subsidies to cattle farmers and bought animals from them. The meat was given cheaply to poor people.
- He also encouraged farmers to switch from raising cattle (arable farming) to growing crops (tillage farming). This was to encourage self-sufficiency and increase the number of jobs in agriculture.
- He guaranteed the prices farmers got for wheat and sugar beet and compelled bakers and animal feed producers to use Irish-grown grain. The sugar beet industry was expanded and new sugar factories were set up. Imports of wheat, sugar, bacon and butter were also restricted.

The impact of these policies was limited:
- The area growing wheat increased from 24,000 acres in 1932 to 254,000 in 1936. The area growing sugar beet also increased. But not many arable farmers switched to tillage. Much of the change was due to farmers, who previously grew barley and other crops, switching to wheat and sugar beet to get the subsidies. In 1936, only 10 per cent more land was tilled than in 1931. That fell to two per cent by 1939.
- Not many new jobs were created because farmers used labour-saving machinery, like tractors and reapers, rather than farm labourers.
- The farmers who gained most from the subsidies were the bigger farmers of Leinster and east Munster.
- The damage to small farmers was eased by Fianna Fáil's decision to cut annuity payments and give them unemployment assistance.

PAYING FOR FIANNA FÁIL'S AGRICULTURAL POLICY

Fianna Fáil's agricultural policy was not good for taxpayers and consumers. Taxes rose to pay the grants and subsidies, while the tariffs on foreign flour, bacon, sugar and butter made these items more expensive for people to buy. This pushed up the cost of living for urban consumers particularly, many of whom were poorly-paid workers.

FIANNA FÁIL'S PROTECTIONIST INDUSTRIAL POLICY

Fianna Fáil wanted to protect Irish industries with tariffs and to develop new ones. That meant the government would interfere more with business

Lemass opened so many new factories that Dublin Opinion joked that he needed a factory to make keys for opening new factories

than before. McElligott objected but the policy had de Valera's backing, so his protests were ignored. The depression and the economic war made these policies popular. In his 1932 and 1933 budgets MacEntee imposed restrictions on the import of over one thousand items. Behind the barriers this created, Seán Lemass encouraged companies to set up factories making textiles, footwear, cutlery, ropes, cement, and a wide range of other items.

Between 1931 and 1938 industrial output rose from £55 million in 1931 to £90 million. They also created 11,000 new jobs, a good record during a world economic crisis. The new industries supplied the Irish market only. No one expected them to export the things they made.

IRISH OWNERSHIP

As nationalists, Fianna Fáil leaders wanted the new companies to be Irish-owned. To achieve that, Lemass introduced **Control of Manufactures Acts** in 1932 and 1934. They decreed that all new firms must be Irish-owned.

But Lemass was flexible in the way he applied this rule. To get around the tariff barriers, some foreign firms like Rank's flour milling or Cadbury's chocolate set up subsidiary companies in Ireland. So long as there were a few token Irishmen on the boards of these firms, Lemass turned a blind eye to the fact that the 'Irish companies' were actually controlled from the companies' headquarters in Britain.

LACK OF CAPITAL

Finding the capital to set up a new company was always a problem. Although there were rich people in Ireland, few of them were willing to risk their money to start a business. Irish banks, whose headquarters were in London, were also slow to invest in Irish ventures.

In 1933 Lemass set up the **Industrial Credit Company**. It made loans to industries but was unable to finance big projects. For them Lemass developed '**semi-state companies**' which were modelled on the ESB (see page 132). The government provided the capital and owned the

company. Semi-state companies included the Irish Sugar Company to develop the sugar beet industry, Aer Lingus to develop air transport, the Turf Development Board (later Bord na Móna) to develop the bogs and Irish Life to develop an Irish-controlled insurance sector.

MONOPOLIES

Another problem was the size of the Irish market. With only three million people, many of them poor, it was not worth a businessman's while setting up in Ireland if he had to compete with others selling the same goods. To remove this objection, Lemass gave many firms, including the semi-state companies, monopolies on the supply of particular items in Ireland.

This was bad for the consumer. Without competition, prices rose and quality was often poor but consumers had no alternative but to buy from the monopoly supplier.

FAILURE TO REFORM THE BANKS

Irish banks seemed an obvious target for change. They were mostly dominated by people of a unionist outlook and opposed any change in the Irish currency's link with sterling. Their reserves were kept in Britain and not invested in Ireland. Fianna Fáil promised a commission to look into this situation, but did not set it up until 1938. It advised against any change. A Central Bank was set up in 1942 but it had limited powers.

JOBS AND EMIGRATION

Fianna Fáil achieved some success in its aim of protecting existing jobs against the economic depression and creating new ones. Between 1931 and 1939 the number of people working in industry rose from 111,000 to 166,000. People in the new industries were better off but unemployment remained high. Wages were still low, falling from 60 per cent of the British average in 1931 to 49 per cent by 1939.

Fianna Fáil had promised to end emigration. For a brief period in the early 1930s, emigration almost ceased but that was mainly because there were no jobs in Britain or America either. Once the depression began to lift in the late 1930s emigration resumed as people went abroad to find work. Even some people with jobs left to get better pay in Britain. In 1937 26,000 people went and the numbers leaving continued to rise during the war.

FIANNA FÁIL'S SOCIAL POLICY

Fianna Fáil's social policy was more generous than Cumann na nGaedheal's:

- The 1933 **Unemployment Assistance Act** increased unemployment benefits and extended them to small farmers and farm labourers.
- The 1933 **National Health Insurance Act** improved the provision of health insurance.
- Old age and blind pensions were also improved and in 1935 pensions for widows and orphans were introduced.

They also wanted to improve housing and clear the slums. Under their 1932 **Housing Act**, the central government paid between a third and two-thirds of the cost of houses built by local councils. Between 1932 and 1940 they spent almost £10 million on housing. Councils built an average of 12,000 houses a year, compared with just 2,000 a year under Cumann na nGaedheal. This improved the living conditions of many families, especially those in the worst city slums, as well as creating jobs in the building industry.

EASING THE ECONOMIC WAR: THE COAL-CATTLE PACT

The economic war with Britain damaged the economies of both countries. Between 1932 and 1934 the trade deficit (i.e. the gap between imports and exports) doubled. Britain's businesses were suffering too. The Free State was their third biggest customer and in the depression they could not afford to lose their Irish markets. They urged their government to heal the breach.

In 1935 the two governments agreed on the **Coal-Cattle Pact**. It raised the quota of Irish cattle allowed into Britain by a third and the Free State took an additional 1,250,000 tons of British coal. The pact was renewed in 1937 and 1938, but a return to normal trade had to wait until de Valera had introduced his new Constitution in 1937 (see page 114).

THE 1938 ANGLO-IRISH AGREEMENTS

In 1938, as Hitler threatened war in Europe, both Ireland and Britain needed to sort out their local quarrels. De Valera, accompanied by Ryan and Lemass went to London for talks on 17 January. The result was the Anglo-Irish Agreements which were signed on 25 April (see page 125 for the political results).

The economic war ended with a three-year trade Agreement. The duties each country had imposed on the other's goods were lowered. Britain gave Irish agricultural produce privileged access to the British market and Ireland did the same to British coal and some other goods. An enquiry was to be set up to look into Irish import restrictions. This part of the Agreement was overtaken by the second World War which broke out in September 1939.

ASSESSING FIANNA FÁIL'S ECONOMIC POLICIES

Fianna Fáil's economic policies were suited to the depression years of the 1930s. During it every country was implementing protection. To survive, Ireland had to do the same.

The industrial policy was more successful than the agricultural policy. Lemass had not just protected jobs, he had created new ones. But the new industries were neither big enough nor efficient enough to survive if protection was removed.

On the other hand, Fianna Fáil's early agricultural policy, which had more to do with nationalism than economics, did not last long. The 1935 Coal-Cattle Pact was a recognition that the dream of self-sufficiency was an illusion. Like Cumann na nGaedheal in the 1920s, Fianna Fáil had grasped that that Ireland had to export to survive.

QUESTIONS

1 Name the three ministers with responsibility for economic policy in the Fianna Fáil government in the 1930s.

2 Explain the factors which influenced Fianna Fáil policy.

3 What caused the 'economic war' and what were its consequences?

4 Explain what Fianna Fáil meant by 'self sufficiency' and describe how that affected their agricultural policy.

5 Outline the aims of the Fianna Fáil industrial policy and explain how Seán Lemass sought to achieve them.

6 What were the terms of the Anglo-Irish Trade Agreement signed in 1938?

7 Compare Fianna Fáil's social policy with that of Cumann na nGaedheal.

8 Do you think Fianna Fáil's economic policy was a success or a failure? Give reasons for your opinion.

LEAVING CERTIFICATE QUESTIONS

Higher Level

1 What were the main economic problems which faced the government of the Irish Free State in 1922 and what was done to deal with them by 1932?

2 What factors influenced Fianna Fáil's economic policies in 1932 and how far had it achieved its objectives by 1939?

3 Compare the economic and social policies of Cumann na nGaedheal and Fianna Fáil between 1922 and 1939.

Election results 1923 to 1938							
	1923	1927 June	1927 Sept.	1932	1933	1937	1938
Cumman na nGaedheal/ Fine Gael	63	47	62	57	48	48	45
Sinn Féin/ Fianna Fáil	44	44	57	72	77	69	77
Labour	14	22	13	7	8	13	9
Farmers	15	11	6	4	8	15	11
Independents	17	16	14	16	9	8	9
Others	–	15	3	2	–	–	–

Study these election results and answer the following questions:

1 Which party won the most seats in the 1923 election? Which was the main opposition party in the Dáil? Explain your answer.

2 Explain Cumann na nGaedheal's results in June 1927. Which other party gained most in that election? Can you explain that?

3 Why were there two elections in 1927? Compare the results that Cumann na nGaedheal, Fianna Fáil and Labour got in September with their results in June and account for the differences.

4 Which party won most seats in 1932? Explain why and say what happened as a result.

5 Look at the number of seats Fianna Fáil won in 1933 compared with 1932. What happened to explain the differences?

6 How well did Fianna Fáil do in the 1937 and 1938 elections? What events account for the differences you see?

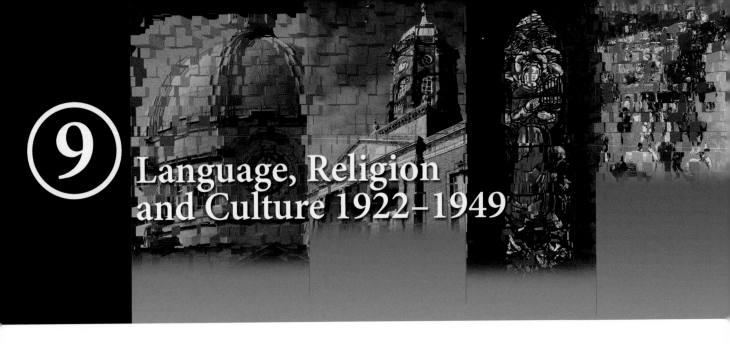

9 Language, Religion and Culture 1922–1949

9.1

BUILDING A GAELIC STATE

INTRODUCTION: WHAT KIND OF AN IRELAND SHOULD BE BUILT?

In December 1922 the British left the Irish Free State. For the first time Irish people were free to build the kind of Ireland they wanted. We have already looked at some of the decisions they took in politics, economics and foreign policy. But many idealistic nationalists thought these things were of secondary importance. Far more urgent was the need to develop the cultural and spiritual side of the Irish nation.

But what did that mean?

- Most leaders of Sinn Féin were strongly influenced by the Gaelic League. Like Patrick Pearse, they dreamed of building an Ireland not just free but Gaelic, where Irish would once more become the language of the people.
- Many of them were also devout Roman Catholics as were 93 per cent of the people in the Free State. Urged on by Catholic priests and bishops who had great influence with the voters, it was inevitable that they would also try to build a state that would reflect Catholic moral values.
- Not everyone shared these dreams of an Ireland that was Gaelic and Catholic. Their dream was a liberal Ireland, free, democratic and open to the ideas and influences of a wider world.

WHY THEY WANTED TO REVIVE IRISH

Both Cumann na nGaedheal and Fianna Fáil were committed to reviving the Irish language. For them it was a spiritual mission. They had a semi-mystical belief that speaking Irish would give Irish people an understanding of the wisdom and culture of their ancestors. Without Irish, they believed, the Irish nation would lose its soul and their claim to independence would be undermined.

CHANGING NAMES

They began this as soon as the British left in 1922. One of the first things they did was to change place names. Kingstown, which got that name when King George IV visited it in 1821, went back to its old name of Dún Laoghaire. Queenstown became

To celebrate its first ten years, the Cosgrave government published this 'Official Handbook'. What does the design of the cover tell us about the image of Ireland which the authors wanted to convey?

Courtesy: Allen Library

Cove again (though now it is spelled Cobh). Maryborough became Portlaoise. New Irish words were developed for modern inventions like *Oifig an Phoist* and *Telefón*. But these were just symbols.

USING THE SCHOOLS TO REVIVE IRISH

The real goal was to revive Irish as a spoken language. Nationalists believed that Irish declined in the 19th century because the schools taught English. Now they planned to revive Irish by making schoolchildren learn it.

In 1922, the Free State government ordered that Irish was to be taught for at least one hour each day in all primary schools. In 1924 the Minister for Education, **Eoin MacNeill** (one of the founders of the Gaelic League) ordered that Irish must be used to teach infants entering primary schools and used as widely as possible in higher classes.

Later Irish was made a compulsory subject in secondary schools and students had to pass in it to get the Intermediate and Leaving Certificate examinations. Extra grants were given to schools which taught all subjects through Irish and extra marks were awarded to students who answered their examinations through Irish.

SOLVING THE PROBLEMS

Several practical problems had to be solved before Irish could be taught in schools:

- One problem was the shortage of teachers. In 1923 only 3,000 out of 12,000 had any qualification in Irish. To solve it, Irish was introduced into the training colleges. Free Preparatory Colleges where Irish was the language of the school were set up. Grants were given to pupils from Gaeltacht areas to go to these schools and they got priority in admission to teacher training colleges.

- Textbooks were another problem. Few of them existed and there were problems about the way the language in them was written. In the 19th century, when other European languages developed standard forms of spelling and grammar, Irish did not. In the 1920s many common words could be spelled in different ways, which was very confusing for pupils. Work on standardising the language began in the 1930s and was completed in the 1950s.

> An example of spelling differences is in the names of *Cumann na nGaedheal* and *Fine Gael*. Think how confusing that would be for small children learning to write.

- Irish also lacked words needed to study science, geography or history. A start was made on dealing with this problem in the 1920s and it speeded up after Fianna Fáil came to power in 1932.

REVIVING IRISH IN OTHER WAYS

The governments also tried to revive Irish in other ways:

- They gave grants to Irish-speaking households in the surviving Gaeltacht areas.
- Schoolchildren got grants to spend holidays in the Gaeltacht.
- Radio Éireann broadcast several hours of Irish programmes each week.
- Those who wanted jobs in teaching, the civil service, the Gardaí, or the army had to pass a test in Irish.

The peak of the language revival came in de Valera's 1937 Constitution, *Bunreacht na hÉireann*, when he made Irish the 'first official language' of the Irish state.

ASSESSING THE REVIVAL POLICY

The revival policy had some successes. By the 1940s:

- The number of primary teachers qualified to teach through Irish had risen to over 70 per cent.
- 14 per cent of primary schools used only Irish in class.
- 64 per cent of secondary students studied other subjects through Irish.

But although more people could speak and understand Irish, most continued to use English in their everyday lives. Even in the Gaeltacht areas the number using Irish as their main language continued to shrink. In 1926, 238,000 out of a Gaeltacht population of 427,000 were Irish speakers; by 1946 there were only 193,000 Irish speakers out of 398,000.

WHY WAS IRISH NOT REVIVED?

The failure to revive Irish was partly due to a misunderstanding of the reasons it declined in the first place. Irish people did not adopt English because the schools made them. They adopted English because it was useful if they had to emigrate to English-speaking countries. After independence poverty still forced many to emigrate, so the preference for English remained.

Even for people who stayed in Ireland, Irish was of little use after school. Government departments, law courts and businesses all continued to use English. And from the 1920s new forms of entertainment – cheap books, films and radio – all in English, made that language more attractive than Irish, which had few of these to offer.

Making Irish compulsory in school could never outweigh these disadvantages. In fact it probably did more harm than good. Parents resented the time teachers spent teaching Irish rather than basic skills like writing and maths and they transferred their resentment to the Irish language itself. Much of the good will towards the language, which existed when the Irish Free State was set up, was lost as a result.

CRITICISM OF THE REVIVAL POLICY

By the 1940s many people realised that the revival policy was failing. In 1941 the Irish National Teachers' Organisation (INTO) published a report that showed that teaching so much Irish was hurting children's general education and damaging Irish itself. The government ignored

Politicians hoped to win votes by appealing to 'Ireland's glorious past'. How does the cartoonist mock this attitude?

Ingenious candidate goes the 'whole hog' in appealing to the sentiments of the people.

Courtesy: Trinity College Library

them but in the 1950s the insistence on the use of Irish eased.

A NEW REVIVAL

Some people who loved Irish realised that a new approach was needed:

- In 1943 they set up *An Club Leabhar* to publish interesting and original books in Irish.
- A number of new magazines also appeared, including *Comhar*.
- A number of poets like Seán Ó Ríordáin and novelists like Máirtín Ó Cadhain, began to produce serious literature in Irish that could stand comparison with anything in English. One of the most popular books was *An Béal Bocht* by the satirist, Brian O'Nolan (also known as Myles na gCopaleen). It was a savage attack on the stupidities of the revival movement.

These people took a more realistic approach to Irish than had been common in the 1920s and 1930s. Through them Irish and the Gaelic culture associated with it, took their place alongside other influences as part of the common inheritance of all the people of Ireland.

QUESTIONS

1   What organisation hoped to revive Irish? Name three leaders of the revolution who belonged to it.

2   What were the first things the Irish Free State did to emphasise the importance of the Irish language?

3   Explain why it was decided to revive Irish through the schools? List three problems which had to be solved first and in each case say what was done to solve it.

4   Describe some other ways in which the government tried to revive Irish.

5   Was the plan to revive Irish through the schools a success or a failure? Explain your conclusion.

IRISH AND CATHOLIC?

THE RELIGIOUS DIVIDE

Partition in 1920 left the Irish Free State overwhelmingly Catholic. Almost 93 per cent of the population belonged to the Roman Catholic Church. Other religions made up the remaining seven per cent, with the Church of Ireland the biggest among them.

PARTITION AND THE PROTESTANT COMMUNITY

In Ireland, religious divisions had long reflected political divisions. While almost all Catholics were nationalists, almost all Protestants were unionists. They had opposed self-government for Ireland ever since Home Rule was proposed in the 1880s.

Before partition, Protestants were a 25 per cent minority in the whole island of Ireland. Then in 1920 Northern Ireland was set up to protect the Protestants in six Ulster counties. The tiny number of Protestants in the remaining twenty-six counties were abandoned by Carson and Craig to make whatever deal they could with the triumphant nationalists.

At first they feared for their existence, especially after the Treaty when violence increased. In places, mainly along the border and in Cork, the anti-Treaty IRA mounted sectarian attacks on them. In May 1922 the Church of Ireland Synod sent a delegation to ask Collins *'if they were permitted to live in Ireland or if it was desired that they should leave the country?'* (T. Brown, *Ireland: A Social and Cultural History, 1922–79*, London 1981, p. 109)

Collins urged them to stay and promised that the Free State army would protect them. It did its best but republicans burnt 192 landlord houses during the Civil War and killed or expelled numbers of Protestants.

THE PROTESTANT COMMUNITY AFTER INDEPENDENCE

In an attempt to reassure the Protestant community, Cosgrave appointed twenty-four Protestants to the

Free State Senate, almost all of them unionists. Among them were the poet W.B. Yeats, Sir Horace Plunkett, the founder of the Co-operative movement and Lord Midleton who had been the leader of the southern unionists before 1920.

Proportional Representation in elections also let a small number of former unionists win seats in the Dáil as independent TDs. But Protestants were too few to have a political impact. They did, however, have economic power. In 1922 they still controlled much of the wealth of the country. The heads of most big businesses and banks were Protestants, as were a third of lawyers and a fifth of doctors.

PROTECTING PROTESTANTS

Cosgrave's government needed Protestant money and expertise and had no reason the discriminate against them. Legally it treated them with scrupulous fairness. Protestant property was not touched. Protestant schools and hospitals received the same grants as Catholic schools and hospitals. Cosgrave also attempted to ensure that they did not suffer discrimination over jobs.

The best example of this was a dispute over the appointment of a librarian in Co. Mayo in 1931. The independent body in charge of making local appointments gave the job to a Protestant woman. Local Catholic clergy and Mayo County Council objected on the grounds that she would not understand Catholic moral principles.

But Cosgrave stood firm. He even suspended the County Council when it refused to make the appointment. The woman became the librarian, though she was later moved to another position because of local hostility. To embarrass Cumann na nGaedheal, Fianna Fáil backed Mayo County Council but when they came to power, they followed a similar policy.

THE DECLINE IN THE PROTESTANT COMMUNITY

In spite of being fairly treated, the number of Protestants in the twenty-six counties fell steadily. A third left between the census of 1911 and the census of 1926. That was understandable in the years of violence and British withdrawal. But after peace was restored, the downward trend continued. Between 1926 and 1936 the Protestant community declined by 12 per cent and between 1936 and 1946 by a further 14 per cent.

A number of factors explain the decline:
- One was the insistence of the Catholic Church that the children of mixed marriages must be brought up as Catholics.
- Another was the poor performance of the economy, which encouraged many to emigrate.
- But in the 1920s and 1930s the Free State also became a less comfortable place for those Protestants who valued their connection with Britain.
  — The cherished symbols of their British identity vanished. Their flag, the Union Jack, was replaced by the Tricolour; their national anthem, *God Save the King*, was replaced by *The Soldier's Song*; the king's head vanished from stamps and coins.
  — The role of the king, to whom many Protestants felt a strong personal loyalty, was steadily undermined in the government of the Free State until it disappeared completely in de Valera's 1937 Constitution.
  — Their schoolgoing children were forced to learn Irish, a language to which many of them felt no connection.
  — The growing power of the Catholic Church and the introduction of laws supporting Catholic moral teaching (see below) added to their discomfort.

THE CATHOLIC CHURCH AND THE CIVIL WAR

Cosgrave, de Valera and most other nationalist leaders were devout Catholics. That did not mean they obeyed the Catholic Church in everything. On political issues, they felt entitled to make up their own minds.

This was clear during the civil war. The Catholic bishops condemned the anti-Treaty side and excommunicated its leaders. But de Valera and other republicans simply ignored the excommunication. When de Valera came to power in 1932 both he and the bishops pretended it had never happened.

THE INFLUENCE OF THE BISHOPS

This experience made the Catholic bishops reluctant to interfere in purely political matters. But they believed they had a duty to guard the moral standards of ordinary Catholics. To fulfil that duty, they felt entitled to interfere in areas like education, health, public order and sexual morality.

Many Catholic voters and most of their elected representatives shared the bishops' view. Both Cumann na nGaedheal and Fianna Fáil passed laws on these matters which were in line with the Catholic Church's teaching. Anyone who disagreed with these policies found it was easier and safer to keep quiet.

WORRY ABOUT DECLINING MORAL STANDARDS

The First World War was followed by huge social changes:

- New forms of entertainment like cheap magazines, public dance halls, films and radio appeared.
- New forms of transport like cars and motorbikes allowed people to move around more, so that parents lost some of their power to control what their children did.
- Women gained political and economic freedom. The outward signs of this change were short skirts and make-up, which had not been worn by 'respectable women' before the war.

Conservative groups in Europe and America worried that these changes were undermining moral values. They demanded, and in places wrote, laws imposing censorship on books and films and restrictions on individual freedoms.

THE CAMPAIGN TO IMPROVE MORALS

In Ireland too, these changes produced a moral panic. Conservative groups, like the clergy, saw them as an attack on their traditional values. Irish nationalists thought these developments threatened the qualities that made Ireland special and different.

Even before 1914, Gaelic Leaguers and devout Catholics had campaigned against English newspapers and books, which they blamed for lowering moral standards in Ireland. Once an Irish government was in place, the campaign against various 'moral evils' intensified. Bishops denounced dance halls, cinemas and modern music, especially jazz. Zealous IRA gunmen seized and burned English papers that they considered morally doubtful or culturally dangerous.

Political leaders from all parties sympathised with these campaigns. The new Ireland, they felt, must set a good example to a world where Christianity was in decline. They brought in laws to exclude dangerous influences and uphold Christian moral principles:

- In 1923, they set up a system of film censorship. Only films passed by the censor could be shown in cinemas.

Courtesy: Trinity College Library

TRAGEDIES OF CENSORSHIP.
The Film Censor's assistant takes the " Sex " out of " Sexton Blake."

This cartoon from the 1930s mocks the excesses of the Censorship Board

- In 1924, the hours during which public houses could remain open were reduced and in 1927 the number of public houses was cut by half.
- In 1929, the Censorship Act set up a **Censorship Board** to keep out books and magazines which were considered 'indecent or obscene' or which advocated contraception.
- In 1933, a tax was placed on imported newspapers and magazines.
- In 1935, dance halls were regulated. As a result, many closed down or were replaced by local parish halls which were under the supervision of the local parish priest.
- In 1935, the sale of contraceptives was outlawed.

CENSORSHIP IN OPERATION

Censorship had a huge impact. The Act did not spell out what 'indecent and obscene' meant and the Censorship Board was soon banning books for the flimsiest of reasons. Irish people could no longer buy books by internationally respected authors such as Thomas Mann and Ernest Hemingway. The Board also banned Irish writers who attempted to give a realistic account of Irish life. This made it almost impossible for them to make a living.

The rigidity of the Board was highlighted in 1942 when it banned a book called *The Tailor and Ansty*. This was a collection of stories and sayings by a country tailor and his wife, Ansty. They were exactly the kind of country people that Gaelic Ireland claimed to admire but in real life their language was too broad and racy for the censors. After it was banned, their book was burned in their home village and the old couple were humiliated.

This led to a heated debate in the Seanad. Most politicians still supported censorship but at least a debate had begun. It was helped along by *The Bell*, a literary magazine edited by Seán Ó Faoláin, one of the writers whose books had been banned. In 1946 an appeal system was established but only in the 1960s was censorship eased.

Irish censorship was not unique. Many countries, including Britain and the United States, censored books and films at that time. But few carried it to the extremes of narrowness that the Irish Censorship Board managed.

DIVORCE OUTLAWED

Marriage was another area in which the law imposed Catholic moral principles. Up to 1922 a wealthy person could get a divorce by having a special bill passed through the Westminster parliament. In 1922 the Free State government was asked if it planned to continue this practice. Cosgrave consulted the Catholic bishops who replied:

> 'it would be altogether unworthy of an Irish legislative body to sanction the concession of such divorce, no matter who the petitioners may be.' (Dermot Keogh, *The Vatican, the Bishops and Irish Politics, 1919–39*, Cambridge 1986, p. 128)

Cosgrave agreed and told the Senate that:

> 'the majority of people in this country regard the bond of marriage as a sacred bond which is incapable of being dissolved. I personally hold this view.' (R. Fanning *Independent Ireland*, Dublin 1982, p. 56)

In the Senate, W.B. Yeats complained that this decision infringed the Protestants' civil liberties. But at that time he had little support. Divorce had only been available to the rich, and the Protestant Churches were almost as opposed to it as Catholics.

In 1937, de Valera included a ban on divorce in his Constitution. He did so, he explained, because divorce damaged society and the family, not to uphold Catholic teaching. His decision aroused little opposition because the Protestant Churches shared this view.

A CATHOLIC STATE FOR A CATHOLIC PEOPLE?

In the 1930s, the Irish Free State had begun to take on the appearance of a Catholic state for a Catholic people. A vocal minority spoke of the Irish as a 'Catholic nation' and in 1931 at the Fianna Fáil Ard Fheis, de Valera said that he was 'a Catholic first'. A clear sign of the state's Catholicism was the Eucharistic Congress in 1932.

1 What proportion of the Irish Free State was Catholic and what proportion was Protestant in 1922? What were the likely consequences of these figures?

2 Outline the way in which the Protestant community was treated in the Irish Free State. How do you explain the decline in their numbers?

3 There was a 'moral panic' in many countries after the first World War. Explain what caused it. List the measures taken in the Irish Free State to deal with the 'evils' that caused it.

4 Write a paragraph about censorship, explaining what it means and how it operated in Ireland.

5 Explain how the issue of divorce was dealt with by both governments.

6 Having read this chapter, do you think that the Irish Free State had become 'a Catholic state for a Catholic people'? Explain your answer.

9.3

THE EUCHARISTIC CONGRESS OF JUNE 1932 (CASE STUDY)

WHAT IS A EUCHARISTIC CONGRESS?

A Eucharistic Congress was like a Catholic Olympic Games. Held every three years in a different city, the Congresses brought together thousands of Catholic clergy and pilgrims to study and celebrate the Eucharist, the central mystery of the Catholic faith. In 1929 Cosgrave's government established diplomatic relations with the Vatican. That helped them persuade Pope Pius XI to have the 1932 Eucharistic Congress in Dublin. It would bring huge numbers of visitors to Ireland and, they hoped, show the world how successful Irish independence had been.

Courtesy: RTÉ Stills Library

Street decorations in Dublin for the 1932 Eucharistic Congress

PLANNING FOR THE CONGRESS

Cosgrave and his ministers were determined that everything must run smoothly. They gave the task of organising the Congress to Eoin O'Duffy, the Garda Commissioner. For a year he made plans to house, feed and organise the hundreds of thousands of people expected to flood into the city.

At the same time in parishes around the country, priests and people also prepared. They held prayer meetings and discussions on the Eucharist and collected money for flags and bunting to decorate their areas.

An election was due late in 1932 but to avoid it clashing with the Congress, Cosgrave decided to call it in February. To his surprise, he lost and it was de Valera and Fianna Fáil who presided over the Congress and basked in its reflected glory.

LAST-MINUTE PREPARATIONS

The Congress was to begin on 20 June with the arrival of the Pope's special representative, the **Papal Legate**. In the week before, people in

Dublin worked feverishly to decorate the city. Flower baskets were hung from every lamppost; flags and bunting were strung from every home, shop and church. In the slum areas, where the city's poorest people lived, whole communities were involved in painting their houses, making small altars and hanging flags.

THE PILGRIMS ARRIVE

At the same time the pilgrims poured in to the country:

- Catholic groups came from Holland, France and other parts of Europe. Many stayed in the large tent encampments that were set up on the outskirts of the city. Others chartered liners that anchored in Dublin bay and acted as floating hotels.
- The highest proportion of pilgrims came from the United States. Most were Irish-Americans whose parents or grandparents had emigrated in the previous century. Now prosperous and successful, they had come to celebrate the independence of their ancestral country.
- Clergy, including over 200 bishops and eight cardinals, arrived from all over the world. Many were Irish or descended from Irish emigrants, but others came from more exotic locations. One bishop who aroused great interest was an American Indian.

THE CONGRESS BEGINS

On Monday 20 June, the sun shone brightly. From early morning, the streets were lined with people, waiting to see the Legate, Cardinal Lauri. As he came off the boat in Dún Laoghaire, he was greeted by de Valera and other dignitaries. Overhead, Air Corps planes flying in the form of a cross, saluted him. Then he drove into Dublin, loudly cheered by the waiting crowds.

CONGRESS WEEK

The Congress lasted for a week and the sun shone throughout. Each day there were different activities. There was a huge garden party in Blackrock College and a big reception in Dublin Castle. Visiting speakers gave lectures on the Eucharist and on various aspects of Catholic doctrine. Masses were said in city churches and in the Phoenix Park where men, women and children each had a special day.

The climax of the week came on Sunday with mass in the Phoenix Park. Every day the papers reported on the preparations for it. A huge crowd was expected and loudspeakers (then a novelty) were rigged up to ensure that everyone could hear. Even more of a novelty was the fact that it would be broadcast on radio. It was reported that the Pope hoped to listen in, if a connection with Rome could

The strange case of de Valera's hat:
In the 1920s Fianna Fáil had accused Cumann na nGaedheal leaders of aping the British by wearing top hats at state functions. When they came to power they wore soft hats, although at that time men normally wore a top hat on formal occasions. This proved embarrassing during the Congress. When de Valera and his ministers greeted the Legate, he almost walked past them, thinking they were detectives sent to guard him. In pictures of the Congress, Cosgrave has a top hat but de Valera is always bareheaded or has his hat in his hand.

Courtesy: National Library of Ireland

Courtesy: National Library of Ireland

Procession of the prelates on the High Altar in Dublin's Phoenix Park, during the 1932 Eucharistic Congress

be established and perhaps even broadcast to the assembled pilgrims. Around the country, priests urged the few people who owned radios to let their neighbours listen in.

THE 'MIGHTY INVASION'

On Saturday night and Sunday morning people flooded into Dublin from all parts of Ireland. Under the headline *The Mighty Invasion*, the *Irish Times* reported:

> *'The multitude, which invaded Dublin yesterday, reached the city by road, rail and sea. Every available passenger-carrying vehicle was brought into commission for the occasion … The number travelling by rail alone numbered 142,000 … Many thousands also travelled by omnibus … A very big proportion of country visitors also came by car. Not many in Dublin had seen such a varied collection of these conveyances at one time. They were of all makes and all ages.' (Irish Times, 27 June 1932)*

Many Catholics travelled from Northern Ireland. During Congress week, Catholic areas had been brightly decorated and this had stirred up sectarian hostility. A number of trains and buses carrying pilgrims to or from Dublin were stoned. Craig later condemned these actions.

MASS IN THE PARK

An enormous crowd gathered in the Phoenix Park. An *Irish Times* reporter, who said he was not a Catholic, wrote:

> *'It would be idle to attempt to estimate the size of that awe-inspiring crowd … It was an ocean*

> *of humanity … men and women marshalled into their places with consummate skill, ordered, decent and reverent, setting an example to the world of popular piety and behaving with a quiet dignity that was worthy of the occasion which evoked it.' (Irish Times, 27 June 1932)*

Mass was said on a specially built altar. The purple robes of the bishops and the scarlet of the cardinals, the flowers and the music, the sense of awe and worship, all made it a memorable experience for those who were there. Later, they recalled three things in particular:

- The first was St Patrick's bell. Over a thousand years old, it had been lent by the National Museum. At the consecration its ancient clang broke the silence that had descended on the huge crowd. Thanks to the miracle of radio, it was also heard by a much bigger multitude listening at home and abroad.
- The second was the hymn *Panis Angelicus*, sung by Ireland's most famous tenor, John McCormack.
- The third was the voice of the Pope, successfully broadcast from Rome. For devout Catholics it was awe-inspiring to hear, for the first time, the voice of the head of their Church.

After Mass, the Eucharist was carried in procession from the Park to O'Connell Bridge where Benediction was given from a special altar. It was the final act of a memorable week.

International Eucharistic Congress, 1932. Benediction at O'Connell Bridge, Congress Sunday

ASSESSING THE CONGRESS

The Congress passed off without a hitch. Even the weather co-operated, with blue skies and bright sunshine showing Ireland at its best. Everyone agreed it had been a great success and people felt proud of that. The new Irish state had shown that it could organise a big international event with the best of them. People also pointed to the huge turnout and the devotion of the people as proof that, in an increasingly pagan world, the Christian faith was still strong in Ireland.

FIANNA FÁIL AND THE CONGRESS

The Fianna Fáil leaders played a prominent part in the Congress. It helped them to bury the memory of their excommunication and the accusations of communism made during the election. It also provided an opportunity to show their commitment to the Catholic Church and its doctrines. After it, they proved even more willing to enforce the Catholic moral code than Cumann na nGaedheal, outlawing the sale of contraceptives and enshrining the ban on divorce in the Constitution.

JOHN CHARLES MCQUAID

It could also be argued that after the Congress the power of the Catholic bishops increased. One man who typified this power was **John Charles McQuaid**. As headmaster of Blackrock College, he held a huge garden party for the Congress. He carefully organised things so that there were no embarrassing encounters between de Valera and the Governor-General, James MacNeill, whom Fianna Fáil was then boycotting (see page 123).

This increased McQuaid's influence with de Valera. He encouraged de Valera to give the Catholic Church a privileged position in the 1937 Constitution (see page 115), though de Valera's final version did not go far enough for him. In 1941 de Valera urged the Pope to appoint him Archbishop of Dublin. In that role, McQuaid exercised enormous power over Catholics in particular and the Irish state in general. He used this power to discourage contacts between Catholics and people of other faiths and to resist change as much as possible.

Archbishop McQuaid reviewing the Irish army. While he was archbishop, the Catholic church exercised far more power in the South than any time before or since

QUESTIONS

1 What is a Eucharistic Congress? Who persuaded the Pope to hold the 1932 Congress in Dublin?

2 Who was put in charge of organising the Congress? Describe some of the ways in which people prepared for it.

3 What government was in power when the Congress was held?

4 How did the Congress begin? Describe the main events of the week that followed.

5 The climax of the Congress was the mass in the Phoenix Park. Describe what happened during it.

6 'Irish people were proud of the success of the Congress.' Give two reasons why they were proud.

7 How did the Congress affect Fianna Fáil and the role of the Catholic bishops in Ireland?

DOCUMENTS: A, B AND C

1: DUBLIN DURING THE CONGRESS

A: The country visitor arriving in Dublin during Congress Week is liable to imagine that he knows what to expect … multitudes of tourists, decorated streets and a general air of festivity. But five minutes after I stepped off the train I realised that … the old familiar Dublin that we knew has vanished for the week. One can no longer stroll easily down Westmoreland Street or O'Connell Street. Instead a crowd of visitors breaking into every language under the sun swarms upon the footpaths. Dublin seems to have doubled its population already and still the pilgrims come by every train and boat. I saw a huge liner disgorging some of them … today, her huge hull towering over the quayside. It was somehow a very strange sight to see her there. Dublin Bay is not used to these leviathans. (*Irish Times*, 22 June 1932)

B: It is in the poor districts, however, in the lowly tenements and the tumbledown back streets that one observes the most impressive tokens of the faith which animates the poor and needy. For every single flag in the better class districts there seem to be at least half a dozen in humble districts … Where the money came from, what added hardships have been endured, to enable the poor people to make this fine display, it is difficult to know … Never, in the lifetime of Dublin have these tumbledown streets, usually the sad sore in our midst, assumed a note so bright and joyful. (*Irish Times*, 17 June 1932)

C: Wherever we went one saw in the poor places of the city the same ungrudging self-sacrifice of the people to make a welcome for their Eucharistic King. Take Long Lane off Dorset Street. Its history is the history of a hundred little streets. On Saturday its women and children were contemplating its narrow hundred yards of beauty with proud eyes … Collections in pennies for its decoration were begun as long ago as January and the actual work of making a rainbow out of slum greyness took a full week. 'The men were great', I was told … 'Every bit of painting they did at night when their work was over …' A little shrine had been set up on the wall, bordered with a crochet fringe with 'IHS' worked into it. Holy pictures and statues showed at windows and doorways. Streamers and banners hung across the Lane … Paper roses in the Papal colours framed the doorways. 'There isn't an inch of it that hasn't been painted and cleaned, inside as well as out.' And I was taken to see the bedrooms with their newly papered walls. (*Irish Press*, 20 June 1932)

QUESTIONS ON THE DOCUMENT

1 What makes the writer of Source A say that the old familiar Dublin 'has vanished for a week'? List the things he expected to see and what surprised him.

2 Where, according to Source B, are the most impressive decorations to be found? What was it about them that impressed him?

3 Source C gives a detailed account of one poor area. Where, according to it, did the money come from for the decorations?

4 Sources B and C agree that the decoration of these areas is evidence of the people's deep faith. Do you find that convincing? Explain your answer.

DOCUMENTS: A AND B

2: EVALUATING THE CONGRESS

Here are two comments on the Congress; Source A is from the Irish Times, traditionally the paper of the Protestant and unionist community. Source B is from the Irish Press, owned by de Valera and set up to present the Fianna Fáil point of view.

A: Ecclesiastics from other lands know how decadent is the state of the modern world. They know that … the grip of religion is being loosened. Indifference and even atheism prevail and increasing millions are taking their cheerless rule in life from the words: 'eat, drink and be merry, for tomorrow we die.' Ireland remains an oasis in this wilderness of unfaith. (*Irish Times*, Editorial, 25 June 1932)

B: These scenes must bring to every Irish citizen and every Irish guest thoughts it would be difficult to express. But what amazement must they bring to those who have learnt of Ireland from corrupt and hostile agencies. The Ireland of disorder, of lawlessness, of communism, of incapacity for self-rule: now at last the world learns the truth, that it was a figment of malicious minds.

Instead they see an Ireland which, with a genius for detailed organisation and a capacity in the people for ready obedience to authority, has produced without a single hitch or a major accident, one of the most superb spectacles the eyes of man has looked on. They see too an Ireland of spiritual strength, of nation-wide devotion to Christianity, of fervent practice of religion. Combined in us, therefore, they find the qualities of heart, of mind and of spirit, which they ask for in most civilized nations. We can pray, we can welcome, we can organise, we can govern.

These things we have been trying to say to the world for a hundred years. They have not been believed because of the poisonous fumes of anti-Irish propaganda. But now comers from the four corners of the earth have knowledge of our full maturity as a nation … (*Irish Press*, Editorial, 26 June, 1952)

QUESTIONS ON THE DOCUMENT

1 What, according to the *Irish Times*, is to be learnt from the Congress? Do you find this a surprising conclusion? Explain your answer.

2 What, according to the *Irish Press*, is 'the truth' the world will learn from the Congress?

3 List the things the writer of source B thinks the world will now know the Irish can do. Why does he think they did not know that before?

4 What do these two sources tell us about what Irish people hoped the Congress would achieve? Can you see advantages or disadvantages in these hopes?

Suggestions for further reading for this case study

Dermot Keogh, *The Vatican, the Bishops and Irish Politics, 1919–39*, Cambridge 1996

WRITERS AND ARTISTS IN THE NEW IRELAND

CREATING AN IRISH IDENTITY WITH WORDS AND PICTURES

At the start of the 20th century the Gaelic League and the GAA were part of a movement to assert an Irish identity, separate from that of Britain. This movement also influenced writers and artists:

- A number of painters tried to create a new image of Ireland and Irish people which was inspired by the remote Irish-speaking districts of the west.
- Writers involved in the Anglo-Irish literary revival tried to create distinctively Irish literature using the English language.

Both of these movements continued after independence. By then the work of the older artists and writers was accepted as good, but when younger artists tried out new ideas and new forms of expression they did not always please the increasingly conservative public of the Irish Free State.

PAINTERS OF THE NEW IRELAND

Two painters were especially important in creating a visual image of Ireland: Paul Henry and Jack Yeats.

Paul Henry was a Belfast-born painter who went to live in Achill in 1910. The images he produced of peasants working in stone-lined fields, of fishermen, of sea and mountain and tiny whitewashed cottages became hugely popular. For many nationalists this was exactly the image of Ireland they wanted. In the 1930s Henry's pictures were so popular that they were used on tourist posters (see below left).

Jack Yeats, the brother of the poet, grew up in England but spent his holidays with his grandparents in Sligo. This drew him to the west of Ireland. He illustrated books about it for his friend, the playwright, J.M. Synge and produced prints for Cuala Press which was run by his sisters. These present images of strong Irish country folk working and playing, which appealed to nationalists and Gaelic Leaguers for whom such people were the 'real' Irish.

In the early 1900s, Yeats returned to live in Ireland. A committed nationalist, he opposed the Treaty and his picture *Communicating with Prisoners* is a tribute to republican prisoners during the Civil War. But in the late 1920s Yeats changed his style of painting. The pictures he produced were among the most wonderful of the 20th century, but they did not appeal to the conservative Ireland of that time and few of them sold.

What will it be? *A typical late work (1952) by the artist Jack B. Yeats*

EVIE HONE AND THE INTRODUCTION OF MODERNISM

In the 1920s younger painters like **Seán Keating** went on painting western landscape though Keating was also commissioned by a proud Free State government to paint the Shannon Scheme. But other young painters were influenced by new artistic movements in Europe, like cubism and abstraction.

Two women, **Mainie Jellett** and **Evie Hone** were among the first to bring these ideas to Ireland. After studying in France, they held an exhibition of their pictures in Dublin in 1923. So unfamiliar were the images they presented that one commentator called them 'sub-human'.

Evie Hone (1894–1955): Born into a prosperous Dublin family, which included several well-known artists, she was crippled by polio at eleven. Despite this she studied art in Paris with her friend Mainie Jellett. They were influenced by modern trends in painting like cubism, fauvism and abstract art. She briefly entered an Anglican convent but later converted to Roman Catholicism.

Evie Hone was deeply religious and this inspired her to abandon painting and start working in stained glass (right). She joined an Túr Gloine, a glass making co-operative set up in 1903 by Sarah Purser, a successful portrait painter.

She won many commissions from churches and religious communities to make windows for their

Stained glass by Evie Hone

churches. One of her finest windows, called *My Four Green Fields*, was commissioned for the Irish Pavilion at the New York World Fair in 1938. Today it is in Government buildings in Merrion Street. Her last commission was a huge window for Eton College in England.

WRITERS OF THE NEW IRELAND
W.B. YEATS AFTER 1922

The most important Irish writer of this period was W.B. Yeats. Although from a unionist background, Yeats became a moderate nationalist and supported the struggle for independence. This made him acceptable in the new Ireland and Cosgrave appointed him to the Free State Senate in 1922. By then his status as one of the greatest poets of the period was generally recognised and in 1923 he was given the Nobel Prize for literature.

Until his death in 1939, Yeats dominated the literary scene in Ireland. He produced his best

W.B. Yeats (1865–1939): The Dublin-born son of a painter, Yeats became involved in the cultural revival in the 1890s and early 1900s. With Lady Gregory he was one of the founders of the Abbey Theatre in 1904.

poetry after 1922, some of it reflecting on the new Ireland that had emerged. He used his position in the Senate to oppose censorship and the ban on divorce. He also sat on the commission that approved the design for the new Irish coinage.

THE ABBEY AFTER 1922

In 1904, Yeats and Lady Gregory had founded the Abbey Theatre and they continued to manage it. In 1924 they persuaded the Minister for Finance, Ernest Blythe, to give it an annual subsidy of £850. This made it the first state-subsidised theatre in the English-speaking world.

In the early 1920s the Abbey discovered a brilliant new playwright, Seán O'Casey. Lady Gregory had encouraged him to write and in 1923 they put on his first play, *The Shadow of a Gunman*. It was followed by *Juno and the Paycock* in 1924 and *The Plough and the Stars* in 1926.

All three plays were set in Dublin's slums in the years between 1916 and 1922. In them, O'Casey did not show the idealised Ireland some wanted to see and there were protests when a tricolour (flag) was carried into a pub during *The Plough and the Stars*.

Yeats and Lady Gregory supported him against the protesters but they had their own ideas about the 'right' kind of writing. When O'Casey's next play, *The Silver Tassie*, experimented with different forms of story-telling, they turned it down. An angry O'Casey left Ireland and spent the rest of his life in England. Though he wrote more plays, none were a major success.

After O'Casey, the Abbey opted for safe plays, mainly domestic dramas set in rural Ireland. After Yeats' death, Ernest Blythe became director and his conservative approach kept the Abbey from experimenting with new forms of drama until the 1960s.

AN IMAGE OF IRELAND

Conflicts such as those over Jack Yeats' painting or O'Casey's plays arose because their work did not fit with the mental image of Ireland, which many of the founders of Irish independence had. That was a rural image of an Ireland whose main

Seán O'Casey (1880–1964): A Protestant from a poor Dublin family, O'Casey worked as a labourer until his plays succeeded in the 1920s. Involvement in the Gaelic League made him a nationalist. He was also a socialist, strongly influenced by James Larkin. For a time he was very involved with the Irish Citizen Army but left after a quarrel with Constance Markievicz, whom he intensely disliked.

inhabitants were farmers, especially the poor farmers of the west. Gaelic Leaguers saw them as the heirs of an ancient Gaelic world. Uncorrupted by the modern materialism, they were poor in worldly things but rich in their store of Gaelic story, music and song. They did not need the material wealth that people in industrial cities craved.

In a talk broadcast in 1943, de Valera described this ideal:

> 'The Ireland that we dreamed of would be the home of a people who ... were satisfied with frugal comfort and devoted their leisure to things of the spirit; a land whose countryside would be bright with cosy homesteads, whose fields and villages would be joyous with the sounds of industry, the romping of sturdy children, the contests of athletic youths, the laughter of comely maidens; whose firesides would be the forums of the wisdom of serene old age.' (T. Brown, *Ireland, a Social and Cultural History*, 1922–79, London 1981, p. 146)

THE REALITY

In reality, of course, this Ireland never existed. 40 per cent of Irish people lived in towns and cities, not in the country. And most country people were not content with 'things of the spirit'. Like everyone else, they could be good or bad, generous or money-grubbing, kind or cruel.

Younger writers wanted to show this complex reality, as J.M. Synge had in *The Playboy of the Western World*, where the hero murders his father. Nationalists were outraged when it was put on in the Abbey in 1907, but by the 1920s it was accepted as a masterpiece. After independence a new generation of writers emerged who wanted to write of their own real Ireland, not de Valera's mythical one.

THE NEW WRITERS

Three of the younger writers had been involved in the War of Independence and they used their writing to try to understand their own experiences and the new Ireland now emerging:

- **Frank O'Connor**, a native of Cork, wrote short stories about townspeople whose lives were narrowed by poverty and religion.

Courtesy: National Gallery of Ireland

MR. W. B. YEATS: "Of course, Mr. O'Casey, you must on no account take this as being in the nature of a rejection. I would suggest that you simply tell the Press that my foot slipped."

Yeats kicking O'Casey out of the Abbey

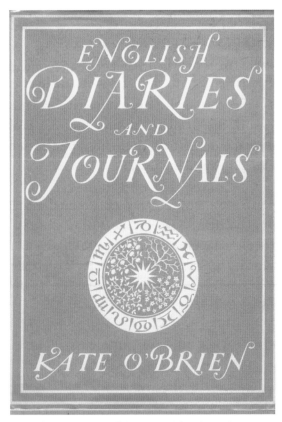

Kate O'Brien was one of the many Irish writers whose books were affected by the Censorship Board

- **Liam O'Flaherty** a native of the Aran Islands, published novels which took a very unromantic view of the independence struggle and of Irish rural life.
- **Seán Ó Faoláin**, in his novels, journalism and historical works, rejected the Gaelic myth and stressed how much contemporary Ireland was a part of modern Britain and Europe.

Other writers like **Francis MacManus**, **Mary Lavin**, **Mervyn Wall**, **Kate O'Brien** and **Maura Laverty** were also at work, teasing out the social tensions within Irish society.

Among the younger poets, an outstanding name was **Austin Clarke**. He began, under the influence of the Gaelic revival, to use themes from ancient Irish history in his poems. Later he used the same themes to satirise the narrow and clerically-dominated Irish society.

Another fine poet was **Patrick Kavanagh**. In his poem *The Great Hunger*, published in 1942, he showed the bleak reality behind de Valera's dream. Writing of his native Monaghan with its poor small farms, Kavanagh brought out the bitter loneliness and frustration of a life of rural poverty dominated by the land and the church.

CENSORING THE WRITERS

But official Ireland, whether political or clerical, did not welcome the insights which these writers provided. It saw their work as corrupting a pure and Catholic people. The Censorship Board banned their books for the flimsiest of reasons (see page 146). This meant that Irish people could not read commentaries on the Ireland of their own time and that the authors found it extremely difficult to make a living from their writing.

QUESTIONS

1 List two painters who helped to create the visual image of Ireland in the early 20th century and describe their paintings.

2 Write a brief account of the life and art of Evie Hone.

3 Write a brief account of the career of W.B. Yeats after 1922.

4 What happened to the Abbey after 1922?

5 Why did writing by young writers cause so much controversy in the 1920s and 1930s?

6 List and briefly describe the work of three writers in the 1920s and 1930s. Have you read any works by any of them?

7 Look back at the section on censorship (see page 146). What kind of literature was it supposed to stop and why was it used against so many Irish writers?

LEAVING CERTIFICATE QUESTIONS

1 What was the attitude of Irish leaders towards the Irish language? What step did they take to revive it after 1922?

2 What was the influence of the Catholic bishops in the Irish Free State after 1922?

3 Many Irish Protestants had opposed Home Rule because they feared that 'Home Rule would be Rome Rule'. To what extent did the fate of Protestants in the Irish Free State between 1922 and 1949 justify these fears?

4 Describe the main events of the Eucharistic Congress and assess its impact on the Irish Free State.

5 What was the role of Irish visual artists in creating an image of an ideal Ireland in the first half of the 20th century?

6 What was the main developments in literature in Ireland from 1921 to 1949 and assess the impact of censorship on writers during that period?

Northern Ireland 1920–1939

10.1

THE FOUNDATION OF NORTHERN IRELAND

THE ORIGINS OF NORTHERN IRELAND

In 1920 Lloyd George decided to solve the quarrel between Irish nationalists and Irish unionists by giving each of them home rule. As a result, the Westminster parliament passed the **Government of Ireland Act** in December 1920. It divided Ireland into two states:

- ○ 'Southern Ireland' containing twenty-six counties with its capital in Dublin.
- ○ 'Northern Ireland' containing six counties with its capital in Belfast.

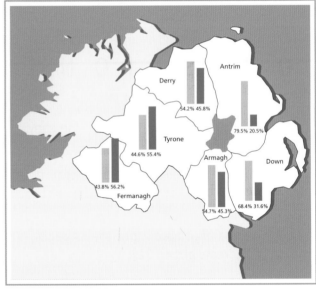

Northern Ireland, showing the distribution of Protestants and Catholics across the six counties

AN UNJUST PARTITION

The British claimed that they did this to keep two irreconcilable communities, unionists and nationalists or Protestants and Catholics, apart. But the way in which they set up the two states in 1920 was neither just nor fair.

Ulster unionists asked for six counties. That, they believed, was the largest area over which they could retain permanent control. Lloyd George gave them what they wanted even though parts of the six counties had Catholic majorities. No one

asked the nationalists where they wanted to be. The result was to leave a far higher proportion of discontented Catholics in the north than there had been Protestants in the whole of Ireland (Table A).

Table A

Religious minorities, North and South	
Irish Free State	**Northern Ireland**
3,000,000 Catholics	430,000 Catholics
225,000 Protestants	820,000 Protestants

THE CONSTITUTION OF NORTHERN IRELAND

The Constitution of Northern Ireland was contained in the Government of Ireland Act:

- It had a parliament of two houses. There was a **Commons** with fifty-two MPs elected by Proportional Representation (PR), and a **Senate** containing the mayors of Belfast and Derry and twenty-four Senators elected by the Commons.
- Northern Ireland was still part of the United Kingdom, with the Westminster parliament keeping supreme authority over it. Only Westminster could change the constitution or deal with the crown, the armed forces, trade, currency, war and peace. All laws passed at Westminster applied to Northern Ireland unless otherwise stated.
- In addition, certain powers in relation to taxation, postal services and the courts were 'reserved' to the Westminster parliament until they could be handed over to a joint **Council of Ireland** that Lloyd George hoped could be set up with the agreement of the South.
- Because of the power the Westminster parliament retained, voters in Northern Ireland were to elect twelve MPs to represent them in it.

CRAIG BECOMES PRIME MINISTER OF NORTHERN IRELAND

The Government of Ireland Act gave Ulster unionists what they wanted. They remained within the United Kingdom. That could be seen as a triumph for Sir Edward Carson who had led the Unionist Party since 1910. The party offered him the option of becoming the first Northern Ireland Prime Minister, but he refused. By then he was almost seventy and wanted to retire.

The position went instead to his deputy, **Sir James Craig**. He left a promising political career in London to set up the new state. Craig remained Prime Minister of Northern Ireland until his death in 1940. The attitudes and policies he adopted did a great deal to shape its future.

Sir James Craig (1871–1940): A millionaire businessman, Craig had been the main organiser of the Ulster Volunteers in 1912–14. He fought on the Western Front during the war and was a minister in Lloyd George's Coalition government from 1919–21.

VIOLENCE IN 1920

The birth of Northern Ireland in 1920 was marked by violence. It began in the early summer. In May and June there were elections for local councils. For the first time, voting was by Proportional Representation (PR). Nationalists won control of Fermanagh, Tyrone, south Down, south Armagh, Derry city and other councils. Nationalist councillors then transferred the allegiance of these councils to the Dáil government. Their success also strengthened the IRA.

These developments frightened unionists who began to revive the Ulster Volunteer Force. After clashes in Derry in which eight Catholics and four Protestants were killed, the British army was sent in in June. But the IRA attacked it and it tended to side with the UVF rather than remaining neutral. Violence spread to Belfast in July after the annual Orange Order marches. The sectarian rhetoric of Orange speakers raised passions, already inflamed by reports of IRA violence in the south.

Tension was increased by competition for jobs. By 1920, the wartime boom in shipbuilding had ended. During it, Catholics got jobs with firms that before the war had only employed Protestants. On 21 July Protestant trade unionists demanded that 'disloyal workers' (i.e. Catholics) be sacked and the jobs be given to soldiers returning from the war.

In the riots that followed, about 10,000 Catholic men and 1,000 Catholic women were forced out of work. Mobs also attacked and burned Catholic houses and shops. Defensive action by the IRA led to nights of violence that spread to neighbouring towns like Banbridge and Lurgan. Eighty-two people died, hundreds of houses were burned and thousands of people, most of them Catholics, were driven from their homes. In Dublin, the Dáil ordered a boycott of northern goods in retaliation for the attacks on Catholics.

SETTING UP THE SPECIAL CONSTABLES

Unionist leaders wanted to arm the UVF but the British army commander, General Macready, did not approve of giving guns to civilians. To get around his objections and also to impose some discipline on the UVF, whose activities were damaging the image of unionism in Britain, Craig proposed an **Ulster Special Constabulary** to assist the RIC. Lloyd George agreed since it gave him additional forces to use against the IRA.

The 'Specials' came into existence in September 1920. There were three classes: Class A were to serve full time, Class B were part-timers who supplemented police patrols in their own areas, and Class C acted as a reserve for emergencies. Later the 'A' and 'C' constables were disbanded, but the '**B Specials**' remained in existence until 1970.

B Specials on patrol

Courtesy: National Library of Ireland

By the end of 1920 over 20,000 men had enrolled as Special Constables. The vast majority had been in the UVF. Although it was never stated officially, the Specials were a Protestant paramilitary force. Their local knowledge made them an effective weapon against the IRA in border areas, though their often-undisciplined behaviour earned the hatred of Catholics. Until they were finally disbanded in 1970, nationalists regarded them as the part of the repressive machinery of the unionist state.

ELECTING THE BELFAST PARLIAMENT

Even before the Government of Ireland Act had passed in December 1920, the British government had begun to transfer power over the six counties from Dublin Castle to the new Belfast government. Early in 1921 Craig was appointed as acting Prime Minister and elections to the first Northern parliament were held on 24 May 1921.

Nationalists refused to recognise the existence of Northern Ireland but rather than allow unionists a walkover, they decided to contest the elections. They were divided between the old **Nationalist** (Home Rule) **Party**, now led by **Joseph Devlin**, and **Sinn Féin**. The two parties co-operated during the election campaign.

Almost 90 per cent of voters went to the poll and the Unionist Party won a decisive victory (Table B). On 22 June, King George V arrived to open the Northern parliament but only unionists attended the opening ceremony. Nationalists still hoped that permanent partition could be avoided.

CRAIG AND THE TREATY NEGOTIATIONS

In July 1921 de Valera agreed to a truce between the IRA and the British army, so that talks could begin

Table B

Results of first Northern Ireland election, May 1921	
Party	**Seats**
Unionist	40
Nationalist	6
Sinn Féin	6

between Sinn Féin and the British government (see page 85). That worried the unionists, who knew that Sinn Féin would try to end partition.

Craig refused to be involved in the negotiations in London. He insisted that they were between the British and the southern nationalists and had nothing to do with him. Northern Ireland existed, he maintained, and nothing would change that.

But the final version of the Treaty dismayed the unionists. It recognised the unity of Ireland. Unionists were allowed to opt out but if they did so, a Boundary Commission would redraw the border between North and South.

Like Collins, though for opposite reasons, Craig thought Northern Ireland would lose the areas in which nationalists were a majority. He hurried to London to protest but Lloyd George calmed him down. In spite of what he had told Collins and Griffith, he now assured the worried unionist leader that the Boundary Commission would do no more than tidy up the line of the border.

VIOLENCE AGAIN

The truce, which ended fighting in the South, had not brought peace to the North. Violence continued in the second half of 1921. It grew worse after the Treaty was signed, especially in border areas where the proposal for a Boundary Commission raised nationalist hopes and unionist fears.

In an attempt to restore order Collins and Craig met in January and again in March 1922. Collins promised to end the boycott of Belfast goods and Craig promised to protect Catholics and encourage them to enrol in the Specials. But Craig was unable to control his own extremists. Only days after the March agreement, attacks on Catholics in Belfast reached a new intensity. In one incident, men wearing police uniforms murdered a Catholic family, but Craig refused to hold an inquiry.

Collins believed Craig had betrayed him and that a pogrom was being launched against northern Catholics. He began to send arms to the northern IRA that, unlike its southern equivalent, was not split by the Treaty.

Sir Richard Dawson Bates (1876–1949): A solicitor, he became secretary to the Ulster Unionist Council in 1906. He was one of the leaders of those who resisted Home Rule from 1912–14 and Craig appointed him Minister for Home Affairs in the Northern Ireland Government.

DAWSON BATES AND THE SPECIAL POWERS ACT

Craig appointed **Sir Richard Dawson Bates** as **Minister for Home Affairs**. A committed unionist, his aim was to establish control over the whole six counties and suppress all resistance to unionist rule.

In March 1922, Dawson Bates got the Belfast parliament to pass the **Civil Authorities (Special Powers) Act**:

- It allowed the Home Affairs Minister 'to take all such steps and issue all such orders as may be necessary for preserving peace' (P. Buckland: *Irish Unionism 2: Ulster*, Dublin 1973, p. 158). He could delegate these powers to any police officer.
- It laid down stiff penalties for certain offences (e.g. the death penalty for throwing bombs, and flogging for carrying arms).
- It allowed the Minister to introduce internment without trial.

The Special Powers Act gave the Northern government almost dictatorial powers. At first it was intended to be temporary, so parliament had to renew it each year. But in 1933 it was made permanent. It was used almost exclusively against nationalists. They resented that bitterly and this added to their alienation from the Northern state.

THE ROYAL ULSTER CONSTABULARY (RUC)

In May 1922 Dawson Bates reorganised the police. He replaced the RIC with a new force, the **Royal Ulster Constabulary**. It was to consist of 3,000 men and, like the RIC, it was armed. Craig, who was not a bigot, insisted that one third of the places in it be reserved for Catholics, hoping in this way to win the confidence of nationalists.

But his hope was never fulfilled. In 1922 about a quarter of the RUC were Catholics but most of those were men who had transferred to it from the RIC. As they retired, few Catholics came forward to replace them. From the 1930s less than 10 per cent of the RUC were Catholics. This was partly because their own community did not approve of them joining but also because the unionist government did little to encourage them. As a result, nationalists saw the RUC too as part of the unionist machine, which aimed at suppressing them.

Dawson Bates also reorganised the Special Constables to assist the RUC. To impose a more military discipline on them, he recruited Sir Henry Wilson, who had recently retired as chief of the Imperial General Staff, to act as their military adviser.

By the middle of 1922, the unionist government had 50,000 full-time or part-time policemen at its disposal. That was one for every two Catholic families. They could also call on thirteen battalions of British troops, who were controlled by the London government.

GROWING VIOLENCE

The violence got steadily worse throughout the early months of 1922. The IRA attacked police and military barracks and, in places, the business premises and private homes of Protestants.

This provoked retaliation from the unionist side and the death toll mounted. On 24 May, after the IRA murdered an MP, Dawson Bates used the Special Powers Act to impose internment. That night over 500 people were rounded up, all of them nationalists. Many of them were interned on a prison ship in Belfast Lough. On 1 June a curfew was imposed and the police, 'Specials' and the British army were given wide powers of search and arrest.

These tough measures had their effect but even more significant was the civil war in the south and the death of Collins. He had given support to northern nationalists but the Cosgrave government was not interested. It encouraged northern IRA men to come south and join the Free State army. By the second half of 1922 a sullen peace had descended.

THE COST OF PEACE

The nationalist community had suffered most in the violence. As Table C shows, over half of all those who died between July 1920 to July 1922 were Catholics even though Catholics made up only one third of the population of Northern Ireland. In addition, over 23,000 Catholics were forced out of their homes, between 8,000 and 11,000 were driven from their jobs and over 500 Catholic businesses, mostly shops, were destroyed. The memory of these years left a deep mark on the northern state from which it has never fully recovered.

Table C

Violent deaths in Northern Ireland July 1920 to July 1922			
Total dead	Catholics	Protestants	Security forces
557	303	172	82

QUESTIONS

1 Write a paragraph about the Constitution of Northern Ireland. Mention the method of election, what the Belfast parliament could do and the powers which were retained by Westminster.

2 Describe the position of Catholics and nationalists within Northern Ireland in 1920–22.

3 Write a short account of Sir James Craig and the establishment of Northern Ireland.

4 Who was Sir Richard Dawson Bates? What steps did he take to establish unionist control over Northern Ireland in 1922? What outside event helped him?

5 'The way Northern Ireland was founded made it unlikely that Catholics would find it easy to give their allegiance to it.' Set out at least four developments which support this view.

10.2

CONFIRMING THE RELIGIOUS AND POLITICAL DIVIDE

THE UNIONIST PARTY

In 1921, the Unionist Party formed the government of Northern Ireland. Most of its leaders were wealthy and powerful men. Craig himself was a millionaire businessman and Dawson Bates a wealthy solicitor. Craig's other ministers included two big landlords and three company directors.

Craig also needed the support of working-class unionists. In 1918 the **Ulster Unionist Labour Association** was set up to encourage the election of workers as MPs, but it had little success because the party leaders were hostile to the idea. Despite this, many Protestant workers remained loyal to the Unionist Party because they felt the links with the United Kingdom were vital to their jobs and their safety.

THE ORANGE ORDER

The Orange Order helped to bind Protestants of all classes to the Unionist Party. The Order, an explicitly anti-Catholic body, had been at the centre of unionism ever since the party was set up in 1886. In the 1920s about two thirds of Protestant men belonged to it. Membership gave them a sense of common purpose and identity, most clearly seen in the colourful marches on 12 July.

It was almost impossible for a unionist politician to be elected to office without being an Orangeman. In 1934 Craig told the Belfast parliament, *'I am an Orangeman first and a politician and Member of Parliament second'*.

ENDING PR IN LOCAL GOVERNMENT ELECTIONS

After the local elections of 1920, nationalist control of councils in border areas worried the unionist government. In 1922 Dawson Bates suspended twenty-one councils which refused to recognise the Northern Ireland government. He then changed the method of electing them from the fairer PR to the more discriminatory 'first past

An Orange march by the painter John Lavery. It is called 12 July, Portadown, 1928

Courtesy: Ulster Museum

the post' system. The change was also aimed at Labour Party candidates who had done well in some council elections, especially in Belfast.

Lloyd George had included voting by PR in the Government of Ireland Act to make sure that minorities were fairly treated. When Dawson Bates proposed changing it, Collins protested to the British. He feared that the changes would influence the Boundary Commission by making nationalist areas appear unionist. Lloyd George spoke to Craig who threatened to resign if they were not allowed to have their way. In the end Lloyd George did nothing.

Dawson Bates then set up the Leech Commission to redraw the constituency boundaries in local councils. Nationalists refused to attend, then found that the boundaries were redrawn in a way that seriously reduced their chances of winning seats. This process (called 'gerrymandering') meant that nationalists lost control of most local councils, even in areas like Derry city and Fermanagh where they had clear majorities. In Fermanagh, for example, where 56 per cent of the population were Catholic, nationalists won only 37 per cent of the seats after the boundary and voting changes.

THE RESULTS OF THE CHANGE

The change in the voting system gave the Unionist Party unchallenged control of most local councils until the 1970s. This led to widespread corruption which Craig and Dawson Bates, though honest themselves, did nothing to stop. Unionist-dominated local councils also made life more difficult for Catholics. They controlled public housing, some aspects of social welfare and many jobs and made sure that Catholics got less than their fair share of these.

HOPING FOR THE BOUNDARY COMMISSION

Up to 1925 northern Catholics hoped that partition would be short-lived. The Boundary Commission, they believed, would transfer many of them to the Irish Free State. While waiting for that, they refused to recognise Northern Ireland:

- Nationalist and Sinn Féin MPs would not take their seats in the Belfast parliament.

- Nationalists refused to take part in any of the inquiries which the northern government set up to decide on future policy.
- Catholic national teachers refused to recognise the Northern Ministry of Education.

UNIONIST ATTITUDES TO NATIONALISTS

Unionists bitterly resented this attitude. They saw Catholic boycotts of their new institutions as proof that Catholics were disloyal and were plotting to overthrow Northern Ireland. They were always conscious that there was a hostile Catholic majority in the island as a whole and a large Catholic minority within their own borders. IRA activity and the rhetoric of southern politicians like de Valera reinforced this sense of threat.

That made it easier for unionists like Dawson Bates, who always disliked Catholics, to discriminate against them. And it made it more difficult for others like Craig who had intended to treat Catholics fairly, to do so.

THE DELAY IN THE BOUNDARY COMMISSION

The Treaty had assumed that the Boundary Commission would begin work at once but it was delayed until 1924. There were a number of reasons for that:

- The Civil War in the south between June 1922 and May 1923 and the death of Collins who had always taken a keen interest in developments in Northern Ireland reduced pressure on the British to see that it was set up.
- Craig, fearing the Commission would take away large areas of Northern Ireland, refused to name a unionist representative to the three-member body.
- In Britain, Lloyd George lost power in December 1922. The new Conservative government saw no need to push their unionist friends to do something they did not want to do.

When the civil war ended in the South, Cosgrave's government demanded action. It had already appointed its Minister for Education, **Eoin MacNeill**, a Catholic from Co. Antrim, to represent the nationalist point of view (see page 98). In 1924

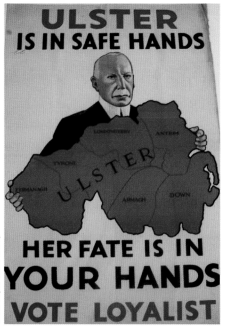

A Unionist Party election poster. Who is the man and what is he holding?

a newly elected Labour government in London listened to their demands. It took power to appoint the unionist representative. They chose a staunch unionist, **J.R. Fisher**, a Belfast lawyer and a friend of Craig's. They also appointed Judge **Richard Feetham** of the South African Supreme Court as the neutral chairman.

THE BOUNDARY COMMISSION AT WORK, 1924–25

Article 12 of the Treaty said that these three men would decide:

'in accordance with the wishes of the inhabitants so far as may be compatible with the economic and geographical conditions, the boundaries between Northern Ireland and the rest of Ireland.'

They set to work in November 1924. First they heard legal arguments about the meaning of Article 12. Then they toured the border areas to get evidence from individuals and groups. They had to decide:

- Whether to redraw the 1920 border completely or merely to alter small parts of it.
- Which of the two conditions, 'the wishes of the inhabitants' or 'economic and geographic conditions', should matter most.

Feetham's decision on these points was vital and he decided to give more consideration to economic and geographic conditions than to the wishes of the people. That meant he would change the 1920

border as little as possible. Two things may have influenced him:

- By 1925 people believed that too much attention to 'the wishes of the people' had caused great economic difficulties in eastern Europe after the first World War.
- The border had been there since 1920; to redraw it extensively would add to the economic disruption which it had already caused.

MacNeill does not seem to have objected to this decision. He also faithfully kept the promise all Commissioners made not to tell anyone what they were deciding. Fisher, on the other hand, made sure Craig knew what the decision would be. This was comforting to the Unionist government, which had feared it might lose a lot of territory.

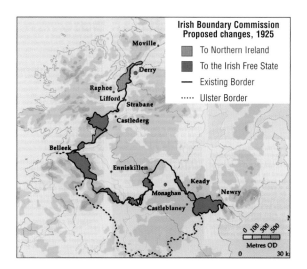

THE COMMISSION REPORT IS LEAKED

Late in 1925 the report of the Commission was leaked to a London newspaper. It showed that it proposed only minor changes, including the transfer of parts of Donegal to Northern Ireland. It was impossible for Cosgrave to accept this (see page 102). He went to London where he met Craig and the British government. On 3 December 1925 they signed the Anglo-Irish Agreement which left the border of 1920 unchanged.

NATIONALISTS ENTER THE BELFAST PARLIAMENT

This was a bitter blow to nationalists. It forced many of them to rethink their attitude to the northern state.

- Those in Belfast and the east took a moderate approach because they were conscious of being a minority and had painful memories of the events of 1920–21. Led by the former Home Ruler **Joseph Devlin** (see page 160), they decided to enter the Belfast parliament so that they could highlight Catholic grievances, especially in relation to education.
- In the west and south, where Catholics were more numerous, the Sinn Féin policy of abstention had more appeal. But even there some nationalists favoured a compromise. In 1928 a former leader of Sinn Féin from Fermanagh, **Cahir Healy**, joined with Devlin to form the **National League of the North**. Although its aim was to work for the 'national reunification of Ireland' it supported Devlin's policy of entering parliament.

By 1928, ten nationalist MPs had taken their seats. But the unionists were not inclined to respond generously to this gesture.

ENDING PR IN ELECTIONS TO THE BELFAST PARLIAMENT

In the 1925 election, which Craig called while the Boundary Commission was in session, divisions appeared among unionist voters. Economic hardship encouraged some working-class unionists to vote for Labour or Independent Unionist candidates. To Craig's dismay, the Unionist Party lost seven seats while four Independent and three Labour MPs were elected.

Stormont: The unionist government built itself a magnificent parliament building at Stormont Castle. It was opened in 1931. After that the parliament which met there is usually called the 'Stormont parliament'.

Craig blamed this result on PR. He feared it would split the unionist vote and let the nationalists in.

In 1929 he abolished PR for elections to the Belfast parliament and replaced it with the 'first past the post' system. The Westminster parliament, which was supreme over the Belfast parliament, could have stopped this because PR was intended to protect the interests of minorities. But it did nothing.

THE RESULT OF THE CHANGE

The abolition of PR had three main effects:
- As Craig and Dawson Bates had hoped, all elections became a straight fight between unionists and nationalists. Other parties such as the Labour Party were squeezed out.
- That forced unionist voters to rally behind the Unionist Party. As a result, it remained in unshakeable control of Northern Ireland until 1972 when the Belfast parliament was abolished.
- Most constituencies had clear unionist or nationalist majorities, so everyone knew in advance who was going to win. That meant that parties did not bother to put up candidates who were sure to lose. As a result, by the 1930s only one third of seats were contested in general elections. This produced a very stagnant political scene in which important issues like economic policy or social reform were seldom seriously discussed.

NATIONALIST FRUSTRATION

With PR gone there was little reason for nationalist MPs to remain in Stormont. Devlin tried to act like an opposition leader but he had no hope of doing what opposition leaders in democracies hope to do – become the government. The unionists either ignored the nationalist MPs or treated any protests they made as an attack on the right of Northern Ireland to exist.

Devlin attempted to reassure them but they would not listen. Finally in 1932, frustration drove him and his followers out of the Belfast parliament again.

Joseph Devlin died in 1934 and none of the nationalist leaders who followed him had anything like his stature or experience. Up until the 1960s nationalists MPs attended parliament only occasionally. The Catholic community withdrew into itself, forming its own schools, clubs and charitable institutions, depending on its own resources to survive in the increasingly hostile environment of the Orange state.

FIANNA FÁIL AND NORTHERN NATIONALISTS

Fianna Fáil's victory in the 1932 election briefly raised nationalist hopes. De Valera talked a great deal about ending partition and encouraged them to abstain from Stormont. In 1933 he stood for the Belfast parliament as an abstentionist candidate. But when northern nationalists suggested that northern MPs be allowed to take their seats in the Dáil he refused. They soon realised that his anti-partitionist language had more to do with winning votes in the South than with helping them.

SECTARIAN IDENTITIES NORTH AND SOUTH

The gap between North and South grew wider as the years passed and took on a more sectarian tone. At first leaders on both sides tried to reassure their minorities with promises of fair treatment. But as time passed, both governments adopted policies that matched the prejudices of their majorities.

In the South the Cosgrave government rejected divorce and censored books and films. These policies were clearly influenced by the Catholic Church. Fianna Fáil went further. De Valera told the Fianna Fáil Ard Fheis in 1931 that he was 'a Catholic first' and his government treated the Eucharistic Congress in 1932 as a Catholic triumph. These developments allowed Craigavon to claim that he was merely responding to southern trends when he spoke of Stormont being 'a Protestant parliament for a Protestant people'.

Thus, by 1939 the actions and attitudes of the two governments had strengthened and reinforced the sectarian basis of partition.

CRAIGAVON, A SKILFUL POLITICIAN

Craig (whom the king made **Lord Craigavon** in 1927) remained as Prime Minister of Northern Ireland until his death in 1940. He was a skilful politician who used threats from nationalist politicians in the South to unite unionists behind his government and to stifle criticism of its policies. Three times he used the slogan of 'the Union in danger' to call elections:

- The first was in 1925 while the Boundary Commission was in session.
- He did it again in 1933 when de Valera was consolidating his power in Dublin and making anti-partitionist speeches. The Unionist Party gained an extra boost from de Valera's decision to stand as a candidate in one northern constituency.
- Finally he repeated the trick in 1938 when de Valera was making his peace with the British government and expressing his hope of ending partition.

Each time Craigavon won decisively and each time he destroyed other unionist groups whose economic or social ideas might have posed a challenge to the Unionist Party.

NORTHERN IRELAND AND THE 1938 ANGLO-IRISH AGREEMENTS

In 1938 in the Anglo Irish Agreements (page 000) de Valera got rid of the land annuities in one easy payment, gained the three Treaty ports and a promise of better trade relations with Britain. After that Craigavon went to London and demanded compensation for Northern Ireland. Chamberlain agreed to increase agricultural subsidies to northern farmers and bring Northern Ireland social services up to the level of services in Britain. While this was not very significant at the time, it paid off handsomely when Britain boosted spending on its social services after the war.

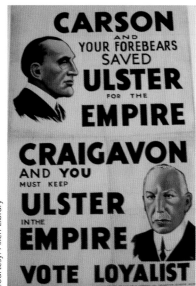

A typical unionist election poster

Courtesy: Allen Library

ASSESSING CRAIGAVON

Although Craigavon was successful in maintaining unionist power he did little to change Northern Ireland. The ministers he appointed in 1921 were wealthy older men (their average age was over fifty) and most of them were still in office when he died in 1940. The state he left behind was more securely established than might have seemed possible in 1920. But he also left it with two deep problems which he did nothing to solve – the decline in its major industries and the sectarian divisions in Northern Ireland society.

Craig himself was not a bigot but he was surrounded by those who were. He turned a blind eye to the injustices suffered by Catholics in employment, housing and other areas. Although Catholics protested to the Westminster government, Craig was able to convince the British that this was an internal matter for Northern Ireland. British politicians and civil servants, profoundly relieved in 1921 to have the eternal Irish question off their backs, were only too willing to be persuaded.

QUESTIONS

1 Write a paragraph about the Unionist Party after 1920 and its links with the Orange Order.

2 Why did nationalists like the Proportional Representation (PR) system of voting and why did the unionists get rid of it for local government elections?

3 Describe the workings of the Boundary Commission. What did it recommend and what happened to its recommendation?

4 How did nationalists respond to the outcome of the Boundary Commission?

5 Why did Craigavon abolish PR for elections to the Stormont parliament? What was the result of that change?

6 Describe the relationship of the nationalist community to the Stormont government and to the Fianna Fáil party.

7 Assess the performance of Lord Craigavon (Sir James Craig) as Prime Minister of Northern Ireland from 1920 to 1940.

10.3

ECONOMIC AND SOCIAL POLICIES: 1921–1939

ECONOMIC TIES WITH BRITAIN

The Government of Ireland Act did not give the Northern Ireland government much economic independence. It could only decide on a limited range of taxes, like stamp duties. These raised only about 20 per cent of the money the government spent. The rest came from taxes which the London government decided on. These were levied on the United Kingdom as a whole, including Northern Ireland. Then London passed Northern Ireland's share over to the unionist government.

The Treasury (Finance Department) in London feared that the unionist government would use British taxpayers' money to give Northern Ireland better social services than they could afford. To prevent that, the 'principle of parity' was introduced. That meant that taxation and services in Northern Ireland should remain at the same level as in the rest of the United Kingdom:

○ In the 1920s this benefited the North. It was a poor area and paid less in taxes than richer parts of the United Kingdom. Money flowed from them to lift pensions and unemployment benefits in the North to the same levels as in Britain. That was better than anything the Free State, with no subsidy from Britain, could afford.

- In the 1930s the situation was reversed as the depression badly damaged the British economy. The level of social welfare fell sharply.
- In 1938, after the Anglo-Irish Agreements, Chamberlain promised Craig to keep services on the same level as in Britain (see page 138).

These arrangements limited the economic freedom of the unionist government. Most decisions about spending were made in London. After paying for pensions and unemployment, little was left to improve housing, health or schools. Between the wars, local authorities built fewer than 8,000 houses and the standard of housing remained well below that in other parts of the United Kingdom.

THE NORTHERN IRELAND ECONOMY: AGRICULTURE

Although the north-east was the main industrial area in Ireland, agriculture was very important in the Northern Ireland economy. In the 1920s almost 150,000 people, about 26 per cent of the work force, were in farming. Agriculture earned £11 million a year, which was far more than shipbuilding.

Farms were smaller than in the Free State; only 4.4 per cent were over 100 acres, compared with 8.8 per cent over 100 acres in the South. Most farmers owned their farms, having bought them under the Land Purchase Acts passed between 1870 and 1909. In 1925 the unionist government, like Cumann na nGaedheal in the South, brought in a final Land Act which made it compulsory for landlords to sell to any remaining tenants.

In the 1920s, the unionist government also made a determined effort to raise farming standards, hoping to increase sales to the rest of the United Kingdom. The **Livestock Breeding Act** set out to improve the breeding of animals and marketing

boards were set up to improve the sales of farm produce. Attempts were made to educate farmers in new techniques and to raise production standards for eggs, meat, fruit and dairy produce.

When the depression deepened in 1931, the London government took steps to protect United Kingdom farmers from foreign competition. Northern Irish farmers also gained when the economic war cut the South's exports to Britain. Pig numbers rose from 200,000 in 1932 to 844,000 by 1939 and sheep, poultry and cattle numbers had also increased.

THE NORTHERN IRELAND ECONOMY: INDUSTRY

Unlike the Free State, Northern Ireland also had heavy industries. The key ones were shipbuilding, engineering, and linen. They had all done well during the first World War. The boom continued until 1920, then depression set in. Unemployment averaged 23 per cent in the 1920s, and reached 30 per cent as the great depression began to bite in 1931. It did not fall below that level until the second World War.

The linen industry, most of whose workers were women, was very badly hit. In the war the industry supplied heavy linen for uniforms, tents, and aircraft wings, but with peace the demand for these disappeared. Changes in women's fashions in the 1920s also cut the demand for finer linens. As a result, many linen mills closed and the number of workers fell from 74,000 in 1924 to 55,000 by 1930. Those who kept their jobs were forced to accept lower wages.

Shipbuilding was Belfast's greatest industry. It had grown by 6 per cent a year from 1900 to 1914. It expanded even faster during the war as ships were built to replace those destroyed by Germany's U-boats. But the boom ended in 1920. The war was over and a fall in world trade reduced the need for new ships. Production fell by an average of 1.7 per cent a year and the number of jobs declined.

Things got even worse in the depressed 1930s. The number of workers fell from 10,000 in 1930 to 1,500

The Harland and Wolff shipyard was the biggest employer in Northern Ireland in 1920, but the number of workers declined throughout the 1920s and 1930s

Courtesy: Ulster Museum

in 1932. No ship was launched in Belfast between December 1931 and May 1934 and Workman and Clarke, the smaller of the two shipbuilding firms, closed in 1935. Harland and Wolff survived only with government aid, until the threat of another war helped it recover in the late 1930s.

STATE INTERVENTION DURING THE DEPRESSION

As in the south, the Northern Ireland government did not intervene in industry in the 1920s, but that attitude changed with the depression.

To preserve what jobs remained, the Minister for Commerce gave grants, tax remission and interest-free loans to businesses. In 1929 he set up the **Ulster Industrial Development Association** to attract new industries. The government offered loans to build ships and tried to encourage the linen industry to develop new textiles. In 1937 an aircraft building industry was started by Short and Harland with government aid.

THE RESULTS OF THE DEPRESSION

The poor of both communities suffered during the depression. In the early 1930s, 36 per cent of the population were living below the poverty line. The wages of people with work were forced down and welfare payments to unemployed workers were

pitifully small. In Belfast a married man with one child received 12 shillings a week. That was about half of what was needed for bare survival and about half the rate paid in other UK cities.

Even that pathetic amount ceased after a person had been out of work for some time. Then he or she had to apply for 'outdoor relief'. It consisted of handouts of food or vouchers to particular grocery shops. Outdoor relief was not a right. It was granted only after the unemployed people had been subjected to humiliating questions about their possessions and their search for work. This 'means-testing' could easily be used to discriminate against political opponents.

These conditions produced rumbles of discontent, even from unionists. In 1932 there were riots in both Catholic and Protestant areas in protest at the outdoor relief system. They were mainly organised by people interested in communism.

The riots and the possibility that Protestant and Catholic workers might unite in protest, horrified unionist leaders. They increased the outdoor relief payments and called on employers to give jobs to Protestants.

Conditions for Protestant workers improved a little and the old pattern of sectarian strife re-asserted itself. In 1935 Belfast saw its worst sectarian riots since 1922.

DISCRIMINATION IN JOBS

Discrimination in jobs existed in Northern Ireland from the beginning. In the 1920s Catholics who had transferred from the previous government, still worked in the civil service and police. Unionist politicians and councillors objected to that on the grounds that Catholics were disloyal. As these Catholics retired, few came forward to replace them and those who did found it hard to get a promotion.

Craig, who promised in 1920 that his government would treat Catholics fairly, did nothing to stop this development. Dawson Bates never even tried. It was reported that, when he heard that there was only one Catholic in his ministry, who worked as a telephonist, he refused to use the phone.

THE NEED TO REFORM EDUCATION

Education was an area in which sectarian prejudices were easily aroused. All the Churches wanted to control the schools their young people went to and what they learned in them. In the 19th century, the clergy of the various Churches had become the managers of primary schools, though the taxpayers paid the running costs. They would fiercely resist any attempt to change this system.

In 1921, Craig appointed **Lord Londonderry** as his Minister for Education. A liberal man, he wanted to raise educational standards generally without reference to religion. He set up a committee to enquire into the existing system. Catholics, who were still refusing to recognise the Northern Ireland government, boycotted it. The committee found that the old education system was not working. Schools were small, poorly maintained and inefficient. There were also too few of them. In Belfast, for example, there were no primary school places for 12,000 children.

THE 1923 EDUCATION ACT

Acting on the committee's advice, Lord Londonderry brought in an **Education Act** in 1923. It contained a new way of managing and funding primary schools:

- Control of primary schools would be **transferred from the clergy to committees** consisting of four members appointed by the clergy and two by local councils.
- **Transferred schools** would get state grants for all building and repairs. Schools that refused to transfer would only get a proportion of the cost of these services.
- Transferred schools would be open to children of all religions, and religious education would only take place outside school hours.
- Teachers in transferred schools would be appointed by the committees. They must not consider the teacher's religion when making the appointment.

PROTESTANTS CAPTURE THE TRANSFERRED SCHOOL SYSTEM

Both Catholic and Protestant clergy objected to these proposals:

- Catholic bishops refused to let their schools transfer to the committee system, even though this meant less money for them.
- Protestant clergy, who disliked the proposal as much as Catholic priests, then felt able to transfer their schools since no Catholics were involved. After that they campaigned to have more control over the transferred schools. The Unionist Party accepted their demands. In 1925 and 1930 they amended the Education Act to give Protestant clergy control of the appointment of teachers and to permit the reading of the Bible in school hours. After that the transferred schools became, in practice if not in law, Protestant schools.

The result was that the Protestant Churches captured the state-funded transferred schools and shaped the system to suit themselves. Catholics were left with schools that were less well funded than those of the Protestant community and a strong sense of grievance.

SECOND-LEVEL EDUCATION

Most second-level schools were privately owned and controlled by the churches. After 1923, the state paid salaries to teachers in these schools provided they were properly qualified. It also gave grants to build more schools and set up a new examination system. Between 1923 and 1938 government spending on second-level education rose from £51,000 to £194,000, while the number of pupils who stayed on in school after fourteen doubled.

QUESTIONS

1 How much control did the Northern Ireland government have over its own economy?

2 How important was agriculture in the northern economy?

3 What were the North's main industries and how were they affected by the economic depression of the 1930s?

4 How did the depression affect working people in the north?

5 What steps did the northern government take to ease the impact of the depression on industry and workers?

6 Explain what is meant by 'discrimination'. Give two examples of discrimination in Northern Ireland between 1921 and 1939.

7 Describe the attempt to reform education and explain why the attempt failed.

LEAVING CERTIFICATE QUESTIONS

Higher Level

1 Why were unionists opposed to Home Rule for Ireland? Explain how Northern Ireland came to be established in 1921.

2 What part did Sir James Craig play in the foundation of Northern Ireland between 1912 and 1925?

3 Describe the part played by Sir James Craig (Lord Craigavon) as first Prime Minister of Northern Ireland from 1921 to 1940.

4 What were the main political and economic developments in Northern Ireland between 1921 and 1939?

Ordinary Level

A Look at the election poster on page 167.
1 Who was 'Carson'?

2 How did he 'save Ulster for the Empire'?

3 What position did 'Craigavon' hold from 1921 to 1940?

4 Which party produced this poster and how did it do in the election?

B Write a paragraph on **one** of the following:
1 Richard Dawson Bates and elections in Northern Ireland.

2 The Orange Order.

C Answer **one** of the following questions:
1 What was the Boundary Commission and why was its report never published?

2 What were the main economic and social problems that the Northern government faced in the 1920s and 1930s?

11 The Impact of the Second World War on Ireland, North and South

11.1

PREPARING FOR NEUTRALITY

DE VALERA AND THE COMING OF WAR

Europe was peaceful in the 1920s but in the 1930s the aggressive policies of the Italian and German fascist dictators threatened another war. De Valera, like the leaders of other small countries, hoped that the League of Nations could keep the peace. He loyally supported its policies over Ethiopia and Spain, while making it clear that Ireland intended to remain neutral if war did come.

De Valera reviewing soldiers in the Irish army during the Emergency

During the Munich Crisis in 1938 de Valera backed Neville Chamberlain's attempt to avoid war by appeasing Hitler. But in March 1939 Hitler broke the Munich Agreement and invaded Czechoslovakia. After that war seemed unavoidable. Ireland, like other countries, had to decide what to do in its own interests.

WHY CHOOSE NEUTRALITY?

Most Irish people wanted to remain neutral. There were several reasons for that:

- ◉ Choosing to be neutral when Britain went to war was the clearest possible proof of Irish independence.
- ◉ De Valera told Chamberlain that partition was the main reason why Ireland would not join in a war on the side of the British.
- ◉ While very few Irish people supported the Nazis, many still remembered the Black and Tans and resented partition. These things made them anti-British. On the other hand, there were many others who still identified with Britain or supported it against Germany. In this situation, neutrality was the policy that least divided Irish people.

- In 1939 everyone expected that cities would be bombed and poison gas used against civilians. Neutrality seemed a good way to avoid the suffering that would cause.
- There were a few who thought this was cowardly. Ireland, they argued, should join in the fight against the evils of Nazism. But that was never a popular view. As the Secretary of the Department of External Affairs wrote in 1941:

> 'small nations like Ireland do not and cannot assume a role of defenders of just causes except their own ... Existence of our own people comes before all other considerations ... no government has the right to court certain destruction for its people; they have to take the only chance of survival and stay out.'
> (D. Keogh, *Ireland and Europe*, Dublin 1988, p. 118)

Ireland was not alone in hoping to stay out of the war. In 1939 other small European nations, like Norway, Denmark, the Netherlands, Switzerland, Portugal and Belgium, made the same choice. So did the United States. Ireland was one of the few lucky enough to keep out of the fighting to the end.

PREPARING FOR NEUTRALITY

Neutrality might be popular, but would it be possible? The 1938 Anglo-Irish Agreement that gave the Treaty ports to Ireland made it easier. As part of that deal de Valera had assured Chamberlain that he would never allow Ireland to be used as the base for an attack on Britain. But would the British be content with that?

And if Britain or Germany invaded, could the country defend itself? Other neutral countries had strong armies but in 1939 Ireland was virtually unarmed. The army only had 7,000 men, a few out-of-date aircraft and armoured cars and four anti-aircraft guns.

Seán MacEntee and J.J. McElligott in the Department of Finance had turned a deaf ear to the army's pleas for money to buy modern equipment. On the eve of war, they finally gave a small sum. But by then Britain needed all the arms it produced to defend itself and American arms were too expensive to buy more than a small quantity of rifles.

THE IRA'S THREAT TO NEUTRALITY

The biggest threat to neutrality came from the IRA. In 1938 **Seán Russell** became its Chief-of-Staff. He wanted to end partition and, like the leaders of 1916, saw an opportunity in war between Britain and Germany. He made contact with the Germans and got funds from them.

In January 1939 the IRA issued an ultimatum to the British government demanding that they leave Northern Ireland. When there was no answer, they set off bombs in London and other places. One explosion in Coventry in August killed five people. The police soon rounded up IRA members, among them the sixteen-year-old Brendan Behan. Two men were hanged for their part in the Coventry explosion and others imprisoned. The only positive result of the fiasco was Behan's account of his prison experiences in *Borstal Boy*.

THE OFFENCES AGAINST THE STATE ACT

De Valera was horrified by the IRA bombs. They undermined the good relations he had developed with Chamberlain and MacDonald during the negotiations for the Anglo-Irish Agreements. Worse still, the IRA campaign threatened neutrality. Their bombs might give the British an excuse to invade Ireland. He decided he had to take action.

In June 1939, the Dáil passed the **Offences Against the State Act**. It gave the Gardaí power to hold suspects for questioning and allowed the government to intern suspected IRA members without trial.

If the IRA had waited till the war began, their bombing campaign would have been a bigger threat to neutrality. Fortunately they started too soon and de Valera's vigorous response greatly undermined their ability to do more damage to relations between Britain and Ireland.

DECLARING NEUTRALITY

On 1 September 1939, Germany invaded Poland. Britain issued an ultimatum demanding that they withdraw and, when they did not, declared war on 3 September.

On 2 September, de Valera summoned the Dáil and said that Ireland would remain neutral. The Dáil then declared a **State of Emergency**. This gave the Government extensive powers to deal with any problems that might arise in the course of the war. From then until May 1945 the country was neutral in the midst of war and the 'Emergency' affected every facet of people's daily lives.

QUESTIONS

1. How in the 1930s did de Valera hope peace could be preserved? Which incident made it clear that war was inevitable?

2. Give four reasons why Irish people favoured neutrality. Which one do you think mattered most? Give reasons for your answer.

3. How well was Ireland prepared to defend itself against an invasion in 1939? Why were the preparations so inadequate?

4. Outline the way in which the IRA threatened Irish neutrality in 1939. How did de Valera deal with them?

11.2
DEALING WITH THE BELLIGERENTS

DE VALERA IN CONTROL

As a small country with an inadequate defence force, Ireland clearly had little chance of resisting invasion. Remaining neutral, therefore, would depend more on diplomacy and the needs of the big powers than on the strength of its arms.

Being Foreign Minister as well as Taoiseach, de Valera handled this aspect of neutrality himself. He usually acted alone, seldom discussing problems with anyone, even other Fianna Fáil leaders. The only person he consulted frequently was **Joseph Walshe**, the Secretary of the Department of External Affairs. In other countries, coalition governments were formed so that all parties could contribute to the war effort. But in Ireland the wounds of the Civil War went too deep for this to happen. De Valera did set up an all-party Conference on Defence, but it had no power.

DIPLOMATIC LINKS

To keep in touch with the belligerent countries, de Valera relied on Irish diplomats abroad and foreign diplomats in Dublin.

Ireland had diplomatic representatives in Britain, Germany, Italy, Spain, France and the United States all through the war. They passed on de Valera's views to their host governments and reported back to Dublin on developments they heard about and the gossip they picked up. Almost from the start the British broke the code in which their communications were sent and made use of the information they supplied.

Foreign diplomats in Dublin were even more important to de Valera. They told him what their governments wanted and through them he sent messages back. The most important were the representatives of Britain, Germany and the United States.

● **Sir John Maffey, the British representative**
Because of the disagreements between them, the

British did not send diplomats to Ireland in the 1930s. But when war began they hurriedly appointed **Sir John Maffey**, as 'United Kingdom representative for Éire'. An experienced diplomat who knew Ireland, he soon developed a good working relationship with de Valera. While always putting over the British point of view, he understood that neutrality was popular in Ireland and that the Irish government was co-operating as much as it could with the British.

● Edouard Hempel, the German representative

From 1938 the German minister in Dublin was **Edouard Hempel**. He was a career diplomat and not a Nazi. Before the war began, de Valera met him and explained that Ireland depended on trade with Britain and that Britain could easily invade us if its interests were threatened. This, he told Hempel, *'rendered it inevitable for the Irish government to show a certain consideration for Britain'* (M. Bromage: *Churchill and Ireland*, Indiana 1964, p. 134). Hempel understood this position. Throughout the war his reports to Berlin urged his government to avoid any action that would justify a British invasion of Ireland.

● David Gray, the American representative

The American government appointed **David Gray** as their representative in Dublin in 1940. Then over seventy, he was related to President Roosevelt's wife and had good personal contacts with the President. In Ireland he mixed mainly with an Anglo-Irish set who were very pro-British. So he did not understand how popular neutrality was or how impossible it would be for de Valera to abandon it.

Gray believed that it was vital for Ireland that Hitler be defeated. At first he accepted that neutrality was due to partition and the memory of British rule. But once the United States entered the war, he assumed that Ireland would join on their side. When they did not, he blamed de Valera whom he disliked and distrusted and urged Roosevelt to put pressure on him to force Ireland to join the allies.

SEPTEMBER 1939–MAY 1940: A 'PHONEY WAR'

When war began everyone assumed that, as in the first World War, most of the fighting would be on the border of France and Germany. But when the winter passed without any significant action in western Europe, people began to speak of a 'phoney war'.

The main activity was in the Atlantic where German U-boats attacked British ships. On 3 September 1939 a liner was torpedoed off the Donegal coast with a loss of 112 lives, and a further twenty-eight ships were lost in the following two weeks. The Royal Navy organised armed convoys to protect them and the British asked de Valera to let them use the Treaty ports. He refused, but indicated that he would not protest if British planes from Northern Ireland flew over Donegal on anti-submarine patrols off the Irish coast.

The 'phoney war' created a false sense of security. The government did little to build up stocks of food or other supplies. The army had called up reserves and reached 19,000 men late in 1939. But McElligott objected to the cost and 5,000 had been let go by May 1940.

MAY 1940: WAR COMES CLOSE

This complacency was shattered in April 1940. In quick succession, the German army overran the neutral states of Denmark, Norway, the Netherlands and Belgium. It entered France, drove back the French and British armies and on 20 May trapped a defeated British army at Dunkirk. Would the Nazis invade Ireland next, as a first step to an invasion of Britain?

NEUTRALITY UNDER THREAT

On 10 May, in the midst of the crisis, **Winston Churchill** replaced Chamberlain as British Prime Minister. He had opposed the handover of the Treaty ports in 1938 and since the war began had wanted Britain to retake them. De Valera now faced two threats to neutrality: an invasion by the Germans on the way to Britain or a British invasion to forestall them.

Winston Churchill became Prime Minister of Britain in 1940

On 23 May de Valera sent army officers to London to discuss the situation. The British warned that a German invasion of Ireland was a strong possibility. The two sides agreed that if the Germans came de Valera would invite the British army in to help repel them. The British wanted to go in before the Germans landed but de Valera insisted that they must only come in response to an invitation from him.

JUNE 1940: AN OFFER OF UNITY

In June the French surrendered to Hitler. The Germans now controlled most of continental Europe. Britain stood alone, under heavy attack from sea and air. The ships that carried food and war supplies through the submarine-infested waters of the Atlantic were now vital to its survival. The Royal Navy which protected them had to travel an extra 200 miles because they did not have the use of Berehaven and Cobh.

Churchill considered seizing the ports but other British ministers thought this would cause more problems than it would solve. In the end he sent Malcolm MacDonald to Dublin. He knew de Valera well from their talks in the 1930s (see page 125).

In Dublin, MacDonald made a dramatic offer. If de Valera entered the war and let the Royal Navy use the ports, Britain would declare in favour of the principle of a united Ireland and set up a joint committee of representatives from the Northern and Southern governments to work out the practical details. But de Valera turned down the offer. There were several reasons for this:

- At that moment it seemed that Britain was losing the war, so Ireland could gain little by joining the losers and offending the winners.
- De Valera did not think the unionists would agree to unity or that the British would be able to keep their promise after the war.
- De Valera remembered what had happened to Redmond who had supported Britain whole-heartedly in the last war. It was a fate he was determined to avoid.

BRITAIN DECIDES AGAINST INVASION

Reluctantly the British accepted de Valera's decision. Churchill, who convinced himself that the Irish were helping the Germans, wanted to invade but finally had to give up the idea.

- His generals warned him that holding a hostile Ireland would tie up too many of their troops.
- A friendly neutral would be more useful to the British war effort and an Irish government would be better at dealing with German spies and the IRA.
- The British also feared the impact an invasion of Ireland would have on public opinion in the United States and Commonwealth countries like Canada and Australia.

But Churchill did not let de Valera know about this decision. He tried to make life hard for the Irish by limiting the supplies they could buy from Britain and by refusing to sell arms to the Irish army. Not understanding how popular neutrality was, he thought hardship might induce the Irish to get rid of de Valera and join the war. In fact his policy had the opposite effect. Irish people blamed shortages on Britain, not on de Valera's government.

EXPANDING THE ARMY

The threat of invasion from one side or the other led to a desperate attempt to build up the defence forces. After an appeal for recruits, the army went up to 42,000 men. A voluntary Local Defence Force (LDF) was set up to supplement it and it soon had

148,000 men. A marine service was started, and fishermen and amateur yachtsmen formed a coastal patrol to watch for signs of invasion.

But these forces were very ill-equipped. Attempts to buy arms in Britain were blocked by Churchill, partly in case they fell into German hands, partly to punish de Valera. De Valera sent **Frank Aiken**, the Minister for Co-ordination of Defence Measures, to buy arms in the United States in 1941. But Aiken quarrelled with Roosevelt, who was very pro-British and hostile to Irish neutrality, and came home empty-handed.

In the spring of 1941 there were new fears of an invasion, and co-operation between the Irish and British armies increased. The British sold more arms to the Irish and senior officers from both forces drew up plans for joint action if the Nazis came. But in June, Hitler invaded the Soviet Union. After that a Nazi invasion became unlikely. In the army, boredom, combined with low pay, made some soldiers restless. A substantial number deserted, with most of them quietly crossing the border to seek better pay and more excitement with the British forces.

UNITED STATES PRESSURE

After the Japanese attacked Pearl Harbor in December 1941 the United States finally entered the war. Churchill renewed his offer of unity, but it was so vaguely phrased that de Valera ignored it. In 1942 American troops began arriving in Northern Ireland. De Valera protested about that to Roosevelt but that was merely a gesture, intended to assure the Irish public that the country was still neutral.

Americans were more hostile to Irish neutrality than the British. David Gray fed Roosevelt stories about German spies in Ireland and Irish support for the Nazis. He urged the American government to put pressure on the Irish economy.

A PRO-ALLIED NEUTRALITY

Throughout the war, de Valera was never sure that the Allies would not invade. With the British and later the American armies in Northern Ireland it would have been easy. To make it unnecessary he made sure that Irish neutrality was heavily biased towards the Allies:

- Ireland sold large quantities of food to Britain, which helped to keep the country fed throughout the war.
- De Valera's government turned a blind eye as about 40,000 people from the South went to serve in the British forces.
- About 120,000 men and women went to work in British factories and building sites, making up for the labour shortage there.
- Weather reports collected around Ireland were secretly transmitted to the Allies.
- RAF planes were allowed to overfly Irish air space to reach the Atlantic on submarine patrols and sea rescue missions.
- Allied sailors and airmen who landed in Ireland were allowed to slip away to Northern Ireland, while Germans were interned.
- The army intelligence unit, G2, and the Garda Special Branch shared information they gathered on German activities with British and American intelligence networks. They also made a significant contribution to breaking German codes.
- From 1943 Irish diplomats on the Continent were asked to gather information which was then passed to the United States.
- Irish army officers co-operated in every way possible with their Allied counterparts. In 1945 the Pentagon recommended that three senior Irish army officers be given the American Legion of Merit for *'exceptionally meritorious and outstanding services to the US'*. (R. Fanning *Independent Ireland*, Dublin 1982, p. 124) The proposal was only dropped when it was pointed out that this would embarrass the Irish government.

This close co-operation with the Allies was kept very secret. Even Gray and Maffey and most members of the Allied governments were unaware of what was going on. On the surface, Ireland was strictly neutral to the end.

THE GERMANS AND IRISH NEUTRALITY

Irish neutrality suited the Germans since it deprived the British of the use of the Treaty ports.

Hempel was told to encourage it by suggesting that a German victory would mean the end of partition. He even held talks with some representatives of the nationalist community in Northern Ireland. The Germans also offered to supply the Irish army with captured British arms, an offer which de Valera carefully ignored.

In 1940 a German invasion seemed a real possibility. De Valera's greatest fear was that they might land in Northern Ireland, posing as liberators of the nationalists. If that happened, what could his government do? Contacts between the Nazis and the IRA gave substance to this fear.

77

DEAD MEN WILL HAUNT COSGRAVE TO HIS GRAVE.

HOW MANY WILL HAUNT DE VALERA?

The present intention is to begin by allowing six Irish patriots to die on Hunger-Strike rather than allow him to treat them as criminals.

AT ENGLAND'S WORD!

An IRA propaganda leaflet.

1   What point is it making?
2   Why did de Valera allow the hunger strikers to die?
3   Why do you think this is forgotten today?

THE IRA AND NAZI GERMANY

When the war began the IRA leader, Seán Russell, went from the United States to Germany. He hoped to persuade the Germans to send troops and arms to Ireland. The Germans, who overestimated the strength of the IRA, were interested. In 1940 they sent Russell to Ireland in a submarine, possibly to organise an invasion of Northern Ireland or to receive an arms shipment, but he died on the way.

In 1940 and 1941 several German agents were parachuted into Ireland. Most were quickly rounded up by the Gardaí or G2. The only one who evaded capture for a time was **Hermann Goertz**. He arrived in May 1940 to make contact with the IRA. He found them disorganised, quarrelling and under constant pressure from the Gardaí. Goertz lost his radio when he landed and had great difficulty making contact with Germany. He was finally arrested in December 1941.

DE VALERA AND THE IRA

In December 1939 the IRA raided the Magazine Fort in Phoenix Park where the Irish army kept most of its armaments and cleaned it out. This spurred de Valera to take action against them. The arms were recovered and an internment camp for IRA men was opened on the Curragh.

Only when German spies arrived did the government realise that IRA leaders were talking

to the Germans. It was a nasty shock and de Valera responded ruthlessly. Active republicans were rounded up and about 500 spent the war interned in the Curragh. Others were tried and given prison sentences. Six men were hanged for murdering Gardaí and three who went on hunger strike were allowed to die.

They got little public sympathy. Neutrality was popular and press censorship was too strict to allow much information about these events to emerge. By 1943, with many of their members interned both north and south of the border, the IRA had almost ceased to exist.

HEMPEL'S RADIO CONFISCATED

Hempel disapproved of German involvement with the IRA. He confined himself to his diplomatic duties, reporting to Berlin on developments in Ireland and passing German views to de Valera.

When the threat of invasion receded in 1942, the Irish Government shut down his radio transmitter and they confiscated it in 1943. That significantly reduced his ability to contact Germany. This was done mainly to reassure the British and Americans who insisted that information useful to the German army was leaking through Dublin. In fact no evidence to support this claim has appeared since the war. Hempel seems not to have had any more than stray bits of gossip, much of it from careless talk by British soldiers on leave in Dublin.

QUESTIONS

1 Why was it necessary for de Valera to keep in contact with the belligerent countries during the war? How did he do so?

2 Name and describe the representatives of Britain, Germany and the United States in Dublin during the war.

3 In May/June 1940 Ireland faced invasion. Describe events in Europe and Britain which made this likely.

4 When and why did Winston Churchill become Prime Minister? Describe his attitude to Ireland and say how he dealt with de Valera in May 1940.

5 Why did de Valera turn down Churchill's offer of Irish unity in return for Ireland entering the war? Do you think he was right? Explain your answer.

6 Describe the measures taken to prepare for an invasion in 1940.

7 What was the attitude of the Germans to Irish neutrality? Describe their links with the IRA and their attempts to introduce spies into Ireland.

8 List and describe the measures which the Government took to deal with the IRA and the possibility of information leaking from Ireland to the Nazis.

9 Irish neutrality was heavily biased towards the Allies. Explain the reasons for that and describe five ways in which this was shown.

11.3
IMPACT OF WORLD WAR II ON SOCIETY AND ECONOMY

EMERGENCY POWERS

When the Dáil accepted de Valera's declaration of neutrality on 2 September 1939 it also declared a State of Emergency. This gave the government almost dictatorial powers. It could:

- Regulate the lives of citizens.
- Control the economy.
- Take any steps it felt necessary to protect the safety of the state and its people.

The Government retained and used these powers until May 1945 when the war in Europe came to an end.

LEMASS AS MINISTER FOR SUPPLIES

The war was bound to affect the Irish economy. The country had to import many of the things it needed and in 1939, 95 per cent of imports came via Britain or in British-owned ships. De Valera appointed Seán Lemass as Minister for Supplies, to manage the distribution of fuel, food and other scarce resources. The Dáil gave him power to tell farmers what to grow, to ration supplies of scarce commodities and to punish people engaged in black-marketing.

THE WAR AFFECTS THE ECONOMY

The economic impact of the war was limited until the summer of 1940. After France fell, Britain stood alone against a Nazi-controlled continent. To starve it into submission, German submarines sank British ships. Britain, finding it hard enough to supply its own needs, was in no mood to carry goods for neutral Ireland.

This reduced imports and the effects were soon felt throughout the Irish economy:

- The quantity of fertiliser imported fell from 89,000 tons in 1939 to 7,000 tons in 1941 and to nil in 1942. This affected the fertility of the soil and the farmers' capacity to grow food.
- Imports of maize for animal feed fell in the same time from 400,000 tons to 50,000 to nil. This meant that home-grown grain had to be diverted into animal feed.

- By 1943, the country was getting only 25 per cent of the petrol it needed, 16 per cent of its gas coal and no domestic coal. These fuel shortages hit both industrial and domestic users.
- Many of the new industries set up in the 1930s depended on imported raw materials and parts. Now they were unobtainable. The factories went on short time or closed altogether.

THE IRISH SHIPPING COMPANY

Lemass set up the **Irish Shipping Company** to try to bring in goods the British would no longer sell to the Irish. The company bought eight ships, most of them old, and chartered five more. Manned by brave crews, they kept a vital trickle of supplies coming through.

FEEDING THE PEOPLE

Keeping the people fed was the top priority. Self-sufficiency in food had seemed an unrealistic dream in the 1930s, but now it became necessary for survival. In 1940 Lemass ordered every farmer to till one-eighth of his land. This was raised to three-eighths in 1944. The acreage of wheat rose from 250,000 acres in 1939 to 660,000 in 1945. But without imported fertilisers, the land was less productive and the yield was lower than before.

" WHERE'S YOUR TEA CANISTER ? "

Shortages and rationing drove people to desperate measures, though it is unlikely that many went this far

Home-produced foodstuffs like bread, eggs, potatoes, meat and bacon remained available. Many people also grew vegetables and potatoes and kept chickens in their gardens. To make wheat supplies go as far as possible, Lemass ordered that bakers use wholemeal rather than the more wasteful white flour. This was very unpopular and having to eat brown bread was what many people remembered of war-time shortages.

Supplies of imported food were a bigger problem. Bananas and oranges disappeared during the war years and the small supplies of tea were rationed. Each person received two ounces of tea (later reduced to one ounce) per week. Sugar and clothes were also rationed.

FUEL SHORTAGES

Coal and oil, neither of which Ireland could produce, were a bigger problem than food. Coal was used to generate electricity, heat homes, cook food and power factories and trains. Gas made from coal was also used for cooking and heating in some towns and cities. Oil was essential for cars and buses.

Lemass limited the use of gas and electricity to a few hours every day. To save oil, he banned the use of private cars, though necessary services like buses, ambulances, doctors and the army still got petrol. People went back to using bicycles and even horses.

Lemass tried to replace coal with turf, the only native fuel supply. Country people had always used it for cooking and heating, but now townspeople had to use it too.

They were encouraged to go and cut turf for themselves, and voluntary turf-cutting campaigns were organised with people urged to get involved as a kind of national service. It was also used to power trains. But turf did not generate a lot of heat and a turf-burning train could take up to twelve hours to travel from Dublin to Cork.

SOCIAL EFFECTS OF THE WAR

Shortages of fuel and raw materials undermined some of the new industries set up in the 1930s.

Some closed, others went on short-time working. Unemployment rose while in Britain there was a labour shortage. As a result emigration to Britain increased. On average 18,000 people went each year of the war to join the British armed forces, work in munitions factories or in the building industry repairing bomb damage.

Those who stayed at home suffered a fall in living standards. Prices rose by 70 per cent between 1939 and 1945 but a **Wages Standstill Order** kept wage increases to 13 per cent. The biggest price increases were for food and fuel. That hit poorly-paid workers and people on social welfare especially hard. With less to eat and living in cold damp homes, they suffered from diseases caused by poverty like TB or death in childbirth. These diseases had declined since the 1920s; in the 1940s they increased again.

IRISH FARMERS AND THE BRITISH MARKET

The Germans attempted to starve Britain into submission by torpedoing ships carrying food supplies. This increased the British demand for Irish food which Irish farmers and the Irish government did their best to supply.

The popular British view was that the Irish did well out of this, but that was wrong. The British government strictly controlled the price paid for imported food and protected the British farmers

Courtesy: Father Browne Collection

With private cars banned, old horse-drawn vehicles like this side car were brought back into use

from competition. In 1944 food prices in Britain were lower than they had been in 1939. Irish farmers also suffered from an outbreak of foot-and-mouth disease in 1941 that restricted cattle exports for a time.

THE ECONOMIC IMPACT OF THE WAR

The war damaged the Irish economy but not nearly as much as it damaged the economies of countries which were at war:

- Agricultural exports to Britain earned money for the country but there were few imports available to spend it on. As a result, the country built up a healthy balance of payments surplus. In 1944 external reserves (savings) stood at £103 million, compared with £65 million in 1939.

- Irish industry had suffered badly from shortages of fuel and raw materials but at least it was not bombed out of existence like the industry in so many countries. When times returned to normal, Irish industry was ready to resume work.

CENSORSHIP

Apart from rationing, the most noticeable effect of the war was censorship. The Government used its emergency powers to impose a strict control over all information. Irish censorship was tighter than in any other neutral country:

- The censor stopped anyone publishing any opinion which might seem to favour one side over the other. He stopped newspapers from carrying comments on the progress of the war. Even death notices for Irish people killed in it were banned. Once he suppressed a bishop's pastoral that contained anti-Nazi views.

- He read private letters and suppressed those he disapproved of, sometimes for reasons that had nothing to do with the war.

- Films, almost all of which came from Britain or the United States, were heavily cut or banned if they dealt with the war.

- On Radio Éireann, the news consisted of dispatches from the Allies and the Axis powers, read without any comment. Even the word 'war' was avoided and replaced by the word 'emergency'.

- All public weather forecasts were stopped in

case they helped the planes or ships of either combatant. Secretly the Government continued to collect weather information and hand it to the Allies.

THE IMPACT OF CENSORSHIP

The heavy censorship of the Irish media limited people's knowledge of developments in the war. Some British newspapers were available and people with radios could listen to the BBC and broadcasts from the Continent. From these it was possible to get some idea of what was happening.

But not everyone had radios or could buy foreign papers. People were also sceptical about British reports of German atrocities, remembering the black propaganda they had spread during the War of Independence. It was only when the war ended and newsreels of the death camps could be shown that people became conscious of the full horror of the Nazi regime.

ESCAPING THE BOMBS

Despite rationing, economic hardship and censorship, neutrality remained popular. People knew it protected them from the suffering war brought to civilian populations elsewhere. The bombing of Belfast in May 1941 (see pages 190–191) was a local example of this. A few German bombs fell on the South but only one did serious damage. It was dropped on the North Strand in Dublin, killing twenty-seven people on 30 May 1941. This was almost certainly the result of a mistake by the bomb crew, though at the time some people suggested that the Germans did it deliberately to show the cost of siding with Britain.

NEUTRALITY AND THE POLITICAL PARTIES

All political parties supported neutrality. Only one politician, James Dillon, Vice-President of Fine Gael, suggested that Ireland should go to war. But

North Strand bombing, May 1941

his call was unpopular and Cosgrave forced him to resign from the party.

Agreement over neutrality helped to heal some of the wounds left by the Civil War. Leading members of Fianna Fáil and Fine Gael appeared together on platforms appealing for people to join the army. But after Hitler invaded the Soviet Union in 1941, the fear of invasion receded and normal political rivalries resumed.

THE 1943 ELECTION

The first election of the war was held in 1943. By then, the war had moved far away to Russia, north Africa and Italy. Neutrality seemed safe but the economic and social effects of the war were painful enough to make the government unpopular. Fianna Fáil lost ten seats. But Fine Gael failed to profit from Fianna Fáil's loss, perhaps because people saw it as pro-British. It lost fifteen seats and seemed on the way to extinction. The main gainers were the Labour Party and a newly established farmers party, Clann na Talmhan (Table A).

Table A

Results of the 1943 election (1938 results in brackets)					
Fianna Fáil	Fine Gael	Labour	Clann na Talmhan	Independents	Total seats
67 (77)	32 (45)	17 (9)	14 (–)	8 (7)	138

1943–45: THE LAST YEARS OF THE WAR

After America joined in the war in 1941, the pressure on Ireland to join the Allies increased. When de Valera still refused, hostility to Irish neutrality grew. British newspapers ran stories about German spies operating freely in Dublin and German submarines being welcomed and supplied along the west coast. David Gray, who hated de Valera and fiercely opposed Irish neutrality, reported these rumours to Roosevelt.

The British and American intelligence agencies sent spies to Ireland to check them out. They reported that G2 was very efficient in tracing and stopping any attempt at spying by the Germans. Unknown to the Allied spies, G2 identified them too, but, knowing they would find nothing damaging to report, left them alone. As a result the British and American military were quite happy with Irish neutrality.

THE 'AMERICAN NOTE' AND THE 1944 ELECTION

This did not satisfy Gray. Early in 1944 plans for the Normandy landings were being completed. Gray suggested to Roosevelt that, to prevent any hint of them leaking out, the Allies should demand the closure of the German and Japanese missions in Dublin. Roosevelt agreed.

In February Gray presented an 'American note' with this demand to de Valera. *'Of course the answer will be no,'* de Valera told him. *'As long as I am here, it will be no.'* The Allies then imposed a total blackout on communications out of Ireland and a ban on travel to and from Britain until after D-Day.

De Valera seized the chance to increase support for Fianna Fáil. He publicised the threat to neutrality and called a snap election. Fianna Fáil regained nine of the ten seats it lost the year before.

Fine Gael still declined but the real losers were the Labour Party. A bitter quarrel had erupted between James Larkin who had won a seat in 1943 and the leader of the Transport Union, William O'Brien. Claiming that Larkin was a communist, O'Brien broke away and set up his own National Labour Party. As a result, Labour lost five of the seats it had won the year before (Table B).

DE VALERA'S VISIT TO HEMPEL

By then it was clear that the Allies were winning. Neutrality no longer had any advantages and other neutral countries began to make their peace with the victorious Allies. But to the end, de Valera was stubbornly determined to appear even-handed. On 12 April, when the United States president, Franklin Roosevelt, died, he called formally on David Gray to express his regrets. On 30 April, against the advice of his officials, he paid a similar call on Hempel to express regret at the death of the German head of state, Adolf Hitler.

This was the most serious mistake de Valera made in his handling of neutrality. While his wartime co-operation with the Allies was unknown to almost everyone, the image of him expressing sympathy for Hitler's death spread far and wide. It gave credit to the accusations that had appeared in the British and American papers that the Irish were pro-Nazi.

THE EFFECTS OF NEUTRALITY

At home, de Valera's reputation was saved by an attack from his old opponent, Winston Churchill. In a victory broadcast, Churchill said that during the most difficult part of the war:

> *'owing to the action of Mr de Valera, so much at variance with the temper and instinct of thousands of Southern Irishmen who hastened to the battle-front to prove their ancient valour,*

Table B

	Results of the 1944 election (1943 results in brackets)						
Fianna Fáil	Fine Gael	Labour	Clann na Talmhan	Independents	National Labour	Total seats	
76 (67)	30 (32)	8 (17)	11 (14)	9 (8)	4 (–)	138	

...THAT WAS AN TAOISEACH, EAMONN DE VALERA

June, 1945

" LISTEN AND LEARN "

'Listen and Learn' was the name of a well-known radio show. Why do you think the cartoonist used it for this cartoon, which appeared after de Valera's radio broadcast in May 1945?

the approaches which the southern Irish ports and airfields could so easily have guarded, were closed by the hostile aircraft and U-boats.

This was indeed a deadly moment in our life and if it had not been for the loyalty and friendship of Northern Ireland, we should have been forced to come to close quarters with Mr de Valera or perish forever from the earth. However, with a restraint and poise to which, I say, history will find few parallels, His Majesty's Government never laid a violent hand upon them, though at times it would have been quite easy and quite natural, and we left the de Valera government to frolic with the Germans and later with the Japanese to their heart's content.'
(T.P. Coogan, *De Valera*, London 1993, p. 611)

De Valera's reply, a few days later, was dignified and restrained. He congratulated Churchill on not adding *'another horrid chapter to the already bloodstained record'* of Anglo-Irish relations and asked:

'could he not find in his heart the generosity to acknowledge that there is a small nation that stood alone, not for one year or two, but for several hundred years against aggression ... a

small nation that could never be got to accept defeat and has never surrendered her soul?'
(Longford and O'Neill: *De Valera*, London 1971, p. 414)

In Ireland, this speech touched a chord, even among de Valera's political enemies. At that moment he spoke for all parties. People were relieved that the war was over and proud that their small country had succeeded in remaining neutral against the pressure of powerful neighbours. The test that was neutrality had been successfully passed. Irish independence, conceded in the Treaty, was now beyond doubt.

WHY DID NEUTRALITY SUCCEED?

Many countries declared their neutrality in 1939, but few were still neutral in 1945. Why was Ireland one of them?

It was not due to the strength of the defence forces. Neither Germany nor the Allies would have had any difficulty conquering the country. The main reason, though few Irish people were willing to admit it, was geographical:

- Hitler was ruthless. He would not have hesitated to invade Ireland as he had invaded other, better-armed, neutrals. But Ireland was far away from Germany, on the other side of Britain. The Germans would have found it difficult to reach Ireland unless Britain fell, and it did not. Throughout the war the RAF and the Royal Navy patrolled the air and seas around Ireland and made it unlikely that a German landing could succeed.

- Britain and the United States, with troops in Northern Ireland, could have invaded easily. But they were democracies and their governments were restrained by public opinion. People in these countries would not have approved of invading a small neutral democracy unless the situation was desperate. Fortunately for Irish neutrality, it never was, as Churchill admitted in his speech.

- Another reason Britain and the United States never felt they had to invade was Northern Ireland. After the fall of France in 1940, most ships crossing the Atlantic to Britain went around to the north of Ireland rather than to the south. Bases in Northern Ireland were able to provide cover for them and therefore the need for bases in the south became less acute. It is the final irony that Irish neutrality survived because of the partition that de Valera hated so much.

QUESTIONS

1. What were the 'emergency powers' the Government got at the start of the war?

2. What job did de Valera give Seán Lemass in 1939? List four problems he faced and show how he solved them.

3. Explain what 'censorship' means and describe how it operated during the war.

4. How was Irish neutrality affected by America's entry into the war in 1941?

5. Outline the main political developments during the war years.

6. Why did Ireland succeed in remaining neutral when so many other neutral states did not?

11.4

NORTHERN IRELAND DURING WORLD WAR II

NORTHERN IRELAND ENTERS THE WAR

As part of the United Kingdom, Northern Ireland was involved in the war from the start. The Unionist government welcomed this because it gave them the opportunity to stress their loyalty to Britain in contrast to the neutrality of the Dublin government.

In spite of this, they did little to prepare for war. Craigavon was seventy and in poor health. He could only work for an hour or two a day. Most of his ministers were also elderly, having been in office since 1921. They were sure that Northern Ireland was too far from Germany to be in danger. At first the London government encouraged this view because it did not want to bear the cost of unnecessary defence measures in Belfast.

UNIONIST SHOCK AT CHURCHILL'S OFFER TO DE VALERA

As in the South, German successes in the spring of 1940 and the fall of France disturbed this complacency. A Nazi invasion threatened Britain and Ireland. But unionists were badly shaken when Churchill offered de Valera unity without consulting them (see page 232). Craigavon wrote to Churchill that he was:

'profoundly shocked and disgusted by your letter making suggestions so far reaching behind my back and without any pre-consultation with me. To such treachery to loyal Ulster I will never be a party.' (Thomas Hennessey, *A History of Northern Ireland*, 1998, p. 87)

But some unionists, including Sir Basil Brooke, the Minister for Agriculture, felt they might have to agree to unity if it was needed to save Britain from Hitler. They were relieved when de Valera turned the offer down.

CONSCRIPTION AND RECRUITMENT

When conscription was imposed in Britain in 1939, nationalists and the Catholic bishops protested against it being extended to Northern Ireland. In spite of Craigavon's objections, Chamberlain accepted their arguments. When war began, the Unionist government called on people to join the British forces but to their embarrassment, the response was slow. At first over 2,000 people a month joined up, but by the middle of 1940 that had fallen below 1,000 a month.

In the crisis of 1940, Craigavon again suggested conscription but Churchill decided against it. Craigavon then appointed one of his more energetic ministers, **Sir Basil Brooke**, to organise recruitment. It was an odd choice. Brooke, who was notorious for his sectarianism, was unlikely to attract Catholic recruits and he did not help by basing his recruitment drive around the Unionist Party branches.

Craigavon also agreed to set up a civil defence unit called the Local Defence Volunteers. But, fearing that nationalists might get arms or training through the LDV, he insisted that the B Specials form the basis of this new body. As a result very few members of the nationalist community became involved in civil defence.

In all, 38,000 men and women joined the British forces in Northern Ireland during the war. About half of them were southerners who crossed the border to sign up. It is also likely that many northerners joined up in Britain, but how many is not known.

NORTHERN NATIONALISTS AND THE WAR

Northern nationalists were ambivalent about the war. Unionists did not encourage them to become involved and many were inclined to see it as 'England's war' which had little to do with them. Southern neutrality inevitably encouraged this view. In 1939 nationalists in some areas in Belfast at first refused to observe the blackout and burned their gas masks.

A few nationalists, disillusioned with Fianna Fáil's inaction on partition, even hoped for a German victory. Hempel met some of them who asked for German protection. Although this attitude changed after the Germans bombed Belfast in 1941, nationalists never supported the war as wholeheartedly as unionists.

Nevertheless, many nationalists joined the British forces. The exact number is not known but it is likely that nationalists were over-represented because they had the highest unemployment rate and the fewest 'reserved' jobs. The only man from Northern Ireland to receive a VC, Britain's highest award for bravery, was James Maginnis, a Catholic from west Belfast who served in the Royal Navy.

THE NORTHERN IRA DURING THE WAR

The IRA revived in Northern Ireland in 1937 during protests against a visit by the newly crowned King George VI. Internment was imposed in 1939 after they set off bombs in Britain (see page 228). Over the next year up to 700 IRA men were locked away. But the IRA survived better in the north than in the south because it had more support among the nationalist community. In Belfast it managed to produce a newspaper and to broadcast on a secret radio transmitter, which the RUC never managed to find.

The IRA became more active in 1942 because of new leaders and the arrival of American troops. Throughout the spring and summer it killed five RUC members. After one killing, six IRA men were captured. All six were sentenced to death but the government listened to pleas for mercy and only one was executed.

Internment both North and South made it difficult for the IRA to remain active for long. When some interned IRA men staged a spectacular escape in the North and went to Donegal, the Gardaí arrested them and interned them in the Curragh. By the end of the war the IRA was seriously weakened.

A FAIRLY NORMAL LIFE

After the fall of France in 1940, fears of invasion increased. It seemed most likely the Germans would land in the undefended South and Britain stationed 100,000 troops in the North to be ready for them.

Apart from the presence of soldiers, the war made little difference to everyday life for the rest of 1940. Shopping took longer because of queues and some foods were unavailable. Food and fuel were rationed but cross-border smuggling reduced the shortages. Townspeople began to grow their own vegetables and keep chickens. There was a blackout to prevent German bombers from seeing where likely targets were but it was not strictly enforced. Visitors from Britain, where the Germans were bombing the cities, commented on how relaxed people in Northern Ireland were about the war.

J.M. ANDREWS, PRIME MINISTER, 1941–43

Craigavon died suddenly in November 1940, just as his government's lack of preparation began to arouse criticism. But his death changed little. The Unionist Party chose **J.M. Andrews** to replace him. He had been a cabinet minister since 1921 and was only months younger than Craigavon. Andrews appointed the same men as ministers, two of whom were Presbyterian clergymen. He also seemed more worried about the threat from nationalists than from Hitler and he constantly urged that only 'loyal' people be employed by the government.

Dawson Bates remained on as Minister for Home Affairs. Living in Portrush, he travelled seventy miles to his office every day in his large official car, using up scarce petrol. Still convinced that Belfast was safe from German bombs, he did little to improve the city's defences. He even refused to answer phone calls from the British army commander in Northern Ireland.

WARTIME PRODUCTION

Northern Ireland, unlike the South, prospered during the war but it took a while for industry to adapt to the demands of wartime production. Shipbuilding did well from the start, but the linen industry faltered in 1940 when imports of flax from Europe were cut off by Hitler's conquests. Up to the end of 1940 there were no new war-related industries and unemployment actually rose.

The situation changed after 1941. By then British war production had reached full capacity, so new industries were located in Northern Ireland. This was partly to take advantage of its labour force, partly to put important industries out of reach of German bombers. After that Northern industry made a substantial contribution to the United Kingdom production of war material:

- The shipyards produced 140 warships, including six aircraft carriers, as well as 123 merchant ships.
- Harland and Wolff also produced tanks and aircraft parts.
- Short's, the aircraft firm set up in 1938, built 1,200 Stirling bombers as well as other planes.
- The linen industry revived after a campaign to get farmers to grow flax. It produced parachutes, uniforms, tents and other military items.
- Torpedoes were built in Antrim, aircraft ball bearings in Portadown, and parachutes at Carrickfergus.

JOBS AND WAGES

These war-related industries created jobs but workers were also needed to build and maintain the many army, naval and air force bases for the British and American troops. The number out of work fell from an average of 30 per cent in the 1930s to five per cent in 1942–5. Wages rose substantially. Before the war the average wage was only 60 per cent of the average wage in Britain; by 1945 it was 75 per cent.

The promise of jobs drew in workers from the South, to the dismay of the unionist government. To stop them staying a system of work permits was introduced which limited the time they could remain in the North.

Employment and better wages did not bring industrial peace. Even though strikes were illegal during the war, almost 300 occurred. They were due in part to the autocratic management style of many employers and the poor conditions for workers in many workplaces.

WARTIME AGRICULTURE

Farmers also prospered in the war years. To meet the British demand for food, production increased threefold from 1939 to 1945. Compulsory tillage orders pushed the amount of land under crops from 500,000 acres to over 800,000 acres.

Apart from flax, the most important crops were oats and potatoes. Much of this was used as animal feed. Cattle numbers rose from 750,000 in 1939 to over 900,000 by 1945 and poultry from 10 million to 17.5 million. To improve productivity, farmers got grants to mechanise their farms and the number of tractors went up from 550 in 1938 to over 7,000 by 1945.

The British government gave farmers a guaranteed price for their produce. It was set at a level that gave farmers a reasonable profit. Since prices were the same all over the United Kingdom, Northern Irish farmers were no longer at a disadvantage because they were far from their markets.

The war brought prosperity to people in Northern Ireland. Industrial workers and farmers all benefited from plentiful work and good wages and prices. That widened the gap between the two parts of the island that had such a different experience in these years.

THE FALL OF ANDREWS' GOVERNMENT

Andrews remained Prime Minister for two and a half years. The worst event during that time was the bombing of Belfast (see pages 190–193). When people realised how poorly protected the city was, criticism of his government increased. A wave of strikes in 1942 reinforced the impression of incompetence.

Andrews stubbornly refused to listen when unionist MPs urged him to sack some incompetent older ministers. Finally in the spring of 1943 some members of the party demanded his resignation.

SIR BASIL BROOKE, THE NEW PRIME MINISTER

Brooke, who had done a good job as Minister for Agriculture, was chosen as the new Prime Minister. He replaced almost all the old ministers. To stress the need for unity in the war, he invited a Labour MP to become a minister but he made no gesture towards the Catholic minority. He explained:

> 'I knew I could not invite the nationalists to run in double harness with the unionists. At the time they were entirely non-co-operative especially in regard to any effort during the war.' (Robert Fisk, *In Time of War*, London 1983, p. 457)

Brooke's arrival invigorated the unionist government and contributed to the improvement of Northern Ireland's war effort.

THE STRATEGIC IMPORTANCE OF NORTHERN IRELAND

Northern Ireland's most important contribution to Britain in the war with Hitler was not its industrial production but its strategic location. From the beginning, German U-boats hunted the Atlantic, seeking ships carrying people, food and supplies to Britain. To protect the ships and their vital supplies, the Royal Navy organised convoys and patrols. With southern ports closed to them, they were based in Northern Ireland.

After the fall of France in June 1940, the Nazis controlled the south-western coast of Europe. Ships heading for Britain then began to use the northern route around the north of Ireland. At Derry, a huge naval harbour was built to provide a base for the Royal Navy and a safe anchorage for hundreds of ships. Airfields were also built and RAF planes flew out over Donegal to search the ocean for submarines. De Valera turned a blind eye to this violation of Irish neutrality.

THE AMERICANS IN NORTHERN IRELAND

The United States officially entered the war in December 1941, but even before that several hundred technicians arrived to help build the harbour in Derry. Later they also built airfields,

African-American soldiers receive their rations at a base in Northern Ireland during the Second World War.

and factories to repair aircraft. Early in 1942 over 30,000 troops arrived to train for the North African campaign. Later about 250,000 trained there for the Normandy landings.

The arrival of so many foreigners had a big impact on northern society. American soldiers had chocolate, sweets and other treats which had disappeared since the war began. They introduced locals to novelties like chewing-gum and nylon stockings. They also brought in their racist attitudes with frequent fights between white and black soldiers. They fought with locals too, usually about women.

THE SURRENDER IN DERRY

Derry remained a centre for American naval activity to the end of the war. In recognition of its role, the victorious Allies arranged that the German U-boat fleet would formally surrender in Derry in May 1945.

QUESTIONS

1 What was (a) the unionists' and (b) the northern nationalists' attitude to the war?

2 Outline the main preparations of the Northern Ireland government to defend the north against a possible invasion.

3 Give a brief account of the IRA's activities in the north during the war.

4 Write a short account of the career of J.M. Andrews as Prime Minister of Northern Ireland. Why did he fall and who succeeded him?

5 Explain why Northern Ireland was (a) economically and (b) strategically important to Britain's war effort.

6 Why were American troops stationed in Northern Ireland and how did that affect the area?

11.5
BELFAST DURING WORLD WAR II (CASE STUDY)

THE DANGER FROM GERMANY

In 1939 many people assumed that the violence of war would not touch Northern Ireland. That optimistic view was undermined in June 1940 when the Nazis conquered much of continental Europe. They then launched savage bombing raids on British cities. Their aim was to destroy that country's war industries and to weaken the will of the people to continue fighting.

Belfast, with its important shipbuilding and aircraft industries, seemed an obvious target for German bombers. In November 1940 German reconnaissance planes flew high over the city and pinpointed areas to attack. From their point of view it was an ideal target. The distinctive shape of Belfast Lough would be easy to pick out, especially on a moonlit night.

INADEQUATE PREPARATIONS

Until the fall of France little was done to protect the city. Dawson Bates, the Minister for Home Affairs, did not want to annoy local unionist councillors by insisting on compulsory air-raid precautions, so they remained voluntary. No air-raid shelters were built.

After the fall of France, the London government warned that Germany might bomb Northern Ireland. Craigavon then appointed **John MacDermott** as **Minister for Public Security**. His task was to co-ordinate civil defence but the general complacency and unwillingness to spend money meant he achieved little.

● By the spring of 1941 there were only twenty-four heavy anti-aircraft guns to defend the city and none anywhere else in Northern Ireland. Ships in the harbour did have guns and a squadron of Hurricane fighters were stationed nearby but their ability to fly at night was limited. There were no searchlights and only a few barrage balloons.

Ruined buildings in the centre of Belfast after the Blitz

- The blitz in London, Glasgow and other British cities showed what could happen but northern officials underestimated the damage a bombing raid could cause. They did little to prepare the fire services or hospitals for what they might have to deal with.
- MacDermott attempted to organise the evacuation of 30,000 children but only 7,000 showed up. Within weeks half of them had returned home.
- Public air-raid shelters were built, but only enough for 25 per cent of the population. And they were all above ground, providing little protection if a bomb landed nearby. Only 4,000 homes had private shelters.

7–8 APRIL 1941: THE FIRST ATTACK

Through 1940 and into 1941 the Luftwaffe devastated British cities but did not attack Northern Ireland. That encouraged complacency, which was reinforced when over twenty alerts turned out to be false alarms.

That sense of security was shattered on the night of 7–8 April. Seven German planes dropped bombs on the harbour area. The shipyards and docks were hit, though not badly and thirteen people were killed. Air-raid sirens only went off after the raid ended and anti-aircraft guns failed to hit anything, although one hurricane did bring down a German plane.

The next day newspaper reports tried to reassure people by stressing how little damage had been done. The message got through because only 3,000 people responded to a government call for evacuation. Smoke screens were installed in the harbour to provide cover against another raid.

15–16 APRIL

The Tuesday after Easter was a dull day but towards evening the sky cleared and the moon shone brightly. At 10.40p.m. the air raid sirens started wailing. This time it was not a false alarm. About ninety German bombers, mostly Junker 88s and Heinkel 111s were approaching Belfast. They came in waves, flying at 7,000 feet, well above the reach of anti-aircraft guns.

At 11.45p.m. the first planes dropped flares, intended to light up the city and show them their targets. People who saw them said they were beautiful and sinister, so bright that they turned night into day. Silently they floated down, accompanied by the monotonous drone of the approaching planes.

THE BOMBS

Then the bombs began to fall. Three types were used:
- **High explosives**: 674 of these were dropped.
- **Incendiaries**: They blew up above targets, generating enough heat to melt steel. 29,000 were dropped over Belfast.
- **Parachute mines**: Adapted from naval mines, these terrifying weapons floated gently down on green silk parachutes, only to explode with extraordinary force when they touched the ground. They were a new development and the British government refused to admit their existence for a year after seventy-six were used in Belfast.

Wave after wave of German bombers dropped their bombs on the almost undefended city. Most of them missed the harbour and the docks. They fell instead on the densely packed working-class houses of New Lodge, Lower Shankill and Antrim Road. The reasons for this are not clear. Perhaps the smoke screen in the harbour confused the pilots; perhaps the navigators thought an old waterworks in that area was an industrial complex.

TERROR AND DEATH

The result was a human disaster. People died in their homes, sometimes whole families huddled together for safety and companionship. In one house alone, nine bodies were found. When a parachute mine hit the York Street Spinning Mill, the largest of its kind in Europe, forty-two nearby houses were destroyed. Thirty people died when a parachute bomb scored a direct hit on a bomb shelter.

Others died in the streets where they ran in terror to escape. One doctor said that:

> 'the greater number of casualties was due to shock, blast and secondary missiles such as glass, stones, pieces of piping, etc … There are many terrible mutilations among both the living and the dead … In the heavily blitzed areas people ran panic stricken into the streets and made for the open country. Many were caught in the open by blast and secondary missiles.' (Brian Barton, *Northern Ireland in the second World War*, Ulster Historical Foundation 1995, pp. 45–6)

HELP FROM THE SOUTH

At 1.45a.m. a bomb hit the telephone exchange. That cut communications and made it difficult for the rescue services to make contact with each other. Anti-aircraft guns stopped firing because they feared they might hit the RAF's Hurricane fighters, but in fact these had been withdrawn.

By then there were 140 separate fires blazing. MacDermott, realising how impossible the situation was, phoned Dublin asking for help. De Valera agreed at once. Seventy firefighters from Dún Laoghaire, Dublin, Drogheda and Dundalk, volunteered to go. Through the night they rushed north but when they arrived they found that bombs had cut the water mains. Without high-pressure hoses, there was little they or their northern colleagues could do but let the fires burn themselves out.

THE AFTERMATH

On Wednesday morning Belfast was covered by a pall of choking yellow smoke. Desperate rescue workers dug through the rubble, often with their bare hands, trying to find survivors. Hospitals were swamped with people suffering from wounds, both physical and psychological.

No one knows for certain how many died but it was at least 900. Lorries collected bodies and body parts and brought them to the city morgues for identification. Distracted relatives searched desperately for their loved ones. Many bodies were not identified, perhaps because the whole family had died. These bodies were later buried in mass graves. Attempts were made to identify their religion so that Catholics could be buried in one plot and Protestants in another.

Anger began to grow as the city's unprotected state became clear. But in the immediate aftermath of the bombing Andrews and his colleagues seemed more concerned about how to camouflage the Stormont parliament in case of another attack and protect its statue of Edward Carson.

ESCAPE

Many people sought safety in flight. About 6,000 refugees arrived in Dublin, some with no more than the clothes on their backs. Thousands of others sought safety with relatives in the country. Small towns were swamped with refugees, many paying high rents for a bed out of reach of the bombers. Many of the poor simply left the city each evening to wait out the night in barns, fields and ditches around the city. It was estimated that about half the city's population left, with about 100,000 taking to the ditches each night.

THE GERMANS RETURN

The Luftwaffe returned just after midnight on 5 May. One pilot reported to his superiors: *'Visibility was wonderful. I could make out my targets perfectly.'* In three hours they dropped 95,000 incendiary bombs and 237 tons of high explosives. Most of them fell on the harbour and dockyards. Two-thirds of Harland and Wolff was destroyed, along with several ships it was building. It was almost six months before it could resume production. Other bombs hit the city centre.

This time casualties were lower, partly because the bombs fell in less populated areas, partly because so many people had fled.

OVERVIEW

Between the three raids, Belfast endured about ten hours of bombing. It is impossible to be sure how many died but the likely figure is around 1,100. About half of them were women and children.

Over 56,000 houses were badly damaged or destroyed – 53 per cent of the houses in the city. Over 100,000 people were made homeless. Many of them were from the city's worst slums. People outside the city offered them shelter but were dismayed by their poverty and poor physical condition. In May, Dawson Bates asked for the use of:

'*large houses, institutions or camps for respectable families who are at present billeted at the rate of thirty to a small house.*'

But he warned:

'*there are probably about 5,000 absolutely unbilletable persons. They are unbilletable owing to personal habits which are subhuman. Camps or institutions under suitable supervision must be instituted for these.*' (Jonathan Bardon, *A History of Ulster*, Blackstaff 1995, p. 334)

The blitz of 15–16 April was the most severe experienced by any city in the United Kingdom apart from London, and the bill for damages from Harland and Wolff was the highest submitted by any United Kingdom firm.

For months afterwards, thousands of people continued to leave the city at sunset each evening, fearing another raid. But there were no more. In June, Hitler invaded the Soviet Union and German interest turned away from these islands. The Luftwaffe did not return.

QUESTIONS

1 Give three reasons why Belfast was not well defended against a German bombing raid.

2 Give two reasons why Belfast was a likely target.

3 Who was put in charge of air-raid precautions in 1940 and how successful was he in achieving his aims?

4 What were German aircraft doing over Belfast in November 1940?

5 Describe the first German bombing raid. How many were killed?

6 Why did Belfast make such a clear target for the Luftwaffe on 15–16 April? How many planes were involved in the raid? List and describe the bombs they carried.

7 Describe the effect of the bombing. Where did the bombs fall and how many people died? Overall, how many people died in the three raids?

8 What did Belfast people do (a) to deal with casualties and (b) to escape from future raids?

9 What was the response in the South to these raids?

DOCUMENTS: A AND B

A: Here is how one observer at the time reported the start of the bombing on 15 April:

> Looking out, I saw something like the powerful headlights of a car shining straight down from the sky. I could not understand it and inside I had a sinking feeling. I realised that on this occasion the Germans meant business. More and more flares, intensely white, appeared in the sky and soon the whole sky was as bright as day. During this time one could hear the steady drone of planes high overhead. In the streets cars were being driven at high speed. ARP [air-raid protection] and fire fighting men dashed to their posts whilst others, civilians were getting the hell out of the city and into the country. The steady, monotonous drone of the planes went on and on. More brilliant white flares came gliding down. Some were like huge lights suspended from overhead wires. They did not appear to lose height. It was now after midnight and so bright that I could read the small print on a Woodbine [cigarette] packet. The barrage guns had not yet opened fire and the only sound came from planes high over the city. I did not see a plane … (Brian Brophy, *Blitz on Belfast*, Belfast 1989, p. 41)

B: Twenty-year-old James Doherty was an air-raid warden in Belfast in 1941.

> [In a lull between bombs he and an older constable] moved off and luckily for us, the constable looked up towards the sky. 'What's that, lad?' he asked as he tugged my sleeve and pointed upwards. I did not take time to look … I knew what it was … I shouted 'Down' and at the same time pushed him to the ground … Time seemed to stop … as the mine came swishing down … What seemed like a thousand years was in fact only a few seconds. The mine did not reach the ground but struck the spire of Trinity Street church and exploded immediately.

> The whole world seemed to rock, slates, bricks, earth and flying glass rained down on us. I dug my face into my arms for protection and lay for what seemed like an eternity. I could hear debris still falling but not with the same force … by some miracle, we were still alive. We were caught in a blast of a parachute mine that had reduced a granite-built church to rubble. And devastated the surrounding area. (From James Doherty, *Post 381: Memoirs of a Belfast Air-Raid Warden*, Belfast 1989, pp. 27–8)

1 What did the author of document A note at the at the start of the raid? Was he frightened?

2 Give three things which were happening on the ground as people realised a raid was beginning.

3 In document B, what had the constable seen? How did Doherty react?

4 Describe what happened in the explosion.

5 What kind of bomb exploded near Doherty? What information does he give to show its power?

6 Which of these sources would be most useful to a historian? Give reasons for your answer.

Timeline for Northern Ireland in the Second World War	
3 September 1939	The United Kingdom government declared war on Germany.
4 September	Craig made statement of support in Stormont.
November 1940	Death of Sir James Craig, J.M. Andrews became Prime Minister.
7–8 April 1941	The first German bombers over Belfast. Thirteen dead.
15–16 April	Ninety German planes bomb Belfast. At least 900 dead.
5 May	Last German raid. Over 100 dead.
December 1941	United States enters the war. American troops begin to arrive in Northern Ireland.
April 1943	Sir Basil Brooke replaced Andrews as Prime Minister.
May 1945	German submarines surrendered in Derry.

11.6

PARTITION CONSOLIDATED: 1945–1949

THE SECOND WORLD WAR WIDENS THE GAP BETWEEN NORTH AND SOUTH

The experience of war was very different in the two parts of Ireland:

- By maintaining its neutrality the South distanced itself from Britain; by being part of the war effort, the North strengthened its position within the United Kingdom.
- In the North, the war brought jobs and relative prosperity; in the South it brought economic stagnation.
- In the North, hundreds of thousands of foreign troops brought contact with a wider world; the South had no similar experience.
- The North suffered the horrific bombing of Belfast; the South suffered only minor damage.

These different experiences widened the gap between North and South that had already become apparent in the 1930s. Between 1945 and 1949 decisions taken in Britain and the South widened the gap further. By 1949, when the South finally left the Commonwealth, partition had become entrenched in a way which would have been inconceivable to people in 1920.

THE UNCHANGING POWER OF THE UNIONIST PARTY

In 1945, the unionist government could feel more secure than at any time since 1920. In Britain many politicians, Labour as well as Conservative, resented the South's neutrality and were grateful that Northern Ireland helped them to fight the Germans. There was more support for unionists and less sympathy with nationalists than ever before.

THE LABOUR PARTY'S VICTORY IN BRITAIN

In the British general election, Churchill's Conservatives were defeated and the Labour Party, led by **Clement Atlee**, won a landslide victory. It promised to bring in the welfare reforms which had been proposed during the war in the **Beveridge Report**. Over the next five years Labour kept its promises and set up what became known as the **Welfare State**. This saw old age pensions, unemployment pay and public housing improved. It also meant free health care for all and better educational opportunities to young people. Because Northern Ireland was part of the United Kingdom, it shared in these welfare improvements.

THE UNIONISTS AND THE WELFARE STATE

The British taxpayer helped to pay the cost of extending these reforms to Northern Ireland.

Nationalists and the Southern government wanted Britain to use its power to control the behaviour of the unionists. But, as this cartoon suggests, British leaders were happy to leave the unionists alone

Between 1945 and 1951, the payments from Britain grew sevenfold to £45 million while local taxation only doubled. British subsidies enabled Northern Ireland to have a much higher standard of services than it could have afforded by itself and far better than the South could provide for its people.

The benefits of the welfare state went equally to nationalists and unionists, though being poorer, nationalists gained more than their share from the welfare reforms.

NEUTRALITY PROVES SOVEREIGNTY

In the South neutrality had proved beyond doubt that the independence won in 1921 was real. By 1945, the Treaty was dead and the issues it had raised – the oath, the role of the king, the right of an Irish government to choose its own foreign policy – were no longer relevant. Ireland was still linked to the British Commonwealth by the External Relations Act, but that was an act of the Oireachtas and could be repealed at any time. Partition was the only one of the old nationalist issues that still remained.

FIANNA FÁIL UNCHALLENGED

De Valera and Fianna Fáil remained in power after the war. De Valera gave up control of foreign affairs, but as Taoiseach he still dominated his government. Most of his ministers were the same men who had held office since 1932 and they continued the same economic policies of protection and state-backed industrial development.

Fianna Fáil looked pretty safe in 1945. The main opposition party, Fine Gael had declined steadily throughout the 1930s and early 1940s (Table A). Many thought it was on its way out.

Labour did quite well in 1943, and briefly looked as if it might replace Fine Gael as the main opposition party. But soon after the election the old feud between William O'Brien and James Larkin which had weakened the Labour movement since the 1920s flared up again. The party split in two, with O'Brien forming his own National Labour Party.

The decline of Fine Gael 1932–1944						
Election years	1932	1933	1937	1938	1943	1944
Cumann na nGaedheal/ Fine Gael	57	48	48	45	32	30

A small farmers' party, Clann na Talmhan, had gained some success in the early 1940s but it only appealed to small farmers in the west and was soon to decline.

A NEW PARTY TO CHALLENGE FIANNA FÁIL

Only in 1946, did a new party emerge which seemed as if it might challenge the power of Fianna Fáil. Called **Clann na Poblachta**, it was led by **Seán MacBride** who had briefly been the IRA chief of staff in the 1930s.

The new party spread rapidly in 1946 and 1947. Many commentators saw parallels between it and Fianna Fáil at the time de Valera set it up in 1926. Would Clan na Poblachta, they wondered, do to de Valera what he had done to Cosgrave?

THE 1948 ELECTION AND THE FIRST INTER-PARTY GOVERNMENT

But de Valera was a much smarter political operator than Cosgrave had been. In January 1948 he suddenly called a general election. As intended it caught the new party before it was ready and it only won 10 seats, not the 20 or more some had predicted (Table B).

Fianna Fáil had lost popularity since the last election. People blamed it for the rationing and shortages which continued even though the war had ended. It lost eight seats but it still had enough to form a minority government with the help of a few Independent TDs. Everyone assumed that would happen, but the leaders of the other parties were determined to get de Valera out. He had been in power for 16 years and that was not good for democracy. This determination was strong enough for the republican MacBride to consider a coalition with the pro-Treatyites of Fine Gael to oust Fianna Fáil.

John A. Costello of Fine Gael became Taoiseach. The rest of the posts in the Cabinet were shared out among the various parties according to the number of TDs they had. MacBride became Minister for External Affairs.

> Coalition governments were unfamiliar to Irish people in 1948. They were seen as dangerously foreign. Therefore, the coalition officially called itself an 'Inter-party government'.

Table B

Results of the 1948 election						
Fianna Fáil	Fine Gael	Two Labour parties	Clan na Talmhan	Clan na Poblachta	Independents	Total of seats
68 (76)	31 (30)	19 (12)	7 (11)	10 (–)	12 (9)	147

THE EXTERNAL RELATIONS ACT

An issue that seemed likely to cause problems was Ireland's relationship to the British Commonwealth. By 1948 only one link remained – the 1936 External Relations Act. It gave the king the right to sign the formal papers, which Irish diplomats going to other countries had to present to their host governments.

By 1948 the Act was not working well and de Valera considered getting rid of it if he was returned to power. In the election MacBride campaigned for its removal. Fine Gael was divided. Mulcahy wanted to keep it as a link to the Commonwealth and Costello wanted to get rid of it.

THE PROBLEMS OF LEAVING THE COMMONWEALTH

Once the Coalition was formed in February, the fate of the External Relations Act came up for discussion. MacBride found to his surprise that the other members were quite happy to see it go. But how would Britain react? There were two potential problems, trade and citizenship:

- Irish exports had privileged access to British markets because Ireland was in the Commonwealth. Would that change if Ireland left? This problem was removed in July 1948 when the two countries made a new trade pact, which gave the Irish access to British market, independent of being in the Commonwealth.

- There were hundreds of thousands of Irish people living in Britain and many thousands more emigrated there every year. Because Ireland was in the Commonwealth, they had the same status as British citizens – e.g. they could go in and out freely, did not need passports and could vote in British elections. If Ireland left the Commonwealth, would the British treat them as aliens or even expel them? This concern was also removed in 1948 when the British passed a Nationality Act which granted citizenship rights to Irish people even if they were not British subjects.

COSTELLO'S SURPRISE ANNOUNCEMENT

In September Costello went on a state visit to Canada. Before he left, the Coalition Cabinet decided in principle to repeal the External Relations Act, though it did not decide when or if that meant leaving the Commonwealth.

While Costello was away, the *Sunday Independent* published an article saying that the Act was to be repealed. At a press conference in Canada, Costello was asked if this was true. Unskilled in diplomatic evasion, he replied that it was. He was then asked if that meant Ireland would leave the Commonwealth and he said it did.

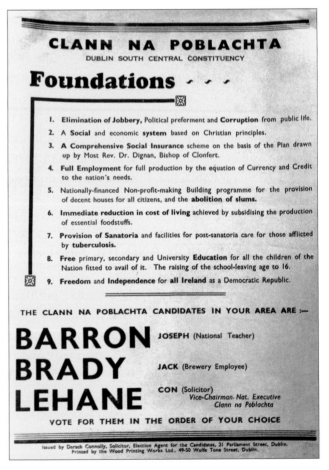

A Clann na Poblachta election poster.

List four of the reasons they give why voters should choose them. Which seems the most convincing in the circumstances of 1948? Explain your choice.

THE BRITISH RESPONSE

This was a most unfortunate way to make the announcement. The British had been expecting it, but it was risky and discourteous to spring it on them like this. Understandably, the Attlee government was annoyed. They warned the Irish of serious consequences for trade and citizenship. But when the leaders of Canada and Australia supported the Irish position, they had to back down.

THE IRELAND ACT SECURES THE UNIONISTS

Brooke was very concerned by these developments. He called an election to show how much support there was in Northern Ireland for the Union with Britain. He also sought reassurances about Northern Ireland's place within the United Kingdom from the British government. Attlee was delighted to give them to him.

In 1949, the Westminster parliament passed the **Ireland Act**. It acknowledged Ireland's departure from the Commonwealth and the establishment of the Republic of Ireland, while guaranteeing that Irish people in Britain would not be treated as foreigners. But it also guaranteed the Unionists that:

> 'in no event will Northern Ireland or any part thereof cease to be part of His Majesty's dominions and of the United Kingdom without the consent of the Parliament of Northern Ireland.' (David McCullagh, *A Makeshift Majority*, Dublin 1998, p. 106)

This gave the unionists more security than they ever had before. No future British Prime Minister could do what Churchill had done in 1940, use them as a bargaining counter in negotiations with the South. The Act consolidated partition, as the Republic's government recognised by protesting strongly but in vain.

CONCLUSION

By 1949 nationalists had achieved their republic, totally independent of Britain. But it was a republic for part of the island only. The area dominated by unionists remained secure within the United Kingdom. It was an outcome that no one could have imagined in 1912 when the first Home Rule Bill was introduced.

" BEGOB, EAMON, THERE'S GREAT CHANGES AROUND HERE ! "

(August, 1948)

Until 1948, a statue of Queen Victoria stood in front of Leinster House where the Dáil met. The government then decided to remove it

1 Who is the statue talking to?
2 List three of the changes to which she refers.
3 Why do you think the statue was removed at that time?
4 Name the leader of the government that ordered its removal.
5 Do you think (a) it should have been removed earlier or (b) it should have been left in place? Give reasons for your choice.

1 List four ways in which the experience of war was different in the North and in the South. Do you agree that these differences increased the gap between the two parts of Ireland? Explain your answer.

2 Explain what is meant by the Welfare State. How did it affect people in Northern Ireland?

3 List the main political parties in the South in 1945 and briefly explain the success or failure of each of them.

4 What new party was set up in 1946? Who was its leader and what kind of people were attracted to it? What party did it threaten?

5 Why did de Valera call the general election early in 1948? Look at Table B and explain the result achieved by each of the main parties.

6 Why did some political leaders form a coalition government in 1948? Who was the Taoiseach and who was Minister for External Affairs?

7 What was the External Relations Act? What problems might arise if Ireland repealed it and how were those problems removed by the end of 1948?

8 How did Costello announce that Ireland would leave the Commonwealth? Was it wise to do it that way? Explain your answer.

9 What was the British response to the Irish decision? Suggest two reasons why the Ireland Act was so favourable to the unionists.

Higher Level

1 Why did the Irish government decided to remain neutral during the second World War and discuss the view that this policy only succeeded because Irish neutrality was heavily weighted in favour of the Allies?

2 What were the internal and external threats to Irish neutrality during the second World War and how did the Irish government deal with them?

3 Compare the impact of the second World War on the society and economy of the two Irish states.

4 Describe the bombing of Belfast in 1941 and assess its impact on the Northern Ireland government.

5 'Between 1939 and 1949, the position of the unionists within Northern Ireland was greatly strengthened.' Discuss the main political developments in Northern Ireland and between North and South in the light of this statement.

6 'Neutrality proved Irish independence. After that declaring a republic was merely putting the final seal on what was already an accomplished fact.' Do you think this is a fair assessment of the relations between Britain and Ireland between 1939 and 1949?

Ordinary Level

A Turn to the cartoon on page 199 and answer the questions.

B Write a paragraph on **one** of the following:
1 Seán Lemass as Minister for Supplies.
2 The IRA during World War II.
3 How World War II affected society in Northern Ireland.

C Answer **one** of the following questions:
1 What problems did de Valera face in keeping Ireland neutral during World War II and how did he overcome them?
2 What did Northern Ireland contribute to the British war effort during World War II?

Abstention: Refusing to enter the Dáil, the Northern Ireland parliament or Westminster because to do so involved taking an oath to the king.

Allegiance: A medieval word for the loyalty that a subject owed to his king or ruler.

Anglo-Irish relations: Ireland's foreign policy in relation to Britain.

Balance of payments: The balance between what a country earns by selling exports to other countries and what it spends by buying imports from other countries.

Belligerent country: A country involved in a war.

Bigot: A person who hates others because of their race or religion.

Blood Sacrifice, see page 36.

Boundary Commission: People appointed to draw a boundary between two states.

British Empire: The parts of the world conquered and ruled by the British. After the first World War, when Britain claimed to be fighting for 'freedom for small nations', the idea of empire became less acceptable and the word '**Commonwealth**' was used instead.

Budget: A government's statement of how much it plans to spend each year and what taxes it has to impose to get the money. The budget has to be accepted by the parliament (Dáil). If it is not, the government falls and an election is held.

Cabinet: A committee made up of the chief minister (President / Prime Minister / Taoiseach) and other important ministers, each in charge of a particular area of government (e.g. justice, finance, etc). The Cabinet usually forms the 'government' of a country, taking the important decisions about how a country is run (e.g. deciding on taxes or spending priorities or relations with foreign countries). Members of a Cabinet are supposed to do what the Cabinet as a whole decides, even if they argued against it during private discussions. This is called 'collective Cabinet responsibility'.

Censorship: Excluding or preventing the expression of certain ideas, images or opinions.

Civil servants: Officials who implement the laws passed by the Dáil and the policies decided by ministers.

Civil war: A war among people of one state/nation.

Commission: A group of people appointed to look into some problem.

Conform/conformity: Falling into line with the prevailing view. Not questioning it.

Conscription: Forcing young men to join the army.

Conservative (to be): To want to keep things as they are; to oppose change.

Conservative Party: British party which appealed to people who were content with things as they were.

Department: The Minister and civil servants who deal with one aspect of a country's government.

Diplomats: The men and women sent to represent their country abroad.

Discrimination: Excluding a person from a job, house or other benefit solely on the grounds of their gender, race or religion.

Dominions: Parts of the British empire which had local self-government. In 1922 they were Canada, Newfoundland, Australia, New Zealand, South Africa and the Irish Free State. After the second World War other countries like India also got 'dominion status'.

Executive Council: The term used in the Irish Free State instead of Cabinet. The **President of the Executive Council** was the official title of the head of the government in the Free State. (Today we would say Taoiseach or Prime Minister.)

Foreign policy: A government's policy towards other countries.

Foreign service/dipomatic service: the civil servants who carry out that policy.

Free trade: Goods going freely from country to country without any interference.

Gerrymander (to): To draw the borders between constituencies in such a way as to make it easier for one party to win.

Home Rule: The limited form of self-government which Irish nationalists asked up to 1918 – a local Irish parliament to deal with local Irish affairs like health, education, transport, etc.

Imports: Goods bought into a country; **Exports:** goods sold out of a country; **Trade deficit:** when a country imports more than it exports.

Internment: Imprisoning people without trial.

King/Crown/Throne: Alternative ways of saying the king as head of state.

Kingdom/monarchy: state whose head is an unelected king or queen.

Labour movement: All the organisations such as trade unions and the Labour Party which aim to improve the living standards of workers.

Liberal Party: British party which appealed to people who supported reform.

Martial law: The army taking responsibility for law and order. It acts as a police force and replaces the normal courts with military courts (**courts-martial**), where army officers act as judges.

Means test: An assessment of people's income to see if they are poor enough to receive social welfare payments.

Minority government: A government formed by a party that is a few votes short of an overall majority. Usually it does a deal with a smaller party or with independents who will vote with it on most issues.

Neutral/neutrality: Not taking sides in a conflict.

Oireachtas: The Irish parliament containing the **Dáil** and **Seanad**.

Official opposition: In a democratic country, the main political party which opposes the policies of the current government. It hopes to persuade the voters to support it and to form the government after the next election. In other words it provides voters with **an alternative government** and gives them a choice of leaders and policies.

Papal Legate: A man appointed to represent the Pope on special occasions.

Partition of Ireland: Ireland divided into two areas, one dominated by nationalists, the other by unionists.

Pogrom: Originally used for attacks on Jewish villages by the Tsar's government in Russia, it was later used for any attack on people because of their religion or race, with the aim of expelling them or wiping them out. Today people would say 'ethnic cleansing'.

Political party: A group of people with a common set of aims who try to get elected to parliament so that they can influence the way in which their country is run.

Protection: Putting taxes (called **duties** or **tariffs**) on imported goods in order to make them more expensive than similar goods made at home. This "protects" local goods (and the jobs of the people who make them) from foreign competition. Protectionism was a popular idea between the two World Wars.

Rebellion/rising: Using force to try to overthrow the existing government.

Recruitment: Encouraging young men to join the army voluntarily.

Republic: a state whose head is an elected president.

Secular: Non-religious; not taking religion into account.

Sectarian: Relating to a particular religion (sect).

Self-government: The right of people living in a country to run their own affairs.

Separatists: Extreme Irish nationalists who wanted a complete separation between Ireland and Britain. They were often called **republicans** though some separatists would have accepted a monarchy, so long as the king was not British. Because they saw no problem about using force to achieve their aims, they were also known as '**physical force' nationalists**.

Sovereignty: The right of a country to control its own laws and taxes and elect its own government without outside interference.

Treason: Plotting to overthrow the state or the government. Until the death penalty was abolished in the 1960s, treason was usually punished by death.

Truce: A ceasefire between warring groups to allow peace talks to take place.

Veto: The right to say no / to block something.

Voting (methods of):

'**First past the post**': The candidate who gets most votes wins. This is only fair with two parties. With more than two, it can mean a party with fewer than half the votes getting all the seats.

'**Proportional Representation**': Dividing up the seats so that they are in proportion to the number of votes won by different parties.

KEY PERSONALITIES

RICHARD DAWSON BATES (1876–1949)

Born in Belfast in 1873, Richard Dawson Bates studied law and became a solicitor. An active member of the Orange Order, he was appointed secretary of the Ulster Unionist Council in 1906. In this post he had played an important part in Unionist opposition to Home Rule from 1910, and in the 1912 signing of the Solemn League and Covenant.

When Northern Ireland was set up, Craig appointed him Minister for Home Affairs. His most important task was to defeat the IRA. He achieved this with the Civil Authorities (Special Powers) Act which allowed him to intern anyone, by having an armed police, the RUC and by forming units of special constables to assist them. Many of the 'Specials' were former members of Carson's UVF and this exclusively Protestant force became a permanent feature of northern life.

Bates also ensured unionist dominance by ending Proportional Representation (PR) in local government elections in 1922 and redrawing the constituency boundaries to ensure that unionists controlled councils in areas like Derry and Fermanagh where there was a clear nationalist majority. In 1929, he abolished PR for elections to the Northern Ireland parliament.

Bates was a religious bigot who refused to employ Catholics in the civil service and encouraged businesses to do the same. When Craig died in 1940, his successor J.M. Andrews kept Bates on as Minister for Home Affairs. He did little to protect Northern Ireland against German attack as became clear in May 1941 when Belfast was bombed. He was blamed for the high loss of life.

This made Andrew's government unpopular, leading to him being replaced as Prime Minister by Sir Basil Brooke in 1943. At that point, Bates finally retired.

MICHAEL COLLINS (1890–1922)

Born in Cork in 1890, Michael Collins went to work in London in 1906. He studied accountancy, joined the Gaelic League, the GAA and the IRB but returned to Ireland in 1915 to avoid conscription. He fought in GPO in Easter Week and was interned in Frongoch camp. Freed in December 1916, Collins rebuilt the IRB and was elected President in 1917. He travelled the country, building up a network of contacts and spies. Having helped set up the 'second Sinn Féin' in October 1917, he was elected to its Executive Council. He was also Director of Intelligence in the Irish Volunteers.

Elected a Sinn Féin TD in 1918, de Valera appointed him Minister for Finance in the Dáil government. As Minister for Finance, he raised £350,000 in the National Loan, using it to pay for propaganda, expenses and guns. As IRA Director of Intelligence, he collected information on British plans and passed it to local IRA units. In Dublin, his 'Squad' intimidated and murdered Castle detectives. He ruthlessly killed British spies on Bloody Sunday. The British offered a reward of £10,000 for him which made him famous. This caused tensions with Brugha and de Valera who were both jealous of him.

Collins reluctantly went with the Irish delegation to London to negotiate with Lloyd George. He soon realised the British would give no more than Dominion Status, but found the Dominions were evolving to full independence. Lloyd George also convinced him the Boundary Commission would end partition. After Lloyd George threatened war, he backed Griffith's decision to sign Treaty on 6 December without referring it back to de Valera. In the Dáil debates he defended it on the grounds that (a) it was the best they could get from the British, (b) it was only the first step to the republic and (c) that the Boundary Commission would end partition.

After the Treaty passed de Valera resigned and Collins became leader of the 'Provisional Government', to which the British were to hand over power. He began (a) taking over from the British, (b) wrote a Constitution for the Free State and (c) set up police, army and civil service. At the same time, he secretly supplied guns to the IRA in the North who were still fighting the Unionist government there.

To avert a civil war, he refused to retaliate when extreme republicans under Rory O'Connor seized the Four Courts. He also tried to isolate extremists by making the Collins-de Valera Pact to fight the June election jointly with the moderate anti-Treaty faction. As part of the pact, Collins left king and Oath out of the Constitution, but the British

MICHAEL COLLINS (1890–1922) *CONT.*

insisted on restoring them. As a result Collins called off the pact on the eve of the election. The pro-Treaty group won a decisive victory (fifty-eight seats to thirty-five).

After that, Collins let Free State army attack the IRA in the Four Courts. This started the civil war. The Cabinet appointed Collins Commander-in-Chief of the Irish army. Within a week he had defeated the IRA in Dublin, then sent the army to attack them in Munster by land and sea. By August, he defeated them there too. On 11 August 1922, Griffith died suddenly. Collins took over as head of government. A few days later, he went to Cork where he was ambushed and killed at Béal na mBláth on 22 August 1922.

W.T. COSGRAVE (1880–1965)

William T. Cosgrave was born in Dublin in 1880, helped to found Sinn Féin in 1905 and was elected a Sinn Féin member of Dublin Corporation. He joined the Volunteers and fought in 1916. Sentenced to death, he was reprieved and freed in June 1917. Elected as a Sinn Féin MP for Kilkenny, de Valera appointed him Minister for Local Government in the first Dáil Cabinet in 1919. When most local councils voted to support the Dáil in 1920, he began to reform them and weed out corruption.

He was one of those who selected the delegates to the Treaty negotiations. After the delegates signed the Treaty, he supported their demand that it be debated in the Dáil and he accepted Collins's argument that it was the best deal they could win at the time. After de Valera resigned, he remained as Minister in the Griffith/Collins government. When Collins was killed in August 1922, a frightened Cabinet chose Cosgrave as President (Prime Minister) because he was the oldest, had the longest political experience and no military connections.

Quiet but firm, Cosgrave backed the execution of leading republicans in retaliation for the murder of a pro-Treaty TD. This hard-line policy helped to end the civil war in May 1923. He then encouraged the restoration of democratic politics by holding free elections in 1923 and freeing most republican prisoners by 1924.

In 1923, Cosgrave turned the pro-Treaty section of Sinn Féin into a new party, Cumann na nGaedheal. It was poorly organised and never won an over-all majority in any election. From 1923 to 1927, with only the small Labour Party to oppose them in the Dáil, Cosgrove's government (a) wrote a democratic Constitution, (b) set up an army, police and civil service, (c) established civilian control over the army, (d) reorganised the courts and (e) made Irish compulsory in schools. When the Boundary Commission failed in 1925, Cosgrave negotiated the Anglo-Irish Agreement which left the border with Northern Ireland unchanged.

In economic policy, Cumann na nGaedheal resisted demands for protection, kept free trade, low taxes and a balanced budget. In foreign policy, they joined the League of Nations and sent diplomats to Washington, Paris, etc. Through their Anglo-Irish policy they expanded the sovereignty of the Dominions by helping to negotiate the Balfour Declaration (1926) and the Statute of Westminster (1931).

In the June 1927 election, Cumann na nGaedheal lost seats but was safe while Fianna Fáil continued to abstain from the Dáil. After the murder of Kevin O'Higgins, Cosgrave brought in the Electoral Amendment Bill which forced Fianna Fáil TDs to take their seats. This was good for Irish democracy, though bad for his party. In another election in September, they recovered most of the seats they lost in June and stayed in power until 1932.

When the Depression hit in 1930, they had no solution to the economic problems. Alarmed by the growth of socialism, Cosgrave put Article 2A into the Constitution, taking power to try them in military courts. This aroused fears about a dictatorship, and Fianna Fáil won the 1932 election. To their surprise, Cosgrave handed over power peacefully and told the British, the army and the civil service to accept the democratic decision of the people.

In opposition, he did not trust Fianna Fáil to uphold democracy. When IRA men broke up Cumann na nGaedheal meetings, he joined with Eoin O'Duffy's blueshirts to form a new party, Fine Gael, with O'Duffy as leader. But O'Duffy soon showed his fascist sympathies. After a year, Fine Gael removed him and Cosgrave took over again. He led Fine Gael from 1934-1943, criticising Fianna Fáil policies. But he never won popular support and Fine Gael declined steadily. Cosgrave retired in 1944 and lived quietly until his death in 1965.

SIR JAMES CRAIG, LORD CRAIGAVON (1927) (1871–1940)

Belfast born, Craig was the son of a wealthy distiller. He served in the British army in South Africa in 1900 and as a Unionist MP from 1906 to 1921. A staunch Unionist, Craig was prominent in the Ulster Unionist Council and the Orange Order. From 1910 he was the architect of Ulster unionist resistance to the third Home Rule bill, working behind the scenes and letting Carson act as the public face of unionism. He co-ordinated a series of rallies, of which the most famous saw 400,000 unionists sign the *Solemn League and Covenant*, promising to keep Ulster within the United Kingdom. He also helped to organise the Ulster Volunteer Force and was involved in the Larne gunrunning.

When the First World War broke out in 1914, Craig encouraged Ulster Volunteers to join the British army to resist German aggression. He served with the Ulster Division in France (1914–1916). From 1916 to 1921, he served in Lloyd George's government at Westminster. He supported the Government of Ireland Act which set up Northern Ireland and was partly responsible for the decision to include six rather than nine counties in it as Lloyd George wanted.

Craig took over from Carson as leader of the Unionist Party in February 1921 and in June he became the first Prime Minister of Northern Ireland. The IRA refused to recognise Northern Ireland and violence there continued even when a truce was agreed in the South. During the negotiations for the Anglo-Irish Treaty, Craig resisted pressure from Lloyd George to make a deal with Sinn Féin. In January 1922, he met Michael Collins to try to end violence against Catholics in the North and the Dáil's boycott of northern goods. They made a pact but it soon fell apart. Tough actions by the Craig's government, which included the establishment of the Special Constables (mostly former members of the UVF) and internment and the civil war in the South in 1922–1923 led to an uneasy peace. Craig refused to name a northern representative on the Boundary Commission. After the Commission report was leaked in 1925, he went to London where he, British Prime Minister, Ramsay MacDonald and W.T. Cosgrave, signed an Anglo-Irish agreement which ratified the border between Northern Ireland and the Irish Free State.

Craig maintained unionist supremacy in Northern Ireland by abolishing Proportional Representation in local elections in 1922 and for elections to the Stormont parliament in 1929. Although not personally anti-Catholic, he allowed ministers to discriminate against Catholics in the civil service and the police. In areas in the west on Northern Ireland, such as Co. Fermanagh and Derry city where Catholics were in a majority, Craig approved of the gerrymandering of local constituency boundaries to ensure unionist control. A skilful politician, Craig called elections whenever there seemed to be a threat to unionist interests and won large majorities each time.

When the Second World War broke out in 1939, Craig gave the United Kingdom his full support. He offered to impose conscription but after nationalists protested, the British refused the offer. His government made few preparations to defend Northern Ireland from a German attack. Craig died suddenly in November 1940.

ARTHUR GRIFFITH (1872–1922)

Dublin born Arthur Griffith trained as a printer and spent two years in South Africa for his health. He returned to Dublin in 1898, the centenary of the 1798 United Irish rebellion. Griffith acknowledged this by naming a small newspaper he set up, *The United Irishman*. The centenary revived interest in republican ideas and Griffith helped this by publishing articles about Wolfe Tone and other republican thinkers. A member of the Gaelic League, he also supported the revival of Irish and the GAA and backed 'buy Irish' campaigns.

Griffith did not like Home Rule because he did not think it would give Ireland enough control over its affairs, but he also knew most nationalists disliked republican violence. In his 1904 book, *The Resurrection of Hungary*, he proposed a middle way between the two:

- Irish MPs would not go to Westminster but would set up an Irish parliament and government in Dublin.
- This would receive the loyalty of Irish people and, Griffith argued, British power in Ireland would just wither away without the need for violence.
- To reassure the British and please unionists, Griffith suggested that nationalists would accept a '*Dual Monarchy*' with Britain, i.e. the British king to be king of Ireland too, like the arrangement between Austria and Hungary.
- British also wanted an Irish government should develop Irish industry behind protective tariffs.

Griffith set up the Sinn Féin Party to achieve these aims in 1905 and changed the name of his paper to *Sinn Féin*. People involved in the cultural revival or frustrated by the delay in getting Home Rule, voted for the party and it won seats on local councils. But after 1910, when political developments in Britain made Home Rule likely, support for Sinn Féin declined. Griffith continued to publish his paper, *Sinn Féin*, supporting nationalist causes other than Home Rule. Gradually the name 'Sinn Féin' became a kind of brand name attached to extreme nationalists, even when they had no connection with Griffith.

When violence broke out on Easter Monday in 1916, everyone called it 'the Sinn Féin Rebellion', even though Griffith and Sinn Féin had nothing to do with it. The British arrested Griffith after the rising but freed him in December 1916. By then, support for the Easter rebels was growing and as a result Sinn Féin became popular too. In 1917, three 'Sinn Féin' candidates defeated the Home Rule Party in by-elections. But deep divisions remained among pro-rising groups until Eamon de Valera acted as peace-maker. To encourage unity, Griffith stepped aside and let de Valera become leader of the new ('second') Sinn Féin.

It promised:
- to abstain from Westminster,
- to set up a parliament (a Dáil) in Dublin,
- to have a republic rather than a Dual Monarchy and
- to appeal to the peace conference which would follow the ending of the war to recognise Ireland's right to self-determination.

The new Sinn Féin grew rapidly. When it opposed conscription, the British arrested the leaders including Griffith for the 'German Plot'. He was in jail during the 1918 election when he was elected MP (TD) for East Cavan and he missed the first meeting of Dáil Éireann in January 1919.

After Lloyd George freed Griffith in March, de Valera appointed him as Vice-President and Minister for Home Affairs in the Dáil Cabinet. When de Valera went to the United States in June, he presided over the Dáil government and was responsible for setting up the Sinn Féin courts. He disliked IRA violence but restrained his protests when faced with violence from the Black and Tans. Arrested in November 1920, he was in jail until the Truce in July 1921.

In October, Griffith led the Irish delegation to London to negotiate with Lloyd George after de Valera refused to go. There he put the case for de Valera's 'External Association' but soon realised the British would insist on Dominion Status. On partition, he accepted that the Boundary Commission would move large areas from Northern Ireland to the South. He was delighted when, during the last day of the negotiations, Lloyd George agreed to let Ireland have full economic independence.

Griffith was the first delegate to agree to sign the Treaty without checking with De Valera. Afterwards during the Dáil debates he argued that the Treaty gave much more independence – an Irish flag, an army, full control of the economy – than Home Rule and that they got the best terms possible.

After the Dáil voted to accept the Treaty in January 1922 de Valera resigned and Griffith became head of the Dáil government. With Collins he began setting up the Irish Free State, but disapproved of things Collins did to try to keep the IRA from splitting. Like everyone, he was heart-broken when the split over the Treaty degenerated into civil war in June. He died suddenly in August 1922, aged 52 years.

EVIE HONE (1894–1955)

Born in Dublin, Hone came from a family that contained several distinguished Irish artists. At age 12, she contacted polio which left her lame and with one weak hand. She studied art in London and Paris with her friend and fellow-artist, Mainie Jellett. In Paris, they came into contact with cubism and studied under Albert Gleizes. Under his influence, Hone arranged her paintings into harmonic abstractions of colour and shape. In 1924, she and Jellett organised Dublin's first exhibition of abstract art, which shocked conservative Irish opinion. Hone also exhibited paintings at art shows in England, the United States and Paris.

Hone was deeply religious, and in 1925 she briefly entered an Anglican convent. Later, in 1937, she became a Catholic. This may have influenced her desire to work in stained glass. In 1933, she joined *An Túr Gloine*, a co-operative for making stained glass and mosaics which Sarah Purser set up around 1900. Her images in glass were simple, bold and often abstract, showing that cubist ideas continued to affect her work. She was soon recognised as a fine and original artist and the Department of Industry and Commerce commissioned her to make a window, *My Four Green Fields*, for the Irish pavilion at the 1939 World Fair in New York. It won first prize for stained glass and today is in the Government Buildings in Merrion Street, Dublin.

When *An Túr Gloine* closed in 1943, Hone set up her own studio in her home. She produced over 100 pieces of stained glass, many of them windows for churches. The most important is a huge window for the chapel of Eton school near London. Although she is best remembered for her stained glass work, Hone also continued to paint. She and Mainie Jellett were founder members of the Irish Exhibition of Living Art in 1943, which aimed to make modern Irish art known the general public. They also exhibited pictures at the avant-garde White Stag Group of artists in Dublin in the 1940s. Evie Hone died suddenly in 1955.

CONSTANCE MARKIEVICZ (1868–1927)

Constance Gore-Booth was born into an Anglo-Irish landlord family. She grew up at the family's mansion in Sligo and studied art in London and Paris. In 1900, she married a Polish Count, Casimir Markievicz and they moved to Dublin in 1903. About ten years later the marriage collapsed and her husband left Ireland for good.

She became involved in the cultural revival and this drew her into nationalist politics. She joined Sinn Féin and *Inghinidhe na hÉireann*, a woman's nationalist organisation. In 1909, with Bulmer Hobson, she set up *Na Fianna*, a scout-type organisation to recruit and train boys to fight for Irish independence. Friendship with James Connolly led to her involvement with the labour movement. She helped to organise the feeding of workers during the 1913 lockout in Dublin. She also joined Connolly's Irish Citizen Army and outraged many in Dublin by appearing in a uniform with trousers and guns.

In the 1916 Rising, she fought in Stephen's Green with the Citizen Army unit led by Michael Mallin. Afterwards she was court-martialled and sentenced to death. But the British did not want to execute a woman and her sentence was at once changed to life imprisonment. Like the other life prisoners she was freed in June 1917.

She then joined the new Sinn Féin Party led by de Valera and along with other prominent members was imprisoned in 1918 as part of the 'German Plot' round-up. In the 1918 election, she was one of two women candidates nominated by Sinn Féin. Her election made her the first woman elected to Westminster and to Dáil Éireann. In line with Sinn Féin policy, she never took her seat in the British parliament but when the Dáil government was set up in 1919, de Valera made her Minister for Labour. But over the next three years she was imprisoned twice which made it difficult for her to achieve much in this role. When the Dáil Cabinet was re-organised in 1921, she was left out of the inner circle of seven Ministers who made the main decisions.

During the Dáil debates on the Treaty, she vehemently opposed Dominion Status. She supported the anti-Treaty side in the civil war and went to America to gather funds. She lost her seat in the 'Treaty election' of 1922 but was re-elected in 1923 as a Sinn Féin TD. When de Valera left Sinn Féin in 1926 and set up Fianna Fáil, she followed him and was elected a Fianna Fáil TD in 1927. She died soon after.

J.J. McELLIGOTT (1893–1974)

Kerry-born James J. McElligott graduated from UCD and joined the British civil service. In 1913, he enrolled in the Volunteers, and fought in the GPO in 1916. After being sacked, he worked in London as a financial journalist. In 1923, he became Assistant Secretary in the Department of Finance and worked with the Department Secretary, Joseph Brennan. In 1927, he replaced Brennan as Secretary of the Department of Finance, the top job in the civil service, a post he held through several changes of government until 1953.

Under Cumann na nGaedheal, McElligott worked closely with Finance Minister, Ernest Blythe. To help big businesses and farmers, they kept government spending and taxes low, while maintaining free trade. But this policy left little to spend on health care, education and housing. Blythe appointed McElligott Chairman of the Tariff Commission to look at requests for tariffs. By 1930, they dealt with twelve requests, but granted only three. McElligott was against government involvement in industry. He opposed spending £5m on the Shannon Scheme or setting up the ESB as a state-run company.

The Depression in 1930 led to a new policy. Blythe removed McElligott from the Commission and imposed more tariffs, even before Fianna Fáil came to power. McElligott was uncomfortable with Fianna Fáil's policy of protection, high government spending and government interference in the economy. He clashed with Seán Lemass, but got on better with Minister for Finance, Seán MacEntee, who came to share his views. He approved of de Valera's decision to talk to Britain in 1938 and he was on the Irish delegation that went to London. He was closely involved in negotiating the end of the dispute over land annuities. When Fianna Fáil set up a Banking Commission in the mid-1930s, McElligott strongly influenced its report which recommended keeping the Irish pound linked to sterling and setting up a Central Bank. This was done in 1943.

McElligott was involved in the government's preparation for war. Wartime conditions forced him to accept more government involvement in the economy, e.g. he supported setting up a government-owned Irish Shipping Company. In 1943, when planning for post-war conditions began, McElligott successfully resisted Lemass's suggestion that the economic ideas of John Maynard Keynes be adopted. He also opposed Irish involvement in post-war international financial organisations like the International Monetary Fund (IMF) and all new economic thinking until 1953 when he resigned to become Governor of the Central Bank.

PÁDRAIG PEARSE (1879–1916)

Born in Dublin in 1879, Pádraig Pearse was the son of an English stonemason. He qualified as a lawyer but never practised. At sixteen, he joined the Gaelic League and became passionate about the revival of Irish. In 1903, he became editor of the League's newspaper, *An Claidheamh Soluis*. He improved its content, publishing news items, stories and poems in Irish. He hoped this would convince more people to learn Irish.

When that did not happen, he turned to education, opening his own school, St Enda's, in 1908. At first it was a success. Friends and family taught in it and many Gaelic Leaguers sent their sons as pupils. Teaching was mainly through Irish. Unlike most other schools at the time, there was no corporal punishment. Students were free to express themselves and were encouraged to admire ancient Gaelic heroes, like Cuchulainn.

But success went to Pearse's head. He moved the school to a bigger house on the outskirts of Dublin. This increased costs while the number of students declined because the school was too far away. By 1912, Pearse was almost bankrupt. He had to beg and borrow money to keep St Enda's going.

Up to then, Pearse concentrated on the revival of Irish and education. He was not involved in politics, though in 1912, he spoke alongside Redmond in favour of Home Rule. But as his school failed and as unionist opposition to Home Rule grew, Pearse became more politically aware. He came to believe that only an independent Irish republic could save Irish, calling for *'an Ireland not free merely but Gaelic as well; not Gaelic merely but free as well'*. In November 1913, he helped to found the Irish Volunteers and, shortly after, took the IRB oath. When Redmond called on the Volunteers to support Britain in the First World War, he sided with the minority who rejected that call. When the Volunteers re-organised soon after, he became Director of Military Organisation. This position allowed him to appoint other IRB men to key positions within the movement.

Although long serving republicans like Thomas Clarke and Seán MacDiarmada at first distrusted him, Pearse won them over with his passionate enthusiasm. He was elected to the IRB Supreme Council and told of the plans for a rising. He developed a theory of 'blood sacrifice',

PÁDRAIG PEARSE (1879–1916) CONT.

i.e. the spirit of Ireland could only be revived if men were prepared to die for it. In 1915, in a speech at the funeral of the old Fenian O'Donovan Rossa, Pearse expressed this idea when he said: *'Life springs from death, and from the graves of patriot men and women spring living nations.'*

The Volunteer Military Committee, which plotted the Easter Rising, appointed him President of the Provisional Government. On Easter Monday, he read the Proclamation of the Republic at the GPO. Throughout Easter week, he was nominally in command, though most military decisions were made by Connolly. On Friday, when it was clear that any further fighting was useless, he signed the surrender. Arrested, he was court-martialled by the British army and executed by firing squad on 3 May 1916.

EAMON DE VALERA (1882–1975)

Born in New York, Eamon de Valera grew up in Limerick, taught maths in Dublin and joined Gaelic League. In 1913, he joined Irish Volunteers and in 1916, was reluctantly sworn into the IRB. During the Easter Rising, he commanded the Volunteers at Boland's Mills and afterwards was sentenced to death. That was changed to life imprisonment when the executions were stopped. In prison he emerged as a leader, healing divisions among republican prisoners.

After Lloyd George freed him in June 1917, he was elected a 'Sinn Féin' MP for East Clare. In October 1917, he united the competing anti-Home Rule groups which emerged after the 1916 rising into the 'second' Sinn Féin Party and was elected its President. Shortly after, he was also elected leader of the Volunteers, thus uniting political and military movements. Imprisoned in 1918 as part of the 'German Plot' round-up, he was in jail for the 1918 election and the first meeting of Dáil Éireann in January 1919. Collins helped him escape and in April, the First Dáil elected him President (i.e. Prime Minister). He appointed a Cabinet, then left for the United States where he stayed until December 1920.

When de Valera returned, he found a guerrilla war and the Sinn Féin Cabinet split between Collins and Cathal Brugha. He sided with Brugha, perhaps through jealousy of Collins. As violence grew in the North, de Valera met the Northern Prime Minister, Sir James Craig, but the talks achieved nothing.

By June 1921, Lloyd George was ready to negotiate with Sinn Féin. He and de Valera agreed to a Truce (11 July) and de Valera went to London. He demanded an independent republic and an end to partition. Lloyd George offered limited 'Dominion Status' to 26 counties. The talks broke down but neither side wanted war and they agreed to reopen negotiations in October. De Valera refused to be part of the delegation, saying that the delegates must have someone to refer back to. He told them to demand an end to partition and offer Britain 'external association' in return. He forbade them to sign anything without his approval.

When Lloyd George offered a Boundary Commission as a way of solving partition, de Valera accepted it but he continued to insist on 'external association' even when the British rejected it. He was furious when the delegates signed a Treaty without consulting him on 6 December 1921 and called on the Irish people to reject it. In the Dáil debates, de Valera opposed the Treaty (a) because it made the king head of state and (b) because the oath would give Britain power in Ireland. His suggested alternative Treaty ('Document no 2') pleased no one. When Dáil accepted the Treaty, de Valera resigned and walked out, leaving Griffith and Collins to set up the Free State. Over the next few months, he made inflammatory speeches and backed the IRA's occupation of the Four Courts but he also negotiated a Pact with Collins to fight the June 1922 election jointly. Collins called off the Pact on the eve of the election.

After the pro-Treaty side won (fifty-eight seats to thirty-five), the Free State army attacked the IRA in the Four Courts and civil war began. Although head of the 'republican government', de Valera did not control the IRA who ignored his pleas for a ceasefire until an extreme IRA leader, Liam Lynch, was killed in May 1923. In elections in August, de Valera's anti-Treaty Sinn Féin Party won forty-four seats, but he was arrested during the campaign and spent the next year in jail.

By 1925, de Valera realised the policy of abstention (staying out of Dáil Éireann) was futile but when the IRA refused to agree, he left Sinn Féin in 1926 and set up Fianna Fáil. It won forty-four seats in the June 1927 election but the Fianna Fáil TDs refused to enter the Dáil because they would have to take the Oath. In July, after the murder of Kevin O'Higgins, Cosgrave's Electoral Amendment Bill, forced Fianna Fáil to enter the Dáil or lose its seats. After this, there was another election in September in which they won fifty-seven seats. From then until 1932, they were the main opposition Party in the Dáil.

Fianna Fáil won the 1932 election. De Valera's main interest was in foreign and Anglo-Irish policy. He appointed himself Minister for External Affairs and left economic issues to his economic Ministers. In 1932, Fianna Fáil quickly abolished the Oath, withheld £5 million in land annuities and imposed tariffs on imports. This led to an economic war with Britain. Up 1937, de Valera dismantled the Treaty, removing the Oath and Senate and downgraded the Governor General. The British could do nothing because the 1931 Statute of Westminster allowed Dominions to change British laws. In 1937, de Valera completed the process with his new Constitution.

In foreign affairs, de Valera supported the League of Nations as the best hope of peace in Europe and often attended its meetings in Geneva. But by 1938, it was clear there was going to be another European war. De Valera and British Prime Minister Chamberlain made the Anglo-Irish Agreements which restored trade with Britain and made neutrality possible by returning the Treaty ports to Irish ownership.

When war began, de Valera declared neutrality. He personally dealt with the representatives of the warring countries in Dublin. After France fell in 1940, he turned down Churchill's offer of Irish unity in return for joining in war but to avoid a British invasion he followed a pro-Allied policy, selling food to Britain, passing on information and allowing Irish people to go and work in Britain or join the British forces. After America joined in December 1941, pressure on Ireland increased. On the eve of D-Day, the 'American Note' demanded de Valera to close German and Japanese missions. When he refused, all travel to Britain was stopped for six weeks. When Hitler died, de Valera visited the German embassy to offer condolences, which gave the impression of support for Germany.

From 1932 to 1948, de Valera dealt firmly with anyone who threatened his government. He (a) banned the Blueshirts and (b) weakened the IRA by enrolling IRA men in the army and police, and giving them pensions. When hard-line republicans returned to violence around 1936, he declared the IRA illegal. In 1939, when the IRA threatened neutrality with bombs in Britain, de Valera passed the Offences against the State Act. During the war, 500 people were interned and he allowed several to die on hunger strike or be executed for murder

An astute politician, de Valera won six general elections between 1932 and 1944. He often called a snap election catching the opposition unprepared. By 1948, post-war economic problems made Fianna Fáil unpopular. De Valera called a sudden election but Fianna Fáil lost seats and he lost power to the first coalition government.

INDEX